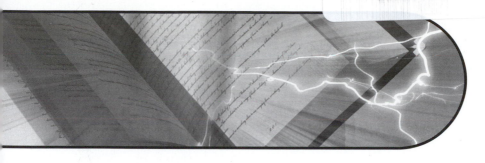

How To Do Things With Cultural Theory

How To Do Things With Cultural Theory

Matt Hills

A MEMBER OF THE HODDER HEADLINE GROUP

First published in Great Britain in 2005 by
Hodder Education, a member of the Hodder Headline Group,
338 Euston Road, London NW1 3BH

www.hoddereducation.com

Distributed in the United States of America by
Oxford University Press Inc.
198 Madison Avenue, New York, NY10016

British Library Cataloguing in Publication Data
A catalogue record for this book is available from the British Library

Library of Congress Cataloging-in-Publication Data
A catalog record for this book is available from the Library of Congress

ISBN-10 0 340 80915 9
ISBN-13 978 0 340 80915 0

1 2 3 4 5 6 7 8 9 10

Typeset in 10/13 point Adobe Garamond by Servis Filmsetting Ltd, Manchester
Printed and bound in Malta by Gutenberg Press.

What do you think about this book? Or any other Hodder Education title?
Please send your comments to the feedback section on www.hoddereducation.com.

For Em, cardy, smiling cat and all the family, with loats of love

Contents

Acknowledgements

My appreciative thanks must go to 'the management' – Terry Threadgold, Justin Lewis and Jenny Kitzinger – for allowing me the time to write this book. At Arnold, Debbie Edwards was unfailingly helpful, so my grateful thanks to her. And Anthony Robinson came up with a stunning cover image, capturing the sense that cultural theory is much more than 'just words on a page'.

If this book was a long time coming, then I have accrued plenty of debts along the way. This seems like a good place to reiterate my thanks to my PhD supervisor, Roger Silverstone. Though the doctorate was quite a few years ago now, its academic debts stay with me, as does all the advice I was given. And many thanks also to Denise Bielby, Will Brooker, Kay Dickinson, Jonathan Gray, Jeremy Gilbert, Sara Gwenllian Jones, Lee Harrington, Henry Jenkins, Catherine Johnson, Alan McKee, Brett Mills, Lauri Mullens, Roberta Pearson, Tim Robins, Cornel Sandvoss, Steven Jay Schneider, John Tulloch, Karin Wahl-Jorgensen and all the many others who have made me think harder about the academic subject matter that I (still!) love.

Discussing new ideas can be one of the most exciting things about being an academic, and in the Cardiff School of Journalism, Media and Cultural Studies, I've been lucky enough to get to do just that with a lot of fascinating folk – among them Bertha Chin, Ben Earl, Inger-Lise Kalviknes Bore, Amy Luther (indexer extraordinaire), Matt Hill (oh, how we laughed), Louise Smith and Rebecca Williams.

Outside academic life – if there is an 'outside' – hello again and 'long time no see' to Russell Bradshaw, Paul Barthram, Ben Morgan, Paul Martin and all my friends and family. I promise *never* to disappear off the face of the earth again while writing yet another book, well, except for that next contract I just signed . . .

This book was written while listening to a range of music – most of it expertly mixed by Tom Lord-Alge – and the writing process was interrupted by occasional visits to watch *Doctor Who* being filmed in Cardiff, and by admittedly less occasional pauses to read Outpost Gallifrey.

First and last, the writing of this book was sustained by Emma Catherine's love, support and kindness. Thanks to Emma for all those things which words of acknowledgement cannot properly express, and for transforming the most quotidian moments of everyday life into the happiest of times.

[T]heory is not only a matter of students learning other people's discourses. It is also about students doing their own theorizing around . . . contemporary issues. Theory has to be *done*, it has to become a form of cultural production and not merely a storehouse of insights drawn from the books of the "great theorists" (Giroux 1997:240).

Doing Cultural Theory

Many academic books are published each year, each of them with its own introductory remarks, some more or less helpful, some more or less inspiring. Here is an introduction from somebody else, and to another book altogether, that helped me to start thinking about the role of this one:

> An introduction to a book is much like an introduction to a person, and similarly, perhaps, not much listened to. None the less, it is worth announcing here that this book is not intended as a directory to all that has recently been written on the topic of culture. . . . What, on the contrary, I have attempted here is . . . an *argument* . . . to *move* the reader with a sense of his and her duties to culture; to call each to the militant colours of the cultures to which we owe our very selves and our keen sense that life is so very worth living (Inglis 2004:vii).

So it is that Fred Inglis begins his textbook on the 'key concept' of *Culture* with a rallying call. For my purposes, his contrast between a 'directory' and an 'argument' is instructive. The former is assumed to recap and reiterate, to tell us things. The latter, on the other hand, doesn't just inform (though it may do that), it also seeks to have an effect on the reader. Inglis's *Culture* (2004) is an attempt to 'move' its readers, not simply to tell them things about culture and its theories. Here is one textbook which seeks to do things. And it does those things, assuming it is successful, with cultural theory.

Inglis's mini-manifesto isn't a million miles away from what I want to explore in this book. His contrast between academic writing that informs or describes, and writing that seeks to provoke or affect its readers, appears at first glance to replay a distinction proposed by the 'ordinary language' philosopher J. L. Austin (1976 and 1979): that of 'constative' versus 'performative'. Austin was concerned with how people used 'ordinary' language, and the subtle shades of meaning that language could create (see Osborne 2000:7; Inglis 1993:96).

Austin set out his ideas in a book whose title may strike the reader as familiar, *How To Do Things With Words* (1976). He coined the terms 'constative' and 'performative', pointing out that 'you are more than entitled not to know what the word performative means. It is a new word . . . but there seems to be no word already in existence to do [its] . . . job' (1979:233 and 235). Constative refers to words that make statements: 'the business of a statement can only be to "describe" some state of affairs, or to "state some fact", which it must do either truly or falsely' (Austin 1976:1). Constatives are hence descriptions of the world or of states of affairs existing in the world. To return to my opening example, Inglis's proposed directory of cultural theory would have been just such an entity, describing a range of views on culture and a series of different theories, and doing this job as truthfully as possible. Set against constatives, Austin explains that performatives 'do not "describe" or "report" . . . and the uttering of the sentence is, or is a part of, the doing of an action' (1976:5). Performatives are acts of speech which achieve something, and make something happen, rather than reporting a pre-existent state of affairs. Inglis's argument and his attempt to move the reader could therefore be broadly described as performative.

In *How To Do Things With Words*, Austin gives a range of examples of performatives such as saying one's wedding vows, naming a ship, bequeathing items in a will, and making a bet (1976:5). These are all 'explicit' performatives. It is evident that they are each parts of a ritual or ceremony, and that in the very act of saying or writing such things, we are committed to and participating in an action. Austin's meaning of performative is very much not a synonym for 'performing' in the theatrical sense of the term, although some writers treat performative in this way. For example, in his *Performative Criticism*, Gerry Brenner says that he calls these essays performative because they ask to be read as texts capable of being variously performed, orally, by a good reader and can be read as if on a stage by an actor (2004:2). Any such 'performing' would be a special case of Austin's performative, and hence a special case of doing things with words, since it would involve the ritual of stage and audience. Performative, therefore, cannot be boiled down to the matter of stage performances. Austin goes on to distinguish the class of explicit performatives from other more 'implicit' examples (1976:32) which resemble statements, but still work to do things. Elsewhere (Hills 2004 and 2005), I have argued that we can approach academic theorizing as a type of implicitly performative act; theory may claim to describe the world, but it also always acts on its readers and hence on the world it purports to reflect. This performativity should not be taken as a failing of theory, however, as if any theory should or could somehow aspire to the purely constative role of mirroring 'the real'. Nor can performativity be identified as a characteristic only possessed by certain types of cultural theory (see Barrett 1999:11). Austin's 'speech act' theory, the theory of performativity, has partly found its way into cultural theory via Judith Butler's (1999 [1990]) work on how gender identities – what it means to be culturally masculine or feminine – don't reflect or describe any true essences of gender, but rather create and cite what they claim to reflect. French (post-)structuralist Jacques Derrida has also applied Austin's work directly to the activities of academics (Derrida 1988, 1992). In an essay tackling the very idea of 'the University', Derrida argues that scholarly debates on the power of language are

> neither simply theoretico-constative [they don't simply describe theory like Inglis's (2004) directory of culture – MH] nor simply performative. This is because the performative is not one: there are various performatives and there are antagonistic . . . attempts to police . . . [language] . . . and use it, to invest it performatively (1992:20; see also 1992:30 and Derrida cited in Readings 1996:205–6n6).

Regarding theory – here, cultural theory – as implicitly performative, while a directory or textbook of cultural theory could be viewed as constative, would be a way of suggesting that theory does things, while textbooks report on those purely theoretical happenings. The action is always somewhere else, it would seem, for the poor, maligned textbook. And when readers expect textbooks on cultural theory to describe key theories, they are assuming that such texts will be purely constative. Yet this contrast between theory-as-performative-act and textbook-as-constative-report becomes unhelpful when it means that we fail to see how reporting on cultural theory is actually another moment of performativity. The constative always also has performative aspects: 'after all, when we state something or describe something or report something, we do perform an act which is every bit as much an act as an act of ordering or warning' (Austin 1976:249). What appear to be distinguishable moments – theory as active/performative, the textbook of theory as passive/constative – are after all both performatives: both do something with words, as Derrida (1992) has observed. In fact, Austin himself concludes that a belief in the dichotomy of performatives and constatives is ultimately untenable (1976:150), and this moment has been crucially drawn on by Judith Butler in her work (see Salih 2002:100).

Although performativity is 'a term arising within linguistic [and Austinian] theory' (Bell 1999:1), Butler's take-up of the term in *Gender Trouble* (1999), *Bodies That Matter* (1993) and *Excitable Speech* (1997) is, as she notes, not a loyal use of Austin (Bell and Butler 1999:164; see Burkitt 1999:91–8). Just as creatively disloyal is Jacques Derrida's reading of performativity in *Limited Inc* (1988), itself drawn on by Butler (1997). Derrida (1988) defends his appropriation of performativity against speech-act theorist John Searle, who in turn positions himself as the rightful defender of, and heir to, J. L. Austin's work (see Mulligan 2003). The term 'performative' has thus enjoyed a varied circulation in cultural theory which has frequently

> invoked Austinian performativity in the service of a . . . project that can be
> roughly identified as antiessentialism. Austinian performativity is about how
> language constructs or affects reality rather than merely describing it. This
> directly *productive* aspect of language is most telling . . . when the utterances in
> question are closest to claiming a simply descriptive relation to some
> freestanding . . . reality . . . [cultural theory seems] to have an interest in
> unmooring Austin's performative from its localized dwelling in a few exemplary
> utterances and showing it instead to be a property of language . . . much more
> broadly (Sedgwick 2003:5).

And in this book I will argue that this includes the language of cultural theory, given that theory is another cultural form which comes close to claiming a simply descriptive relation to some freestanding reality. Even when this reality is viewed as constructed rather than naturally occurring – as anti-essentialist rather than present in worldly essences – the assumption is that theory reflects upon these processes of construction rather than being implicated in them. Theory conceptualises, but we tend to assume that it does so in order to show us the world's underlying skeins of sense anew, and not in order to (re-)construct that world. In other words, theory is common-sensically approached by its practitioners as something constative, something describing reality more or less adequately.

In what follows, this book will therefore necessarily be part-directory (reporting on cultural theory) and part-performative (doing things with cultural theory, just as Inglis promised to in *Culture*). Beginning with the admission that cultural theory does things means that even my reporting on any such theory must pay attention to how theory is constructed, how it seeks to move readers, how it works to achieve things for its writers, and above all, how it is used (produced, distributed and consumed). In other words, I am not approaching cultural theory as a set of pure thoughts or pronouncements. Instead, I will treat cultural theory as a material series of texts which academics and students practise on and carry out practices with: cultural theory does things, it makes promises, provokes meanings, and its writers and readers do things with these theory acts. As producers and consumers of cultural theory (for this is a product mediated and commercialised just as much as film, TV or popular fiction), we can do many different things with it, pursuing and tracing Derrida's many performatives. We can do things with cultural theory such as affecting, authorizing, analysing, annotating, autonomizing, contrasting, challenging, creating, careering, contradicting, deconstructing, defining, devaluing, disciplining, decoding, distancing, encoding, evaluating, fan-worshipping, highlighting, innovating, individualizing, jargon-speaking, legitimating, moralizing, making things matter, mirroring, making ordinary, mediating, making a name, networking, ordering, othering, prescribing, performing, pleasing, poaching, politicizing, publishing, reading, redefining, relating, romancing, see-sawing, setting apart, setting above, succeeding, storytelling, structuring, textualizing, using, valuing and writing . . .

And in this book, I will explore some of these ways of doing things with cultural theory, investigating not just what cultural theory is, but exploring what can be made of it. However, the incessant mixing of constative and performative is managed somewhat through the structure I have used. Part One is most self-evidently constative. It operates more in the manner we might traditionally expect of a textbook. Here, I provide a necessarily schematic overview of how culture has been theorised (Chapter One), but I also address what it means to have a theory of culture (Chapter Two). This is a topic which primers on cultural theory have tended to neglect, with the result that while we might get to know a lot about the 'cultural' in *cultural* theory, we are liable to treat cultural *theory* simply as a vehicle or conveyor belt for different, contrasting ideas, rather than considering how theory is itself a form of culture. Chapter Two therefore concludes by moving towards the notion that cultural theory occurs as a type of *theory culture*: it is an example of what it claims to analyse. Indeed, one early title for this book was *Theory Cultures*, which would have more directly linked and contrasted this text to my own first book, *Fan Cultures*, suggesting that just as we can study fans of media and culture, then so too can we study professional cultural theorists.

Moving on from Chapter Two's end point, Part Two then more significantly and self-consciously mixes constative and performative dimensions of cultural theory, reporting on theories of reading (Chapter Three) while also addressing how to read cultural theory, and analysing how real readers use cultural theory (Chapter Four). In these chapters, and Chapter Five, I turn cultural theory back on itself, applying theories of reading to how theory is read, and applying theories of mediation to how cultural theory is written and mediated. In a sense then, this study undertakes a 'cultural studies of cultural studies' (Hall 2002:111), reflecting on what it means to be a student and a scholar of contemporary culture.

This includes providing 'How to . . .' guides on how to effectively read and write cultural theory in Chapters Four and Five. This is very much not a book along the lines of

How To Get a 2:1 in Media, Communication and Cultural Studies (Williams 2004), although if it were such a thing, its variant title would be *How To Aim For a First* . . . For, where I discuss how to produce and consume cultural theory, my own emphasis is on the challenge of creating innovative theory, and on the importance of challenging established theoretical frameworks. Students facing the practical matters of reading and writing theory may thus want to turn to these chapters, but the reader who traces the book's trajectory sequentially will benefit from its incremental movement from a predominantly constative description of cultural theory (as in Chapter One) to a predominantly performative analysis of theory culture (in Chapter Seven).

Part Three intermixes Austin's constative and performative aspects of language with the greatest emphasis on cultural theory and performativity. It describes and reports on theories of subculture and popular culture (Chapter Six), and fan culture (Chapter Seven) while simultaneously considering how cultural theory performatively enacts a series of relations with these cultural forms. Chapter Six suggests that doing things with cultural theory can involve the creation of theory culture as a subculture in its own right, distanced from mainstream consumption and supported by its own commercial 'niche media' (Thornton 1995) and its own social networks (Becher and Trowler 2001), value systems and constructions of group authenticity (versus 'selling-out'). It also addresses how cultural theory is indebted and related to popular culture (Greig 2004; Hills 2005) even as it theorizes it. And finally, Chapter Seven considers theories of fandom, arguing that scholars are not only rational critics or passionate fans of popular culture, but may also be fans of cultural theory (Lacey 2000). For as Fred Inglis has noted: 'In the lives of middling-poor students and teachers working in the universities of the rich nations, . . . study from time to time . . . ignites the charge between the book and the heart' (1993:247). Hence Part Three suggests that cultural theory is used by professional theorists to do things such as participating in a commercialized academic subculture, telling certain stories about the cultural world, and consuming or celebrating celebrity texts.

Cultural theory is never just a matter of dry words on a dusty page, never just knowledge to be learnt or books to be opened. It is a form of life that far exceeds the page or the pure thought, energizing both. Despite this, it should be noted that exactly what scholarly work 'cultural theory' refers to has proved to be problematic. For example, Judith Butler describes one of the founding fathers of cultural studies, Stuart Hall, as being 'receptive to what she labels "cultural theory"' (in Gary Hall 2002:92), while Ben Carrington observes that 'Scott Lash . . . has argued against . . . cultural studies (or cultural theory in Lash's vocabulary)' (2001:290). These alleged mislabellings or rogue vocabularies are remarked upon by Hall and Carrington as if to chastise the offenders. Yet in each case what is demonstrated, instead, is that the boundary between what some scholars call 'cultural studies' and what others call 'cultural theory' can be crossed or ignored. Bill Readings has identified what he calls a 'dereferentialization' (1996:17) of culture in the contemporary university, by which he means that culture no longer has a fixed or consensual referent (a series of objects that the label 'culture' directs us to). But we might observe that, more than this, cultural theory also has no clearly or fully agreed-upon referent (see Part One). This is not a disastrous state of affairs, however, since it means that books such as this are called upon to nominate examples and exemplars of cultural theory. One of the things that scholars performatively do with cultural theory is ascribe certain boundaries to it by putting forward landmark texts. The reader should therefore be cautioned that doing things with cultural theory involves making and constructing this object. Or as Catherine Belsey remarks: 'distrust all introductions (even mine!)' (2005:157).

Rather than transnational publishers assuming that students constitute a market in need of books on *How To Do Media and Cultural Studies* (Stokes 2003) wherein guidance is provided on doing a research project, this book begins from a different starting point and a different set of assumptions. As José López cautions, there has been a tendency for textbooks to guide the doing of research but not the doing of theory:

> One looks in vain for a book that deals with 'doing . . . theory'. The most obvious
> place to look is, of course, the ever expanding market for introductory . . .
> theory texts. However, a perusal of these texts quickly reveals that they are not
> so much concerned with exploring . . . theory as such, but rather with
> introducing students to the work of particular theorists . . . students are rarely
> asked 'to theorize' . . . [but] . . . are always asked 'to research'! (2003:1–2).

And on those rare occasions where a recipe for theory is given, then this usually occurs far outside the realm of the textbook, such as in Michel de Certeau's influential study *The Practice of Everyday Life* (1988:62; see Chapters Three and Four in this book). Such a recipe is given an ironic twist by de Certeau, as if making theory repeatable as a systematic, conventional gesture immediately renders it inadequate or bad (1988:62–64). De Certeau perceives theory's recipe as to 'cut out and turn over'. That is, it isolates or cuts out objects of study that are '*foreign* to the place in which the theory is produced' and then finds, in these objects, a principle or concept that offers a general explanation, thereby magically turning over the specific into a mark of the general. For de Certeau this is a trick: theory promises only false moments of 'seeing everything' or 'recognizing . . . the same order everywhere'. We are then seemingly led to believe that real and good theory (see Chapter Two) mystically, and ever more magically, evades any recipe.

López's quest for a theory text that helpfully engages with doing theory identifies what Inglis (2004) only assumes: that textbooks are typically construed and viewed as places of constative description rather than of performative engagement (although see Nealon and Searls Giroux (2003) for one useful forerunner to this book). This identification is, however, not a natural one. Instead, I would suggest that it is an artefact of what I will go on to introduce properly in Chapter Two and explore in Part Three: theory culture. Doing theory is all too often restricted to a scholarly elite, and this leads to a situation where students are unnecessarily intimidated by Theory, coming to uneasily share their lecturers' (tacit) definition of it as sacred and extraordinary material to be pored over. Alternatively, students may prematurely dismiss Theory as alien to their experiences and situations.

I will argue that this is a culturally constructed state of affairs, and that it emerges through cultural theory's own role and operation within theory culture. Thus we can suggest counter-constructions and counter-discourses of cultural theory (see Hills 2005). We can investigate how doing theory might work positively for scholars and students, just as

Brunsdon (2000) and Barcan (2003) have begun to do in their respective interviews with cultural theory/studies scholars and undergraduates (see Evans (2004:ix) on the pressing need to investigate contemporary academic life). We can set out from different framing assumptions. Rather than *a priori* – in advance of the facts – decrying students' theory-blindness or theory-rejection, we might instead consider how to support students' theorizing. This book hence tells the story that López could not find when he examined theory textbooks, and the story that Inglis (2004), Neil Larsen (1997) and others ignore as a possibility when they devalue textbooks as passive and purely constative. The following chapters tell a story of cultural theory and theory culture as always simultaneously constative and performative in a variety of ways.

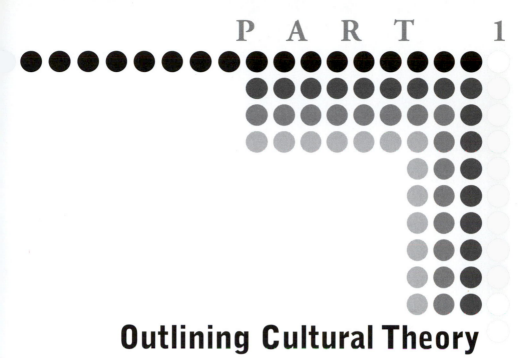

P A R T   1

Outlining Cultural Theory

chapter one

Defining: What is Culture?

Many studies of culture tend to begin with a particular argument. This piece of reiterated scholarly lore is drawn from Raymond Williams's (1983 [originally 1976]) *Keywords*. In this book, Williams traces the meanings attached to specific terms, offering 'an inquiry into a *vocabulary*: a shared body of words and meanings in our most general discussions, in English, of the practices and institutions which we group as *culture* and *society*' (1983:15). It is a very precise moment in Williams's investigation into the concept of culture which is frequently cited in introductions to the subject (see, for example, Jenks 1993:1; Milner 2002:11; Milner and Browitt 2002:2; Payne 1997:1; Smith 2001:1). This is the moment where Williams points out that 'Culture is one of the two or three most complicated words in the English language' (1983:87).

Such has been the academic proliferation of this sentence, where 'reference to Williams is a more or less ritual incantation' (Bennett 1998:23), that no less a cultural critic than Terry Eagleton doesn't even feel the need to attribute it to Williams. The opening line of Eagleton's *The Idea of Culture* reads simply ' "Culture" is said to be one of the two or three most complex words in the English language' (2000:1). Williams's observation is also sometimes supplemented by a citation of Kroeber and Kluckhorn's (1952) cataloguing of at least 77 discrete concepts used under the banner of culture (see Payne 1997:1; Smith 2001:1). Given all this, it is tempting to conclude that if Williams hadn't announced that culture was a murky, difficult and complex word, then theories of culture would have had to invent such a statement anyway.

Why has Williams's observation proved so useful to scholars of culture? For one thing, it lets academia off the hook somewhat. Rather than having to define a single meaning for the term 'culture', academics can content themselves with 'mapping' different meanings, perhaps even announcing that culture is a term which exists beyond any clear definition: 'we want to sidestep the difficulties of defining "culture" as it would take us too far from the issue at hand, and most likely not produce any satisfaction' (Fuery and Mansfield 2000:24).

Noting the complexity of reference underlying culture also means that academics are not then called upon to provide any boundaries to the concept. Culture can be left in place as a concept, and an entity, that is 'porous, fuzzy-edged, indeterminate, [and] intrinsically inconsistent' (Eagleton 2000:96). Failing to fence in and differentiate a notion of culture, the concept shades into a host of other terms. Foremost among these is the 'social', the result being that contemporary cultural theory and social theory are rarely wholly distinguishable. As Barbara Adam and Stuart Allan have pointed out, 'the word "culture" . . . seems to be appearing everywhere [across the humanities and social sciences – MH], its meaning stretched to the point that attempts to specify the non-cultural run into severe difficulty' (1995:xiii). For example, *Profiles in Contemporary Social Theory* (Elliott and Turner (eds) 2001) includes entries on writers often thought of as cultural theorists, such as Theodor Adorno, Roland Barthes and Stuart Hall (see also Miles (2001) on social theory). Observing this state of affairs, Toby Miller argues that 'the "cultural" has become a "master-trope" in the humanities, blending and blurring textual analysis of popular culture with social theory' (2001:1).

This blurring means that a sub-section of the discipline of sociology, 'cultural sociology' (see, for example, Alexander 1992; Archer 1996; Rubinstein 2001; Smith 2000; Spillman 2002) has borrowed from many of the same theoretical sources as what has been labelled 'cultural studies'. Frank Webster (2001:90–1) suggests that cultural studies and sociology can be viewed as working on one another from the 1970s onwards, carrying out a negotiation of knowledge and a re-orienting of scholarly 'authorities' (for instance, Stuart Hall, one of the founding fathers of cultural studies, was actually made a Professor of Sociology in 1979). Webster (2001:92–3) warns against the futility of erecting disciplinary boundaries around sociology as opposed to cultural studies (see also Martin 2001). But such disciplinary defences are not easily overcome or set aside. Although social theory and cultural theory blur together at their edges – sometimes merging far more obviously than this – cultural theory is still often vigorously held apart from cultural studies:

> I want to point out the difference between 'studying culture' and 'Cultural Studies'. The first involves many movements and intellectual traditions . . . It is a mistake to identify (in fact to confuse) these with 'Cultural Studies'. The latter has a distinctive history in Great Britain and subsequently the United States and internationally (Peter Brooker 2003:viii; see also Jenks 1993:151).

This distinction may seem highly counter-intuitive to the uninitiated student or scholar. As a result of various interdisciplinary borrowings of specific theories, social and cultural theory can be seen to leak together, yet cultural studies is supposedly set apart from cultural theory, emerging through the work of its own founding fathers, usually named as Richard Hoggart, E. P. Thompson, Stuart Hall and Raymond Williams (Miller 2001:3, drawing on Maxwell 2000; see also Davies 1995:30–66). But even this is to simplify matters. Just as culture may have many meanings, and studying culture has involved many intellectual traditions, then so too has cultural studies carried a multiplicity of different strands and threads of endeavour (Hartley 2003:13 identifies seven, while Johnson *et al* 2004:10–13 also discuss seven different agendas within which culture can be framed).

The somewhat strange scenario I am gesturing towards here is one where scholars have been less than keen to define 'culture', yet exceptionally keen to define their disciplines against rivals. Working against academic turf wars over exactly who has the right to call their work cultural studies or cultural theory, it may be helpful not to police rigorous lines of division between cultural theory/studies and its disciplinary opponents such as sociology or philosophy (see Osborne 2000; Seigworth and Wise 2000). Rather than patrolling what should really count as cultural theory, we could instead begin by identifying a series of ways in which culture has been defined in cultural studies/theory. I will return to the matter of how Theory is defined in the next chapter, in order to question the assumption that cultural theory can be equated with different ways of thinking about culture, and to argue that such theory also involves ways of doing things, that is, it carries its own characteristic and material practices. In all that follows, however, any reference to cultural studies can be read as a reference to cultural theory, and vice versa. Across this book I will often use the clumsy term 'cultural theory/studies' to deliberately remind readers and myself that disciplinary borders may be of less consequence than the conceptual borders to culture which different writers use or refuse.

With that in mind, in the next few sections of this chapter I will introduce a range of attempted scholarly definitions of culture. I will take into account the argument that:

> restricting the meaning of culture to the projection of a single viewpoint or even placing limits on what counts as cultural knowledge (for example, 'the great novelists', 'serious composers', or 'the works of scientific genius') ignores a great deal of what is of interest [analytically] (Smith 2000:21).

However, by challenging limits to culture, theorists may have created a boundless object of theory. The first defining work I'll address is that of Raymond Williams. As established in the introduction, my approach here will involve considering what Williams's theory describes constatively as culture, and also what his theory does performatively, that is, how it acts on the world.

Making ordinary

Having asserted culture's complexity, Williams then immediately isolates conflictual meanings of the term:

> What I was now hearing were two different senses . . .: first, in the study of literature, a use of the word to indicate . . . some central formation of values; secondly, in more general discussions . . . a use that made it almost equivalent to *society*: a particular *way of life* – 'American culture', 'Japanese culture' (1983:12).

He seems to pit a *hierarchical* and common sense version of capital C 'Culture', viewed as the finely thought expressions and finely wrought forms of art and literature, against a more *anthropological* meaning, as in a 'way of life'. And it is the latter sense – culture as 'ordinary' and as a way of life (Williams 1997 [1958]) – which has tended to predominate in cultural theory/studies. As Jim McGuigan notes, 'Williams's resonant phrase from 1958, "culture is ordinary"' is as good a phrase as any to mark the beginning of cultural studies. In this striking 'three-word catchphrase' (Kendall and Wickham 2001:7), Williams proposes a 'clear and concise rebuttal of . . . "elitist" conceptions of culture' (McGuigan 1992:21; see also Jenks

1993:11–12). Having said this, Williams's conception of culture is rather more complex, since the essay 'Culture is Ordinary' argues that:

> We use the word culture in these two senses: to mean a whole way of life – the common meanings; [and] to mean the arts and learning – the special processes of discovery and creative effort. *Some writers reserve the word for one or other of these senses; I insist on both, and on the significance of their conjunction* (Williams 1997:6, my italics).

Culture may be ordinary, giving us the essence of Williams's culturalist argument (Hall 1996; Smith 2000:26–7), but such a notion still has to engage with hierarchical and elitist conceptions of culture. It cannot simply proceed as if this alternative view has disappeared or can be fantasised away. How then might we best hold on to two apparently contradictory versions of culture? Such a question is made no easier to answer by the fact that a range of writers have reinforced Williams's basic opposition between culture as ordinary, that is, as belonging to everyone in society and being 'in every mind' (Williams 1997:6), and culture as 'special' or belonging only to a cultivated elite.

Williams's meaning of culture as a way of life, where he gives the examples of American culture and Japanese culture, appears to be an idea based at the level of national cultures, but Williams's sense of adding 'culture' as a suffix to an adjectival prefix (for example, Japanese) has been extended in a huge variety of ways by later scholars. Academic books have sought to analyse *Commercial Cultures* (Jackson *et al* 2000), *Advertising Cultures* (Malefyt and Moeran 2003) and *Consumer Culture* (Lury 1996), also taking a further range of nouns as prefixes, such as my own *Fan Cultures*, Sarah Thornton's *Club Cultures* (1995) and Matthew J. Pustz's *Comic Book Culture* (1999). On top of this, the media have proved to be tempting targets for this 'culture-as-suffix' terminology, via books such as *Exploring Media Culture* (Real 1996), *Media Cultures* (Skovmand and Schrøder 1992), *Television Culture* (Fiske 1987) and *Tabloid Culture* (Glynn 2000), not forgetting *Internet Culture* (Porter 1997) or *New Media Cultures* (Marshall 2004). All of these scholarly works proceed from and reinforce Williams's meaning of culture, as something ordinary and a part of everyday life, rather than something creatively or artistically special.

This growth in types of more or less ordinary culture to be studied could be taken as evidence that the word 'culture' has become a 'linguistic weed', spreading into forms such as 'camera culture, gun culture, service culture, museum culture, deaf culture, football culture' (Hartman cited in Milner and Browitt 2002:3). But this weed image suggests rather insidiously that culture has no 'proper' place in the new conjunctions that scholars have championed, and that it is unwanted in such accounts. Seeing the term as having undergone a kind of unruly growth implies that its spread should be checked – after all, one usually seeks to uproot weeds – and that culture should instead be restricted to the elite arena of great literature and art. Such a critique therefore returns us squarely to Williams's other meaning of culture, which still reflects how this term is frequently used in contemporary society. But it seems here as if we are forced to choose between these two meanings of culture as an either/or, whereas Williams insists on taking them *both* into account.

To begin to do this, we need a third way of considering culture, something that is not just the arts and learning approach or the way of life approach. Something akin to this third possibility actually emerged in early cultural studies work, where culture was thought of as '*collective subjectivity*' or an outlook adopted by a community; this was exemplified in studies by the Birmingham School, the pioneers of cultural studies on youth and working-class subcultures (Alasuutari 1995:25–6). Such a perspective may seem to resemble Williams's emphasis on culture as ordinary. However, Tony Bennett has argued that the object of analysis that was established was significantly detached from the way in which the concept of culture as a whole way of life was embedded in Williams' own writing, since the 'collective subjectivity' approach to culture drew far more on sociological subcultural theory (1998:23–4).

This definition of culture, exemplified in the early CCCS collection *Resistance Through Rituals* (Hall and Jefferson 1976), is not after all culture viewed as a whole way of life or culture restricted to art and literature. Instead, it depicts culture as a series of spatially and temporally bounded, but still everyday, practices through which self-identity is generated against 'mainstream' or 'parental' others (for more on the concept of subculture see Chapter Six). Culture in this sense becomes a fragmented field of power relations rather than an organic 'whole', appearing as a series of competing norms or everyday identities (Thornton 1995; Highmore 2002). The appeal of culture defined as a bounded but fragmentary (non-whole or non-totalising) series of practices has been considerable in cultural theory/ studies. This version of the term continues to hold open the democratising and anti-hierarchical promise of Williams's culturalist position (that culture is ordinary), while also holding on to the notion that culture is linked to socially structured communities, some of which may be elite groups linked to more traditional notions of culture-as-art. Nevertheless, all manner of culture-producing and culture-sustaining communities can be identified: culture in this definition amounts to routinized ways of doing things and ways of thinking about the world that work to define any specific, substantial community against other groups.

Such an approach allows us to respond to the question of how we might follow Williams's idea of retaining a focus on culture as elite and ordinary. For, following the 'culture = communal modes of practice' account, both these opposed views of culture – thesis and antithesis – can be incorporated or synthesised into a wider viewpoint. Defined in this way, culture is any social production of a communal identity and value system, whether this is the communally recognised identity and value system of the artist, or the identities and values of, say, football fans. Of course, some communal identities and value systems already self-consciously use the term 'culture' as a label for their formation of values (artists, writers, critics), whereas others generally do not (such as certain class groupings, commercial producers or consumer-based identities like fandom). The distinctive step taken by cultural theory/studies is one of extending the analytical category of culture to cover practices beyond those that are usually nominated and labelled as culture. Again, this isn't just a constative description of culture. It also works as a performative act of theory. It intervenes in relation to how we usually think about culture, seeking to analytically extend the term, hence disrupting views of culture as somehow *only* being special and creative work (though it can still be these things).

Cultural theory/studies' performative and constative defining of culture is well captured in Tony Bennett's book, *Culture: A Reformer's Science*:

> A more open-ended formulation might be to say that cultural studies is concerned with all those practices, institutions and systems of classification through which there are inculcated in a population particular values, beliefs, competencies, routines of life and habitual forms of conduct (1998:28).

Bennett's summary lacks the immediate catchiness of Williams's 'culture is ordinary' slogan, and also carries a problematic sense of inculcation, seeming to imply that populations are manipulated and made to think and act in certain ways by inevitable powers of culture. Writers who have developed the type of culture definition put forward by Bennett, such as Gavin Kendall and Gary Wickham (2001), playfully return to the elegance of well-crafted rhetoric, as well as further addressing issues of agency (individuals' and communities' power to make a difference to their situation) versus structure (forces that transcend the individual or a community, confronting them as a limit on the new actions which can be taken). Kendall and Wickham argue that 'culture is ordering (yes, we like to have a three-word catchphrase)' (2001:24). In the next section, I will move on to consider structuralist as well as (post-)structuralist definitions of culture like Kendall and Wickham's (2001). Structuralism and post-structuralism represent significant schools of thought within cultural theory/studies. In what follows it will be necessary to address these terms (see also Chapter Two) as well as discussing definitions of culture.

Structuring, ordering and mattering

In contrast to 'culturalist' versions of 'culture as ordinary', we can consider 'structuralist' approaches to culture, given that 'without structuralism, cultural studies as we now understand it is all but inconceivable' (Tudor 1999:79). It is customary for cultural studies' textbooks to sequence different approaches to culture in terms of their successive phases of influence in cultural theory/studies. In such accounts, the culturalist work of Williams and others is followed by structuralist work via key theorists, such as linguist Ferdinand de Saussure, and anthropologist Claude Levi-Strauss, and the '(post-)structuralist' theories of Michel Foucault and Jacques Derrida. The 'post-' in this latter label supposedly surpasses 'structuralism', which itself is posited as a move on from the assumptions of culturalism (see Hall 1992 and 1996; Turner 2003:23–4; McKee 2003a). A tidy temporal and logical sequence is thus installed, although it is questionable to what extent any of the approaches actually does definitively surpass its predecessors, making neat narratives of succession difficult to sustain.

Structuralist definitions of culture, as the name suggests, stressed the idea that culture can be defined as a structure of related meanings. Studying culture in this way hence involved first and foremost 'the study of *meanings*' (Badmington 2004:11). Culture was whatever signified – whether this was a crisp packet, a cereal box, an item of clothing, a bestselling novel, a car or a road sign. Structuralism, like culturalism, thus broadened culture out from its usual role as a label for aesthetic objects, and again performatively challenged the idea that culture was a marker only for 'special' artefacts. For the structuralist, culture became more than a whole way of life: it became the system of symbols through which societies understood themselves. These symbols were analysed by structuralists as if they were a kind of language structuring human understanding.

The structuralist view of culture remains partly continued in (post-)structuralist approaches, since both share an emphasis on 'culture as meaning' and 'culture as ordering'. However, for the structuralists, it was culture as a structure of meaning, built out of fixed binary oppositions, that had primacy and reality (binary is a language made up only of 1s and 0s; it has only two options, hence the phrase 'binary oppositions' emphasizes the duality of these opposed terms). It was this fixed or 'deep' structure, supposedly underlying all the manifestations of culture, which was declared to be the proper object of analysis. And it was this 'deep structure' which determined, like a language determining speech, what could be said and produced within a society's culture. Culture as meaning was hence viewed as determinate and as fully recoverable by the properly trained theorist: myths could be analysed for their underlying structures and codes (Levi-Strauss 1972); the fashion system could be analysed for its rules of combination of clothing items (Barthes 1983); and film and television output could be analysed for deep-rooted binary oppositions (see, for example, Tolson 1996).

Structuralism undoubtedly appealed due to the manner in which it enabled cultural theory/studies to tackle culture as being made up of all forms of meaning. It also operated as an unveiling mechanism. Structuralist scholars contended that it was culture, as a system of meaning, which constructed a society's very view of reality. For instance, who do we label 'terrorists' and 'freedom fighters'? Who do we celebrate as heroes and despise as villains? What do we consider socially to be real (the physical, the factual) and what do we label as 'unreal' (fantasy, perhaps even Theory)? What is to be counted as rational and what is irrational? All such binary oppositions – hero/villain, reality/fantasy, rationality/irrationality – are ways of structuring the world that appear to be natural and unquestionable, but they are actually relational and social constructions of meaning that allow us to make sense of the world. So the concept of hero requires its binary opposite of villain in order to mean anything, just as the concept of reality *needs* a counter-concept of fantasy in order to secure itself. Each binary opposition which feeds into the overall structure of culture has a generally-agreed-upon valued term and a devalued term. For example, being aware of reality is taken to be morally superior to being caught up in fantasy (devalued as delusion, hallucination and wishful thinking), while rationality is culturally valued above irrationality (devalued as hysteria or excessive emotion).

By highlighting how culture's meanings construct the world, cultural theorists were challenging a common sense view of the world as naturally *there* (see Chapter Two). Scholars also held out the possibility of challenging the power of culture-as-meaning to determine peoples' world views. If we realize that there is a system of meaning that, say, allocates heroic roles to some (freedom fighters) and villainous roles to others (terrorists), then we can begin to challenge these constructions of meaning. We can question whether the groups and individuals our culture depicts as monstrous really merit such representations: we can start to think differently, and critically, about our own cultural world.

Structuralist approaches to culture, or what Jeff Lewis (2002:13) calls culture viewed as 'an assemblage of imaginings and meanings', carry a number of potential problems.

Somewhat like the culturalist view, there is seemingly no term that could be meaningfully opposed to culture. In structuralist accounts, culture becomes all that there is; even nature is itself a cultural construct. This is profoundly ironic for a theory of culture that so radically and insistently stresses deep-rooted binary oppositions.

Structuralism also tended to stress the fixed 'whole' of structures of meaning: it therefore replayed a version of the problem of wholeness which afflicted culturalism, though there it was a whole way of life that supposedly defined culture. Structuralism's whole structures of meaning proved equally problematic, suggesting that the meanings of culture were fixed in place and could be pseudo-scientifically read by trained analysts. And although culture supposedly had a power to determine peoples' view of the world, this seemed to work without conflicts between different systems of meanings, or without malfunctions or slippages in systems of meaning. The structuralists had in fact envisioned a world resembling the starting point of the film narrative of *The Matrix* (1999, directed by Andy and Larry Machowski), where unwitting dupes are trapped inside a system of representation that they take to be reality (for more on overlaps between cultural theory and popular culture, see Chapter Six). In structuralism's rather dystopian view, people were supposedly not able to challenge culture's structures of meaning unless they were properly trained to do so by Theory in its unveiling, liberating capacity (Barthes 1977:165–9). This implies a massive 'derogation of the lay actor' (Giddens 1979:71), by which is meant any non-specialist or non-expert member of society, hence offering little or no scope for agency beyond that granted to theorists thanks to the magic word of 'theory' (Michael 2000:128–30). Although Tudor (1999:79) has argued that it is only certain inflections of structuralism that lack 'a coherent grasp of the operations of agency' rather than structuralism in total, adequate considerations of agency nevertheless appear to be a recurrent absence in much structuralist thought (Swingewood 1998:178–9).

The 'post' of post-structuralism seeks to rectify this by emphasising that the meanings of culture can be conflictual rather than working as part of a perfect structure. So it is that Jeff Lewis supplements his structuralist view of culture with a (post-)structuralist addition: 'culture is an assemblage of imaginings and meanings *that may be consonant, disjunctive, overlapping, contentious, continuous or discontinuous*' (2002:13, my italics). This development is also evident in the work of Gavin Kendall and Gary Wickham (2001), who are indebted to the theoretical perspective of French (post-)structuralist Michel Foucault. And Bennett stresses the idea, drawn from Foucault's studies (1970 and 1977) of the human sciences and institutions such as prisons, that culture works

> in the organisation and regulation of different fields of conduct [and] is seen to be disaggregated from those singular kinds of politics [and singular kinds of cultural theory – MH] which see all fields of cultural struggle as being connected to a generalised struggle of the subordinate against a single source of power (the state, the ruling class, patriarchy) (Bennett 1998:82).

This notion of culture once again bleeds into 'the social', since as Bennett points out:

> culture . . . goes beyond the influence of representations on forms of consciousness to include the influence of institutional practices, administrative

routines and spatial arrangements on the available repertoires of human
conduct and patterns of social interaction (1998:82).

This definition of culture moves away from the 'culture is ordinary' argument, since
Raymond Williams's culturalist position implies that people in every society possess their own
culture. Williams offers a profoundly democratising stance on culture, whereas (post-)
structuralist followers of Foucault view culture as a network of dispersed practices which
govern our actions, even if this network does not act on behalf of an identifiable group or
system which can therefore be said to hold power. Kendall and Wickham note that their use
of the term 'ordering' in the slogan 'culture is ordering' is 'very similar to the notion of
governance' (2001:27–8), but they mark out the difference of ordering as follows:

> ordering . . . might more accurately be said to treat control of one's own
> behaviour and emotions as an equivalent type of ordering to that involved in the
> rule of a nation state, region or municipal area . . . One crucial aspect of
> ordering that mirrors a crucial aspect of governance is its inherently limited
> capacity. Ordering, like governance, is never complete; it always falls short of
> total control (2001:32).

This Foucauldian position transforms culture into a series of orders: culture can be thought of
as orders in terms of commands or pressures internalized by the self, and also orders as more
general ways of ordering human conduct in space. Following this definition, we could
identify the culture of the university as a matter of ordering spaces (seminar rooms and
lecture theatres) where the lecturer, standing in front of their audience, can monitor students
(O'Shaughnessy 1999:166–7). The university as a cultural institution is also a matter of
ordering through administrative practices; registers are taken, student numbers and email
accounts are allocated, places on modules are taken up. And then there is the ordering of
degree classifications, and the routines and practices of marking.

University culture is patently not a whole way of life. Staff and students can move outside
its parameters, being defined by other aspects of their cultural identities. However, the
cultural ordering of being a student is surprisingly tenacious. It tends to be replayed through a
range of cultural institutions and spatial organizations beyond the university's halls of
learning – in halls of residence and shared student housing, at student nights in student
venues, when returning to the family home and to pre-university friendship circles during
holidays. In these cases, it is difficult to perceive where the limits actually exist to something
defined as 'university culture', since related cultural practices are not only housed in the
academic's office, the seminar room, the committee meeting, the academic registry or the
lecture theatre. Related practices spin in and out of these spatial arrangements, reaching far
beyond the immediate institution concerned (*contra* Kendall and Wickham's examples of
ordering the world of the University, 2001:32 and 40). The Foucauldian, (post-)structuralist
emphasis on culture as ordering appears to work most clearly in cases where we are dealing
with a spatially bounded institution with its own rules and routines, such as an asylum or
prison (Foucault 1967; 1977). Where the identities produced by these institutions, such as
the types of inmate, are fixed to spatial control or occupancy, then it makes sense to treat the

institution more or less as a unit for ordering analysis. But where cultural identities are less self-evidently spatially determined and fixed, this approach becomes less helpful. Some aspects of our cultural identities may be so pervasively reiterated across different cultural institutions that they appear to be almost entirely despatialized, for example, the consumer. And between the extremes of space-bound and despatialized orderings of culture there are identities, such as those of student and academic, which are ordered through a limited multiplicity of sites.

As I have indicated, Kendall and Wickham (2001:32) emphasize how culture's ordering always falls short. No cultural institution can fully determine or order and regulate the actions taken under its auspices. Forms of resistance to culture's institutional orderings always remain possible, even if they may be very limited in scope (Giddens 1979:71–2). The prisoner can go on hunger strike, or the inmate can attempt not to take their medication. The student may sit in a lecture texting friends or spend a seminar doodling on a sheet of paper, while the academic may 'refuse to abide by particular constraints on their teaching or research practice' (Kendall and Wickham 2001:40). Since ordering cannot wholly determine its objects – academics and students are not zombified components of a university knowledge system, which would return us to some dystopian Matrix-esque vision – types of 'counter-ordering' are also possible. But the (post-)structuralist concept of counter-ordering makes it clear that 'objects are given to us, as "the world", only in and through ordering. As such, ordering can be considered characteristic of all human life. . . . we cannot hope to ever find pure "things"' (Kendall and Wickham 2001:40–1). Ordering is, for Kendall and Wickham after Foucault, 'ontological' (2001:47–50): it is an essential quality of the world.

This being so, what sociologists of culture would term 'lay actors' (Giddens 1979:71) cannot magically stand outside of culture as ordering. There is no natural self capable of being contrasted to culture's operations, and there are seemingly no non-cultural phenomena. This all sounds strikingly like the assumptions of structuralism. However, resistance to this imperfect system can emerge through the frictions between different 'technologies of the self' (Foucault 1986; Kendall and Wickham 2001:150–1) and between different orderings. Since one of the ways that culture operates is via internalized practices and routines, the self can carry one institution's technology of self into another's very different ordering. How, for example, might we interpret a student who regularly attended classes dressed as if they were ready for a night out? The 'care of the self' routinized in clubbing and socializing is clearly not the same care of the self and the same, internalized sense of correct practice as would be expected in a university seminar. Presumably such a student might be interpreted as not taking their studies seriously.

A more common type of counter-ordering occurs in the university when students criticize lecturers for 'reading too much into it' when analysing films or TV programmes. Here, a student would be displaying resistance to an academic ordering, but not by referring to some natural truth set against scholarly Theory. Rather, such student comments invoke the technology of the self that characterizes media consumption as a leisure activity. They oppose the labour of academic interpretation with the different ordering of media texts as something non-serious, entertaining and fun which one is *not* supposed to analytically pore over: 'leisure time has strong . . . connotations: freedom *from* work; freedom *to be* one's self; freedom *to do* as one pleases' (Meehan 2000:75). These paradoxically ordered freedoms can also be counter-ordered in other ways, such as in fan responses (Jenkins 1992; Hills 2002; Sandvoss 2005). Fans take particular media very seriously indeed, often within a new type of consumer 'labour' (Meehan 2000), but they don't often academically theorise their favoured media texts (Hills 2002:19). In the media and cultural studies seminar room, fandom can sustain a further counter-ordering or type of resistance to 'a passive learning place . . . in which you absorb information and knowledge from the lecturer, the overheads, the screen' (O'Shaughnessy 1999:166). Students may challenge the legitimacy of academic Theory on the basis of already feeling that, as fans, they possess expertise about the media. Such counter-ordering has its limits. The student who says that 'you're reading too much into it' will most likely receive a very poor grade if they do not develop and internalize the technology of the self presupposed by academic practices of writing and expression, while the dedicated fan is also likely to find that their form of expertise may be devalued in favour of scholarly Theory in the seminar room.

Treating culture as ordering has a number of benefits: it allows us to think of culture not as a unitary, romanticized whole way of life, nor as the expression of one form of power, nor as something limited to what we usually label 'culture'. It also emphasizes culture's institutional qualities, tending to link culture to forms of spatial arrangement and routines of self-identity. On the minus side, culture as ordering appears to leave no meaningful concept of the 'non-cultural' intact (despite the efforts of Kendall and Wickham 2001:37–9), particularly as it fully absorbs the social into the cultural. It shares this type of problem with the cultural theory which it supposedly surpasses – structuralism.

Since structuralism and post-structuralism define culture as structures of meaning or as spaces or patterns of ordering, we can suggest that culture is all too frequently dematerialized in these approaches. Being addressed as meaning and ordering, culture tends to be idealized – that is, viewed in an 'idealist' philosophical framework as systems of ideas about the world – rather than being considered as forms of matter in the world via a 'materialist' philosophy. Although it has not often been commented upon in cultural theory/studies, and hence lacks the canonical status of the work of culturalists, structuralists and (post-)structuralists, Eugene Halton has put forward a rather more materialist definition of culture. Halton continues the (post-)structuralist emphasis on meaning but takes considerations of culture elsewhere:

> Current conceptions of culture and meaning tend towards extreme forms of . . . disembodiment, indicating an alienation from the original, earthy meaning of the word *culture*. I will . . . turn to the earlier meanings of the word and [suggest] why the 'cultic', the living impulse to meaning, was and remains essential . . . Putting the 'cult' back in culture requires a reconception of the relations between human biology and meaning (1992:30–1).

The original meaning of culture that Halton refers to is that of agriculture and thus of tending to crops and livestock (see Williams 1983:87; Kendall and Wickham 2001:6). Halton claims that a wide range of different theories of culture have reduced and narrowed culture to an issue of system/code/meaning, in what amounts to a profoundly 'etherealizing' gesture (1992:31–2). Cultural theory, at least in structuralist and some (post-)structuralist guises, has thereby lost touch with the ground and the emotionality of culture (Real 2001:176). Halton proposes that culture should instead be analysed as '*cultus*, the impulse to meaning' (1992:31). On his account, culture cannot be wholly reduced to any system of conventions, meanings or codes which precede it, being 'a spontaneous, meaning-generating gesture or sign' (1992:41). He goes on to say that the cultic roots of culture are the springing forth of the impulse to meaning which involves the deepest emotional, preconscious and even instinctive capacities of the human body for meaning-making (1992:50).

This restores a type of special quality to culture, since Halton is discussing culture in the sense of works of art, and rescuing these from what he perceives as an attack on their autonomy, creativity and expressiveness. But by returning to culture as special, albeit rooted in experience and expression, Halton is not merely taking us back to an elitist view of culture. He is in fact championing the notion of culture as an embodied interruption to system and code, and as something 'vital, extrarational, incarnate' (1992:41). While sharing the question of meaning with structuralists and (post-)structuralists, Halton distinctively views culture as a series of living acts, not as an 'abstract, depersonalized system' (1992:41). Rather than having no place for agency in culture, he seemingly has no place for culture-as-structure. Halton converts culture into a highly romanticized moment of novelty, a step outside of structure that is then caught up in structures of meaning. Culture spills out of people and their embodied relations to the world, is incarnated and affects that world.

Halton's essay is not a lone voice in contemporary cultural theory. Other writers including Gregory Seigworth have pondered the possibility of a reinvigorated return to Raymond Williams's work after cultural studies' long and winding two-decade structuralist and (post-) structuralist detour and a return to how Williams attended to change, culture-in-process and concept-creation (Seigworth 2000:264n30). However, Seigworth's call to sidestep (post-)structuralist debates on culture is itself significantly indebted to the work of philosopher Gilles Deleuze and psychoanalyst Félix Guattari (see Seigworth and Wise 2000). Like Halton's intervention, an emerging body of work using Deleuze and Guattari in cultural theory/studies has redefined culture as a type of 'impulse to meaning', this impulse being expressive, incarnated and forceful, and not inevitably contained by prior structures or systems.

Deleuze and Guattari surface in cultural theory/studies in commentaries by Ian Buchanan (1999 and 2000b), Lawrence Grossberg (1992a, 1992b, 1997a and 1997b), Brian Massumi (1996 and 2002) and Meaghan Morris (1998a). Exploring the same culture-defining problems as Halton, Buchanan contrasts what he terms 'Deleuzism' to philosophies which emphasize culture-as-system:

> Habit is the supreme paradox cultural studies must confront. The paradox of habit . . . is that it is formed by degrees (therefore it is constituted not constitutive), and, at the same time, it is . . . constitutive . . . An important axiom follows from it, namely that *the subject invents the very norms and general rules it lives by*. Despite appearances, habit is not . . . an acquired system . . . The . . . subject, in contrast . . . is as much a product of self-invention, as it is the consequence of . . . conformity to existing structures. In the

given, the subject is without agency . . . To gain agency, the subject must transcend the given (2000b:86, my italics; see also Osborne 2000:50–1).

The role assigned to Deleuze and Guattari by their commentators in cultural theory/studies has not only been one of challenging post-structuralism and emphases on structures of symbols or codes. 'Deleuzism' has also been embraced for its ability to place affect on the agenda of cultural theory. By affect is meant

> what we often define as the feeling of life. You can understand another person's life: you can share the same meanings and pleasures, but you cannot know how it feels. . . . [D]ifferent affective relations inflect meanings and pleasures in different ways. . . . [A]ffect defines the strength of our investment in particular experiences, practices, identities, meanings and pleasures. In other words, affect privileges volition over meaning (Grossberg 1992b:56–7).

Both Buchanan and Grossberg use Deleuzian thought to emphasize how 'mattering maps' (Grossberg 1992b:57) create differences that matter, whether these are fans' love for *this* band ('fansons' who love the band Hanson, or 'deadheads' who follow the Grateful Dead), or academics' love for *this* theory ('Deleuzians'). Affect leaves open the possibility of performatively creating newly emergent distinctions and differences in the world. It does not merely respect, or conform to, already coded binary oppositions and structures, and it is not about signification or meaning in typically (post-)structuralist ways. Affect is cultic in Halton's sense: it is a powerful impulse to meaning. Yet this is an impulse to make something meaningful not in the sense that it can be interpreted as a sign saying x, y or z, but rather in the sense that it becomes something meaningful to the self as an embodied, felt locus of value. In this account, culture is defined as what matters to us: who we make into our loved ones, and what we make into our loved things. But affect is not a synonym for subjective emotion: 'emotion and affect . . . follow different logics and pertain to different orders' (Massumi 1996:221; see also Kennedy 2000:101 and Grossberg 1992a:82). Where emotion is owned by and belongs to the subject as a 'socio-linguistic fixing' (Massumi 1996:221), affect exists at least partly beyond the subject's capacity to verbally articulate and narrate it. It is hence 'irreducibly bodily . . . [and could] be called "passion", to distinguish it both from passivity and activity' (Massumi 1996:222; see also Williams 2001:88).

If affect has its own value for cultural theory (Shukin 2000:155), it lies partly in attempts to oppose structure-focused accounts in the name of more agency-focused approaches (Grossberg 1992a:126–7). And yet Deleuze and Guattari's work is, to be sure, never directed at defining 'culture'. To take it as the philosophical basis for a new paradigm in cultural theory/studies may, indeed, prove to be 'singularly inappropriate' (Osborne 2000:52), especially given that a restricted view of specific cultural artefacts as special underpins Deleuze's writings on 'high culture' (that which supposedly deserves the label of 'art') versus 'popular culture' (supposedly degraded and mass-produced commodities that are mere entertainments). Deleuze champions cultural producers such as playwright Samuel Beckett, while attacking pop videos. He accords aesthetic value to film but not to other popular media, 'despite the fact that film really has no special claim to . . . artistic separation from the capitalist machine' (see Buchanan 2000b:177). The conceptual productivity of Deleuze's philosophy is thus, it would seem, traversed by those very forms of elitism that Raymond Williams set out to challenge via something that became cultural studies. Deleuzism's interests in experience, affect and the body, its attacks on structuralism (Goodchild 1996:112–4), and its investment in 'cultus' as an impulse to meaning may all seem to potentially ally it with recent re-imaginings of cultural studies. But any such alliance should perhaps take care not to return to the notion that culture is special and thereby install an elitist aesthetics under the guise of opposing other theories and other problematic definitional assumptions.

So far in this chapter I have, necessarily schematically, worked through key definitions of culture, definitions which have launched and sustained the enterprises of cultural theory/studies and which have developed through different schools of thought in cultural theory. Despite the notable differences between these definitions, a number of common problems and issues emerge:

- Where exactly are the limits to culture? Can culture be restricted to special processes of creativity and production, or should it be thought to include processes moving beyond this?

- What possibilities for agency does culture leave open or restrict? (Differing definitions have stressed culture's structuring and ordering powers, or have reacted against these limitations by addressing 'self-fashioning' and the creative impulse to meaning.)

- Can culture be restricted to processes of meaning-making, or should it be thought to include practices moving beyond this?

One way to circumvent the limits to singular definitions of culture (culturalist/structuralist/ (post-)structuralist/Deleuzian) may be to supplement the aspects of any one definition, thereby constructing culture as a kind of *portmanteau*, composite term. This approach is taken by Jeff Lewis, who incrementally adds to the definition of culture he works with. Lewis's concluding outline of culture thus reads:

> Culture is an assemblage of imaginings and meanings [a structuralist argument – MH] that may be consonant, disjunctive, overlapping, contentious, continuous or discontinuous [a broadly (post-)structuralist point – MH]. These assemblages may operate through a wide variety of human social groupings and social practices [a broadly culturalist argument – MH]. *In contemporary culture these experiences of imagining and meaning-making are intensified through the proliferation of mass media images and information* (Lewis 2002:15, my italics).

Not being drawn from a given strand of theoretically informed definitions of culture, the last component added to Lewis's definition is instead one of social and historical context. Contemporary culture is said to draw on general processes of culture that are true for all time, but to draw on these universal or trans-historical processes in a distinctive and highly mediated way. In short, culture in the 'first world' in the twenty-first century both is and isn't the same thing as culture in the eighteenth, nineteenth or even twentieth centuries. I want to follow this element of Lewis's definition here. But in this chapter's closing section, I also want to amend the fact that in his textbook collation of culture as meanings, social groupings and mass-mediated information, Lewis notably leaves out a term that has persisted across different scholarly definitions of culture: the text.

Textualizing culture

Much of cultural theory/studies has been preoccupied with 'texts', indeed the use of this term may be one of the most recognizable contemporary markers that someone is producing cultural theory. Despite the omnipresence of the term, precious little work has been undertaken on the question of 'what is a text anyway?' (Johnson 1996:96). Although Richard Johnson poses this question, he doesn't go on to directly answer it. Others, such as John Mowitt in the book *Text* argues that a textual paradigm (1992:141) has moved out of literary theory (in the (post-)structuralist work of Roland Barthes, Jacques Derrida and Julia Kristeva) and into media and cultural studies (see Hartley 1999). But again, Mowitt never conclusively delimits the text. Texts appear to be everywhere in cultural theory and its analyses of culture, but their limits and existences are not always clearly defined. The text is a taken-for-granted concept in cultural theory/studies, so much so that its very conceptuality and non-self-evidence seems on occasion to be forgotten.

When it is defined, usually in undergraduate 'primers' in cultural theory/studies, a text is said to be 'a combination of signs' (Thwaites, Davis and Mules 2002:77) or 'any form of signification' (Lehtonen 2000:48). This enables us to see why texts have been central to work on culture: the two terms appear to dissolve into each other, especially in (post-)structuralist accounts where texts are meanings are culture. An equation underpinning the majority of work in cultural theory is thus that culture, no matter what its precise definition, is textual in the broadest sense. Whole ways of life are sedimented in texts; cultural structurings or orderings operate in and through texts; culture is cultic through the production of new texts, and affect is expressed through and in relation to texts.

In place of an overly narrow culture and a narrowed set of valued or canonical texts, we thus have a textualized universe of meaning in which speech, adverts, films, TV shows, books, clothes, written sentences, shopping lists, all sorts of consumer goods and commodities and technologies can all be thought of as texts and hence as culture. This all-consuming inclusivity has caused some critics to bemoan the tendency to focus on the text as something that is perfectly suited to contemporary academic life. '[It has] privileged [academics'] activity and legitimized unsubstantiated speculation' (Philo and Miller 2001:48). So-called 'textualists' and the 'textualization of cultural studies' (Morley 1997:123) have been criticized for their failure to focus on real social and cultural inequalities. Cultural theory/studies has recurrently challenged over-narrow definitions (culture is special art and literature) through over-broad notions of culture as ordinary or culture as meaning. These are also over-narrow and over-broad concepts of the text, viewing the term either as something that should be limited to great works of art and literature, or as something indicating any combination of signs. And what these approaches share is that both treat texts as self-evidently found 'units' of either aesthetic brilliance or ordinary meaning, depending on the view adopted.

Artworks are in part defined as texts by their assumed boundedness, being literally framed, or placed in sacred gallery spaces. Art is hence symbolically separated from the ordinary and the mundane, being elevated into a special 'textual' and isolatable status. And moving from the elite to the ordinary, popular TV programmes are either assumed to be already bounded texts via their appearance in schedules, or the question of where their boundaries might lie is suspended in academic study, as researchers focus only on specific TV programmes rather than simultaneously including the study of the adverts in a show's commercial breaks (these being thought of as separate and similarly bounded texts). Likewise, film scholars will tend to focus on groups of specific films rather than simultaneously analysing the trailers selected to precede these films, or the adverts on a videotape. DVD extras might at a pinch be admitted to the study of properly textual materials, but these hover in an indeterminate zone of 'extra-textuality', being associated with a bounded film text but still uneasily existing alongside it. And academics focusing on particular works of literature, novels, plays and theatre performances, again tend to treat these all as pre-bounded texts and/or pre-bounded 'combinations of signs'. Even in relation to Internet culture, researchers tend to pick over and treat online postings as securely bounded units of meaning.

Cultural theory/studies appears to all too often respect specific demarcations of the text, where industry-given and institutionally or communally-constituted constructions of bounded and discrete texts (within art worlds) are typically replayed, and where attempts at studying how boundaries between texts might be eroded nevertheless rely on notions of inter-textuality that construct sets of bounded and discrete or identifiable texts which can then be said to interact. However, instead of treating the text as the unit of culturalist, structuralist, (post-)structuralist or Deleuzian analysis, we could pursue very different research tactics:

> If people in actuality screen out the vast majority of images and texts around them, there will be a great difference between the total textual environment (the field of possible textual interactions for anyone) and the segments of that field with which particular individuals actually intersect. One person's 'textual world' will only partially intersect with another's. Surely, therefore, we should know more about what individuals' 'textual fields' are like – how do people select from the myriad texts around them, what common patterns are there in what they select? Yet this is an area where cultural studies has done little research (Couldry 2000:73).

This absence in cultural theory is hardly accidental; it has occurred as a result of the way that cultural studies/theory has treated texts as naturally bounded and discrete objects of study, tracking audience 'readings' of specific films, TV shows and books, or providing scholarly, (post-)structuralist readings of the same things. Fortunately, the 'apparent obviousness of treating the book, or play, or poem as the basic unit of analysis' has recently been challenged (Couldry 2000:70), given that 'the media are firmly anchored in the web of culture' (Bird 2003:3). Audiences are 'diffused' into everyday life (Abercrombie and Longhurst 1998:68–9); they are 'everywhere and nowhere' (Bird 2003:3). And under these contemporary conditions of media culture it has therefore arguably become impossible to clearly isolate out what the meaning of a single, specific, bounded text would be.

And yet we – cultural theorists as much as non-academics – still talk about watching our favourite soap or TV drama, or going to see a film. Readers still 'come to recognise that they are, in fact, engaging some particular text over which they may quarrel' (Mowitt 1992:18). A quick glance at the Internet movie database (www.imdb.com), or at any one of the Internet's countless film- and TV-based newsgroups, confirms that many, many people frequently engage in such quarrels. The continued prevalence, if not dominance, of this taken-for-granted idea of the text – both inside and outside the academy, and inside and outside cultural theory – has led to a lack of focus on how cultural theory, and other forms of knowledge-production, 'textualise' the world (Hartley 2003:138). That is, isolating texts requires a form of 'symbolic work' (Willis 2000:69). This work may be partly done for us by media and culture industries needing to get a return on their products, and so aiding us to distinguish between texts to render them distinctive in the marketplace. But such symbolic work is carried out by producers and consumers at all levels and scales of textual productivity. To produce and consume a text on this account is not simply to encounter a self-evident thing, though the processes of textual boundary-marking are highly naturalized in contemporary culture. It is precisely to enter into a process of textualization. Through this process a mediated and symbolically bounded entity is rendered recognisably discrete. Opportunities for textualization have, it should be noted, vastly increased through the rise of new media technologies within contemporary culture (Marshall 2004). This implies that culture is not automatically made up of bounded, unitary texts which are necessarily special or ordinary: rather, it is created through how producers and consumers do different things with texts, including breaking the world into certain textual, symbolic bits in the first instance:

> The new individual agent uses not only the telephone, radio, movies, and television, but also computers, faxes, copiers, stereos, portable music players, VCRs [DVDs, mobile camera-phones] . . . and the Internet. . . . As a result individuals are now constituted as subjects in relation to these complex information systems: they are points in circuits of language-image flows: they are, in short, textualized agents (Poster 1998:204).

Mark Poster suggests that this empirical, new-media-technological shift casts us out of debates in which texts as bounded things are pitted against agents (1998:201), and where (post-) structural theories argue in favour of the power of the text, whilst culturalism errs on the side of agents and their experiences. Literary theorist J. Hillis Miller similarly testifies to this change, posing the question 'Why did the massive shift to cultural studies from language-based theory begin to occur when it did . . . around 1980?'. His answer is that

> One crucial force . . . was the growing impact of new communication technologies . . . The younger scholars who have turned to . . . cultural studies are the first generation of university teachers and critics who were brought up with television and with new forms of commercialized popular music. . . . The critics of this new generation have been to a considerable degree formed by a new visual and aural 'culture' (but it is culture in a somewhat new sense of the word) (Miller 1998:60).

In this 'electronic age' (Miller 1998:60), 'technologized culture' (Mackay 1995; Giles and Middleton 1999:248) and the 'media world' (Bird 2003) confront the contemporary theorist of culture. Yet, rather than viewing culture as dissolved into either special or ordinary texts, we can account for this 'new sense' of qualitatively different 'media as culture' (Bird 2003:1–3) by limiting our definition of culture to that which people do with texts, including recognizing certain bounded units, but perhaps not others, as 'texts'. This has a number of consequences for the definitions of culture set out across this chapter:

- When viewed as textualized agency, culture is necessarily both special and ordinary. It is special partly by virtue of mass- and niche-mediation, which confers an elevated status on distributed products (Couldry 2003: 1–2), and it is special via its reliance on processes of textualization, working to construct more or less sealed and symbolic boundaries around texts. Such culture is simultaneously ordinary in terms of confronting the contemporary 'first world' subject as a set of textualized resources through which identity and sociality can be articulated (see King (2004:193–4) on modular texts). Although I am drawing on aspects of culturalism here, I am not thereby indicating that culture is in any way whole.

- Although culture defined as 'textualized agency' can be analysed as a system of meanings, it is not everything that signifies, since not all meanings are caught up in processes of textualization for all agents. In other words, the ascribing of a special status to texts which are bracketed off from everyday life as art is itself an act of textual agency, as is the structuralist's notion that T-shirts, crisp packets or clothes can be treated as symbolically bounded texts. Neither is the correct approach to culture, for each is a different way of performatively doing something with texts, and of recognizing certain materials as fully textual (and/or aesthetic). Textualized agency therefore uses elements of structuralism, while rejecting the structuralist emphasis on pan-textualism (everything is automatically a text, has a meaning and is part of culture). It offers in fact a kind of meta-definition, since it not only draws on a range of previous definitions of culture, but also enables the analyst to consider these prior definitions as forms of textualized agency themselves, as performative culture-in-action rather than as mere accounts or descriptions of culture.

- Culture remains analysable as a matter of institutional orderings, but in my meta-definition these orderings become significant primarily insofar as they intersect with processes of textualization. That is, institutional practices can operate culturally by doing things with texts – setting limits to the types of texts that are ascribed value or legitimacy, nominating or recognising specific textual boundaries but not others, and working on texts in distinctive ways (classifying, reading or interpreting). In this manner, the definition outlined here is also indebted to (post-)structuralist, Foucauldian work on culture as a type of governance. However, unlike the Foucauldian approach, this definition is not tied to spatial dimensions. Rather, textualized agency is inevitably 'multi-sited' (Marcus 1998:79; Willis 2000:110) given the reach, extensibility or disembeddedness of texts.

- Culture remains necessarily and partly cultic in this account of culture as textualized agency, for the very reason that one of the things that can be done with texts in contemporary media culture is the new creation of individualized and/or communal significance. Textualized agents make certain texts matter in a way that allows new, text-derived social groupings to emerge. Media fandom is a leading example of this cultic version of culture, being a specific, pronounced form of textualized agency (see Hills 2005). However, unlike approaches to culture drawing on Deleuzian trajectories, subjective emotion is not entirely displaced from any such account, nor does it stress a celebratory sense of self-fashioning, given that textualized agency remains action performed in relation to, and via, texts – with all the situated limits this may carry.

One outcome of starting to think about culture as textualized agency is that cultural theory can no longer be analysed simply as a set of pronouncements reflecting on what culture is. To assume that theories of culture work in this way is to treat them as set apart from culture itself, existing as pure ideas that do or don't manage to capture the realities of culture. In this chapter I have partly reproduced such assumptions about cultural theory, conveniently carving theories into different schools of thought. But if, as Ioan Davies notes, 'the thrust of any cultural theorizing is partly based on an engagement with the communications institutions within which we all have to work . . . [such as] journalism, television, drama, radio and language' (1995:17) then cultural theorists perform symbolic work within these engagements just as much as all other contemporary cultural groups. Cultural theorists are themselves textualized agents: they are absolutely a part of contemporary culture. They too work on specific texts in specific ways (Smith 2000:110), being consumers and producers of cultural theory's texts (see Part Two). With this in mind, in the next chapter, I will consider what theory is. So far I have treated it as a conceptual window on culture which can give us a better or worse view of the 'thing itself'. As something assumed to bring culture into focus, visually based metaphors for theory involve cultural theory disappearing into perfect transparency as it discloses what culture is. The mediatedness of theory is denied here. In Chapter Two I will therefore question what is meant by theory. Rather than merely considering what counts as culture, leaving the theory of cultural theory in place as a silent, taken-for-granted vehicle for this debate, I want to address what theory has to do to merit the term.

Evaluating: What is Theory?

On the face of it, 'What is theory?' is a simple question to answer. Cultural theory is self-evidently any theory of culture. It does what it says it does. Hence cultural theory is a body of work that exists objectively and can be listed chronologically (Lewis 2002), assessed for its historical turns (Tudor 1999), and canonised by repetition in textbooks (Katz *et al* 2003). Unfortunately, such a circular response – cultural theory theorises culture – fails to address a major difficulty, namely what qualifies as theory in the first place. In this chapter, I want to evaluate the parameters of cultural theory. I shall consider how academic 'Theory' is variously legitimated and attacked, as well as addressing what attributes it is thought to possess. Culture may be a complex, awkward word requiring careful definition, but ' "Theory" . . . is perhaps as difficult to define' (Smith 2001:4). In the following section I will consider how cultural theory is defined against types of non-academic theory circulating outside the university.

Legitimating and authorizing: Theory's Others outside the academy

The term 'theory' actually crops up a fair bit in our daily lives and in media coverage, although of late it has frequently appeared in a specific guise, being caught within the phrase 'conspiracy theory'. Conspiracy theories reverberate through the media, surrounding events such as the death of Princess Diana, the 9/11 attacks, the Iraq War, and even in tales of extraterrestrial activities and government cover-ups (Badmington 2004). Many of the major events of our time are saturated by encircling conspiracy theories:

> It seems that conspiracy theories are everywhere. From *JFK* to *The X-Files*, from the Oklahama bombing to TWA flight 800 . . . the language of conspiracy has become a familiar feature of the political . . . landscape in the last couple of decades (Knight 2000:1).

And yet it is not merely the language of conspiracy which has proliferated here, it is also the language of theory. However, this is depicted as a 'bad' version of theory, and a monstrous form of theorizing, for as Peter Knight observes: 'The term "conspiracy theory" often acts as an insult itself, an accusation of woolly-headed thinking that verges on the mentally disturbed' (2000:11). 'Theory', then, becomes a predominantly negative term when coupled with 'conspiracy', shown as failing to measure up against 'a gold standard of rationality' (2000:111). Conspiracy theory is dismissed or used as a 'discrediting label' (Birchall 1999:140) and 'serves as a strategy of delegitimation in political discourse' (Fenster 1999:xii).

Conspiracy theory is 'Other' to what is counter-posed as more legitimate theorizing, acting as proper theory's corrupt, evil twin. Bad conspiracy theory supposedly misses its mark by seeking to connect everything, by scape-goating specific groups, and by producing an underlying narrative explanation for contingent historical events. Conspiracy theory assumes in a paranoid manner that it has the answer, thereby enacting a moral separation of shadowy insiders who are in-the-know, and duped outsiders who continue to swallow disinformation. By articulating the language of theory with such accusations and ridicule, conspiracy theory threatens to underpin a negative, populist attitude to theory more generally, represented as a paranoid way of thinking, impenetrably focused on its own 'in-group' concerns, and obsessed with its own truth, beyond all evidence.

Now, it would be pleasantly self-legitimating for an academic writing about cultural theory if all the negative connotations attached to the theory of conspiracy theory could be demonstrated to be definitively false in relation to that other theory of cultural theory. And although many cultural theorists would happily and immediately endorse such an argument, it is somewhat problematic. For, as Clare Birchall has argued, conspiracy theory is a specific discourse, a particular way of ordering meaning in the world, and as such it shares qualities with other types of theory:

> Academic discourses perhaps revile conspiracy theories because these conjectures make explicit an implicit structuring element of traditional interpretation. . . . [C]onspiracy theories exacerbate a general condition of reading: any reading will leave a remainder that can be interpreted by a different methodology. We can also observe a continuity between the task of conspiracy theory and the critique of ideology [in cultural theory]: both aim to 'to discern the hidden necessity in what appears as a mere contingency' (Birchall 1999:139, citing Slavoj Zizek).

Conspiracy theory's apparent unendingness, its sense of there always being 'one more clue to chase . . . one more connection to make' (Knight 2000:1), highlights a shared difficulty for proper, good theory. Legitimate theory, here taken to be synonymous with academic theory, similarly cannot have the last word. On this account, all theory attempts to map the world and make it make sense, to 'discern the hidden'. Marxist-indebted versions of cultural theory share conspiracy theory's focus on translating surfaces into a master narrative of hidden meanings, seeking to unmask the operation of social ideas as ideologies which benefit society's ruling class (see, for example, the 'critical theory' of Adorno 1991; Jarvis 1998; Jay 1973).

What bad conspiracy theory and good cultural theory therefore seem to share is a certain power of translation: both do something to everyday thought, received wisdom or dominant explanations of the world and its events. Both produce different, novel ways of viewing the world. Although they may claim to access hidden truths, these are produced through interpretations or readings, and cannot ever fully capture the world being so interpreted. This suggests that theory, by definition – and whether good or bad – is a construction of meaning that tends to be opposed to reality as its very own generalized Other. Conspiracy theory supposedly runs away into flights of fancy by making every little detail of reality part of a secret master plan, while good theory also necessarily fails to master reality, since the real world always exceeds any one theoretical framing. However, recall that we are still dealing with notions of good versus bad theory here, despite certain similarities which indicate a tendency for all forms of theory to be conservatively devalued in opposition to a reality requiring no further explanation (Branston 2000:18).

This good/bad 'moral dualism' (Hills 2002:8–9) of theory means that we need to carefully consider differences and similarities between popular representations of conspiracy theory and theory in its academic incarnations. One major difference between the two has very little to do with the structure of the theorizing involved, or with its carving of the world into insiders and outsiders via the use of specialist knowledge. Instead, we can distinguish between what is labelled 'conspiracy theory' and what's called 'cultural theory' by considering who is authorized to produce them. When Clare Birchall refers to 'academic discourses' as reviling conspiracy theories, she is explicitly contrasting theory produced by professional academics to theory produced by non-academics. These groups and discourses can overlap, however. For example, non-professional-academics may use academic work to attempt to support their conspiracy theories. One of the ways that we can begin to move towards a definition of cultural theory is to observe that it is a type of theory produced by a specific social group legitimated via their possession of educational and institutional credentials (Bordwell 1989). Indeed, what is now generally referred to as 'cultural theory', or simply 'Theory' with a capital T, has been described as the product of a specific generation of scholars, who worked to promote those French schools of thought termed 'structuralism' and 'post-structuralism' within anglophone university humanities departments in the 1960s and 1970s. Theory is thus frequently narrated as something generationally distinctive:

> There are those 'Young Turks' whose work introduced modern French thought to the English-speaking world and whose commitment and courage . . . helped to establish the Anglophone discipline of Theory . . . They are joined by a generation of thinkers who have . . . consolidated Theory's position within the academy and . . . there is a generation of academics who have grown up with Theory and who cannot remember a time when they did not have it (McQuillan *et al* 1999:xvi).

'Theory' has been identified as 'a classy continental number, centrally composed of elements of Louis Althusser, Jacques Lacan and Roland Barthes, often with optional features derived . . . from Michel Foucault, Julia Kristeva, Pierre Bourdieu, Gilles Deleuze, and . . . Jacques Derrida' (Bordwell 1996:37). 'Post-Theory', in relation to this generational account, does not simply mean overcoming or correcting Theory (though this sense occurs in Bordwell and Carroll 1996). It also names the situation of scholars arriving in the profession after the moment of Theory's 1970s emergence:

> The golden age of cultural theory is long past. The pioneering works of Jacques Lacan, Claude Levi-Strauss, Louis Althusser, Roland Barthes and Michel

Foucault are several decades behind us. So too are the path-breaking early writings of Raymond Williams, Luce Irigaray, Pierre Bourdieu, Julia Kristeva, Jacques Derrida . . . Not much that has been written since has matched the ambitiousness and originality of these founding mothers and fathers (Eagleton 2003:1).

Akin to accounts of Theory given by McQuillan *et al* (1999:xvi) and Jeffrey Williams (2000), Terry Eagleton argues that 'we are living now in the aftermath of what one might call high theory' (2003:2). Eagleton also makes this a matter of generational change in academia: 'the generation which came after these path-breaking figures . . . came up with no comparable body of ideas of its own' (2003:2). Instead, in Eagleton's recounted history, this second generation set about applying, critiquing and reiterating the insights of structuralism (represented by the primary work of Levi-Strauss, Ferdinand de Saussure and Roland Barthes) and post-structuralism (represented again by Barthes, along with psychoanalyst Jacques Lacan and philosopher Jacques Derrida). As Peter C. Herman puts it: 'everyone in the next generation received the various approaches . . . signified by the short-hand term *Theory*, second- if not third-hand. Theory is . . . not something . . . we discovered for ourselves at its originary moment' (2000:1).

But the generationality of Theory with a capital T cannot be reduced to a strictly chronological definition of generation, as Herman (2000:1) has pointed out. Instead, the notion of a distinctively 'post-theory generation' is better thought of as institutional (Williams 2000:25). That is, rather than being defined by individual age, it relates to a group of scholars just out of graduate school in the late 1990s (Herman 2000:1), their academic identities formed by confronting a specific field, just as the Theory generation of the 1960s and 70s confronted their specific time and social context (Williams 2000:27). This scenario calls to mind the work of June Edmunds and Bryan Turner on generations, since they

conceptualize generations as alternating between active and passive . . . Thus an active generation that transforms social and cultural life tends to be followed by a passive one that simply inherits the changes wrought by its more successful predecessor (2002:117).

However, Theory cannot be addressed merely as an objectively existent and generational body of work, for it is also work created by those who are, or were, authorized to create it, thus standing in opposition to amateur, non-credentialed theorizing which can be dismissed or attacked as paranoid, irrational, just a bit loopy, or at best in need of refinement and systematic expression. Amateur theory has tended to be defined against expert Theory as 'lay knowledgeability' (Tulloch 1999:32–3) or 'lay theory' in sociology, or even as 'commonsense theory' (McQuail 1987:5) in media studies. Such invocations of the laity imply that academia may occupy a version of the elitist role once occupied by the priesthood, working to read cultural objects and their implications rather than reading God's Word for the faithful (Branston 2000:20; Hartley 2004:132).

Viewed in its material and social context, cultural theory or Theory is work produced by a specialized, professionalized group of experts. A professional distance is taken from other interests, while internal professional debates or power struggles are entered into. In an essay entitled 'Tales of expertise and experience: sociological reasoning and popular representation', Graham Murdock recounts how his professional sense of identity as a theorist was challenged by the alternatively professionalized world view of journalists:

> Contests between conflicting criteria of professional judgement [academics versus journalists – MH] are fought out on the battlegrounds of linguistic and visual signification . . . so many key words – class, culture, community – are in common usage and have to be carefully qualified and defined before they can be used with any degree of precision . . . Some specialist terms are certainly clumsy and inelegant and should be buried, but others are indispensable to clear expression (Murdock 1994:110).

When cultural theorists attempt to engage with the media what they encounter is 'a collision of professional cultures, each with its own procedures and preferred forms of representation and argument' (1994:122). Journalists may request plain speaking and jargon-free discussion, restricting the professional theorist's ability to clarify and define their terms.

'Theory' that merits the label, as opposed to degraded and crank 'conspiracy theory' or degraded and non-expert 'lay theory' is thus the privilege of a professional caste of cultural producers, or a 'Theory club' (Sconce 2003:186). This state of affairs is not an essential one: there is no necessary reason why Theory should be produced by a specialized group of professionals within a division of labour. It is rather an historical outcome strongly linked to twentieth-century modernist notions of the intellectual as a detached, heroic figure critiquing and purifying ordinary thought (Robbins 1993). Theory is professionalized through a social, historical process which divorces the theorist from a wider public and installs him or her as part of an elite, professionalized group.

This professionalization of academia is bemoaned by writers who see the career academic as a betrayal of the role of free-floating intellectual – an idealized figure able to offer entirely unfettered criticism of their society (Jacoby 1987 and 1989). In contrast, professionalized Theory is supposedly partly degraded by virtue of possessing its own social context:

> To conceive of intellectuals as professionals is to put critical thought in social context. To put thought in social context is to accuse it of self-interest . . . But self-interested thought, from the point of view of the ideal . . . is certainly not critical or radical or adversarial thought. This is the fatal logic of the intellectuals' disappearance: the more intellectuals are grounded in society, the less they are seen as truly critical or oppositional, hence the less they are themselves (Robbins 1993:12).

Being placed within an institutional frame, cultural theory becomes visible as a type of thought with its own history and manner of expression as well as its own range of non-academic Others. This constructed distance from multiple Others works to secure and legitimate the professional distinction of the scholar, who thus wins status within the bounded fields of the university and its different disciplines (Bourdieu 1988:40).

The emergence of something generalisable as Theory with a capital T (see also Rabaté 2002:3; Cunningham 2002:14–5) can be viewed as an attempt to secure the professional status of theorists of culture (Michael 2000:3). As Graham Murdock notes, the term 'culture' has some general currency, and hence professional theorists of culture require an armoury of theoretical terms, concepts and self-identities through which they can differentiate their work from, say, journalists evaluating the culture of art and literature as well as popular fiction, film and TV. Bruce Robbins views the new Theory of the 1960s and 70s as 'a renegotiation of the profession's legitimation. New terms like "ideology" . . . "narrative" and "discourse" . . . redefined the professional object. They promised . . . an alternative expertise, an alternative grounding' (1993:81). This was an alternative to previous legitimating claims based on a scholarly ability to police what should be counted as the finest objects of culture, but it also offered an alternative to Othered bids for knowledge of culture from non-academic evaluators and self-appointed, amateur experts – cinephiles and TV fans. John Frow has gone so far as to characterise theorists as one 'local fraction' (1995:131) of a more general 'knowledge class' that is formed

> around the professional claim to, and the professional mystique of, autonomy of judgement . . . [It] acquires legitimacy through the acquisition of credentials, and at the same time achieves a measure of class closure by integrating the community of those with appropriate credentials and excluding those without (1995:125–6).

However, this closure can only ever be provisional. Its exclusionary gesture, whereby journalists, fan-consumers, and even media producers are not fully accorded the honoured status of Theorists (see McKee 2002a; Hills 2002 and 2005) is open to persistent border skirmishes. As Pierre Bourdieu (1988:3) has noted, 'those who frequent the borderland between academic and ordinary knowledge – essayists, journalists, academic journalists and journalistic academics – have a vital stake in blurring the frontier' between these knowledges. Any such border is thus, in actuality, 'far from watertight' (Branston 2000:25). For example, some journalists may begin to draw on the languages of cultural theory by way of distinguishing themselves from their more clearly anti-academic colleagues.

Boundaries between legitimated, authorized Theory and lay theory are also arguably becoming increasingly permeable due to new media technologies such as the Internet. In a discussion of theoretical work on culture that now exists online, Will Brooker notes of cultural studies websites that

> their analysis and debate are 'on' the Web, but they are also 'of' it, immersed in its unruliness, only one jump away from a Barbie fanpage . . . [T]he impossibility of fencing off one site from the next, with no boundaries between the 'culture' and the 'studies', risks an eclecticism sometimes verging on chaos, while the vanity-press nature of the medium may allow open-access to all comers but also threatens any notions of academic 'quality' (1998:416).

Brooker suggests that this 'lack of hierarchy' on the Web 'raises pertinent questions about the received value of . . . different kinds of "research and meaning-making"' (1998:417), but by doing so it also highlights how academic business-as-usual operates: precisely through the exclusion of a range of Others and through a fencing off of academic Theory from popular culture (see Chapter Six) and fan cultures (see Chapter Seven). In a sense, the Web helps to facilitate a shift from consumption activity to production activity on the part of lay users – users not placed within the institutions of academia or properly accredited by its educational schemes. This means that here 'reception [the consumption of media texts] . . . ultimately leads the user or viewer towards self-production' and a 'more producer-like' series of engagements and identities (Marshall 2004:44). It is this form of productivity that can potentially challenge academic Theory's desire to keep itself apart from other genres, narratives and modes of representation, and thus secure its professionalized distance from its objects of study.

What P. David Marshall terms the 'cultural production thesis' (2004:10) in relation to new media therefore partly captures Will Brooker's sense of a threatening and emergent 'chaos' in online theorizing (1998), where students can upload their dissertations to be read alongside work by more obviously accredited post-doctoral researchers, or where theorizing about pop culture can begin to occur 'outside of institutions (you do not have to enrol to study *Buffy*, there is no fee, nor any gatekeepers, guarding entry . . . you do not have to attend a University library to find these articles)' (McKee 2002b:69; see also Vieth 2000). And yet it is all too easy to exaggerate the seemingly magical capacity for online studies, and new media, to collapse or erode the modernist fences around academic Theory. As Alan McKee observes, drawing on John Frow's (1995) work on the 'knowledge class', 'some . . . get paid to employ their expertise and write articles about *Buffy* for [online journal] *Slayage*, while other[s] . . . do not' (2002b:69). The position of the professional scholar is not immediately undone by (debatable) shifts towards popular audiences achieving 'a "read and write" capacity in publicly distributed media via participation . . . in communication where digital equipment for making audiovisual texts and messages is close to achieving the banal . . . status of the pen' (Hartley 2004:136). In a move that resembles an application of Marshall's 'cultural production thesis' to the university, John Hartley has suggested that 'barriers between producers and consumers, currently organised around divisions of labour such as professional and amateur' will be increasingly undermined by 'resources of interactive media' (2004:140). Hartley interprets this as announcing a situation where

> we – modernist intellectuals working in barely post-medieval institutions [recalling academia as a type of 'priesthood' – MH] are no longer self-evidently the source, the provider. One implication of the emergence of the new . . . creativity and consumption is that now 'we' have serious competition. We've dissolved into our other (2004:140).

However, what Mark Andrejevic refers to as a desired and hyped (rather than actual) 'dedifferentiation' of production and consumption via new media technologies (2004:44) is rather difficult to view as a whole-scale dissolution of academic Theory into its Others (such as journalism/fandom/lay theorizing). Professional and modernist academics – intellectuals operating within their own social group and being properly accredited and detached from their objects of study – can recuperate forms of professionalized and distinctive expertise in part by policing the meanings carried by theoretical terms. Via this emphasis on the correct employment of terms, the quality and propriety of academic work is preserved through the use of specific, specialized languages. Even if one doesn't have to pay a fee to study, nor gain access to university libraries, nor be a member of a given educational institution, to evade the degraded label of 'lay' theory or the stigmatised cult of 'conspiracy theory', one still has to observe and reproduce the specialized, professionalized ways of writing that have come to linguistically characterize Theory.

Being materially produced within a given social setting, Theory is not simply a magically enlightening form of thought; that is, it is not merely a pure set of ideas that we can capture more or less accurately by reading textbook commentaries on the great thinkers. Theory is a material product – even a commodity (see Jagodzinski 2004:2; Sconce 2003:186) – that displays its own linguistic modes. This is a crucial point that is well made by José López when he notes that theory is often introduced to students through a visual metaphor or as a conceptual map, rather than as a type of language, and as always language-borne (2003:2–3). Via a reliance on visual metaphors and notions of conceptual mapping, theory is portrayed in textbooks as something that is primarily defined through its logical structures and coherence as a set of pure ideas. Introductions to cultural theory often participate in these guiding metaphors and images of theory by providing overviews that de-materialize theory and transform it into a set of principles, ideas, thoughts and terms rather than approaching it as a series of language practices.

What academic publishers dub 'critical dictionaries' or 'glossaries' of cultural theory stress the need to understand theory as a set of terms, with the reader being positioned as someone called upon to master an A–Z of theoretical terminology (Brooker 2003; Hartley 2002; Lechte 2003; Payne 1997). Yet rather than emphasizing cultural theory as language-borne, and as therefore inevitably interacting – often in marginalized and occulted, occluded ways – with other genres and narratives outside its institutional and educational boundaries, such texts create an image of theory as a set of key concepts and ideas that are carried by their specific words. These words can be learnt by looking up their authorizing, correct meanings. There is an implicit notion here of theoretical ideas as being carried neutrally by words – a vehicular or 'conveyor belt' notion of meaning (Morley 1992:121) – that is strangely at odds with how cultural theorists often otherwise approach meaning. Everyday, non-theoretical words are treated as carrying many meanings, as varying in their social contexts, and as not merely naming a world but working to construct it. By contrast, magic theoretical words are seemingly accorded the honour of naming pure concepts and ways of thinking: there are proper authorizing and legitimating meanings to theory's special words and languages. Such words are privileged by virtue of *not* being considered to carry many meanings. They are, rather, presented as commitments to closed-down, singular meanings. They are commitments that capture the truth of a given way of thinking. Like spells, incantations or passwords of a sort, Theory's words grant access to the proper and legitimate world of the academic. Theoretical terms must be used correctly by apprentice theorists:

Also daunting to newcomers to theory can be its intensely deliberative, *written* mode, as they come to realise that its debates are often registered in small nuances of phrasing. . . . Theory being usually a written discourse (unfortunately even when it is spoken as a conference paper) it is necessarily denser than speech, a contrast which students can find slow and irritating: 'Why can't s/he just put it simply?' It takes a time for the apprentice theorist to realise that a single word or naming ('postmodernism', 'thick accounts') can imply allegiance to whole continents of emphasis; that outdated models can be returned to, unwittingly, via 'slips of the tongue'. . . and that these habits take time to work through and change (Branston 2000:27).

The written-ness of Theory is an important part of its character. John Shotter notes that 'conversation . . . and academic discourses' can be powerfully contrasted. Where conversation is 'rooted' in a given, embodied situation, academic discourses 'claim somehow . . . to have floated free of such an embedding and to be "based" in certain supposedly undeniable properties of a "subject matter" ' (1993:139). Theory, as written, presupposes lone producers and readers, partly fixing a myth of the academic writer as a detached, heroic, modernist figure, but also simultaneously feeding into a counter-myth of the abandoned reader who feels frustrated and alone by virtue of struggling to comprehend specialized terms, and who is unable to engage in clarifying, explicatory dialogue with the writer ('what does this mean?').

Another crucial aspect of Theory is its commitment to intertextual connections and histories that necessarily require time and labour to trace, as Branston also observes. Steven Miles stresses the time taken up by theorizing when he asks 'in a world which appears to be changing so rapidly . . . do we even have the time to theorize?' (2001:1). It could be suggested the temporality of Theory is drastically out of step with the temporal rhythms and shifts of contemporary networked, hyper-mediated societies, existing instead as a remnant or residue from an earlier age where the scholar was sheltered from issues of (economic) need, and where scholarly practices emerged through a 'long process of autonomization' (Bourdieu 2000:25) from state, religion and the market. Although some writers may seek to reconnect Theory with just-in-time social worlds by reiterating theoretical arguments in 'sound bites' rather than 'longer narratives' (Jagodzinski 2004:2), and others may lament that academic theory has collapsed into being just another bit of information in an information society (Lash 2002:76), Theory typically continues to be defined against a range of Others. And that means Othered temporalities as much as Othered non-professionals. For instance, Theory does not – even where it becomes akin to a brand and even where it is commodified – promise to produce immediate results, instant gratifications, or a rapid assimilation to lifestyled consumer 'tribes' (Maffesoli 1996). Emphasising the relative slowness of producing and consuming the written word, and the *longue durée* of lineage that comes with defining specialist terms, Theory is rampantly intertextual, but in a very precise manner. It involves the citation and quotation of approved, institutionally legitimated and legitimating sources. This can occasionally seem to resemble a game of self-referentiality or citation for citation's sake, but it nevertheless functions as part of the professionalization and distinction of Theory. Invoking an authorizing series of prior sources and debates, Theory thus always refers the reader to a set of texts beyond what is currently being read, gesturing towards a vast intertextual web of material. The process of sifting through a range of preceding material and synthesizing it into new shapes, contesting its assumptions and challenging its limits, is perhaps one attribute which makes Theory an unusual form of cultural production. Lay theory is not required to name its sources or define its terms, and conspiracy theory also tends to circulate without those processes of naming and citation that characterize Theory.

One of the strangest aspects of Theory is its apparent reliance on the already said or the already argued, and its seeming tendency to discipline thought into established structures via its use of specialist terms. However, although Theory can be described as normative, perhaps even small-c conservative at times, its re-readings and rewritings nevertheless

> vacillate between citation, reproduction, system-integrated innovation . . . and the production of something not entirely new, but 'undisciplined' . . . which effects 'revolution' or radical change of a type that cannot be easily contained within the existing structures of the integrated system (Threadgold 1997:33).

By dispersing into a range of inter-related sources, Theory poses a challenge to what I have elsewhere termed the 'fallacy of internality' (2002:68). This can be taken to suggest that the value of any one academic study supposedly resides wholly in that study itself. The fallacy of internality, where value supposedly inheres in a bounded text, is an approach to value that we often employ outside academia, such as when we dismiss or praise a specific film, book or TV series, or even when we consume ranges of branded commodities. Value seems to inhere in a bounded unit, whether it is the singular text or the unitary brand. By contrast, while Theory certainly attempts to fence itself off from a range of non-professionalized Others, within its institutionally patrolled borders it is surprisingly indiscrete or lacking in boundaries. Although Theory appears in articles and books which seem to have the character of symbolically bounded texts, these texts presuppose one another – via considerable amounts of direct quotation – in ways which render them meaningfully part of an intertextual matrix or system. And it is knowledge of this matrix, listed in an alphabetised bibliography at the end of each new academic study, which constitutes the value system of Theory, not evaluating responses at the level of individual texts (see Green 1997:206–8). It would make little sense, for example, to give any particular Theory book a rating out of five stars. But it would make sense, within the value system of Theory, to discuss how original or rigorous a certain academic study was, since these evaluations are ways of relating an individual act of theory to the legitimating, authorizing intertextual matrix of prior theoretical sources. Rigorous work makes a show of covering as broad a range of references as possible, while original theoretical work may combine this with re-readings of preceding theory acts. This underlying value system indicates that new, emerging Theorists are most likely to establish themselves as significant scholars by initially challenging and critiquing the work of already well-established figures. Such a gesture works to confer value on the new Theorist as well as placing him or her firmly in relation to preceding work. Then, once they are established, the new Theorists can then begin to write in more free-form and less matrix-focused ways, having already won a space or niche within which to produce and write.

The ever-growing and ever-shifting web of theoretical sources, where patterns in citation can be discerned – certain sources or references becoming more important and oft-cited than others – is what lends Theory such a daunting sense of scale and scope. There is always another University Press book that can be read, or another academic journal article to be tracked down. Theory is thus a dispersed system of thought produced materially via specialized terminologies. Navigating its byways calls for time, care and effort. But Theory thereby also offers the lure of an intertextual matrix that can never be completed or finished. Like many forms of cult media (Hills 2002), or like the collector's acquisition of infinitely serialized objects, Theory is by definition unfinishable and non-forecloseable. It represents an 'endlessly deferred narrative' which nevertheless possesses an ongoing structure and order.

Whether the bibliography to any one Theory book is actually owned as a material stack of books and essays littered about its author's desk, Theory nevertheless resembles the collecting of knowledge. Academics' places of professional work are often framed by walls of book-lined shelves, where 'a collector's attitude . . . stems from an owner's feeling of responsibility toward his property' (Benjamin 1992:68). Knowledge is accumulated and displayed as property, and along with this comes a sense of responsibility to Theory's unending, intertextual matrix. Just as the 'objects of a hobbyist's collection have significance only in relation to one another and to the seriality that such a relation implies' (Stewart 1993:153), so too do the objects of Theory gain their significance in relation to each other. Theory is a 'serial game' (Baudrillard 1996:90) as much as a 'language game' (Lyotard 1984:46).

No two acts of Theory addressing the exact same topic are likely to carry the exact same bibliography. And as a thought experiment, we can consider what would happen if an aspiring author read all the books or articles taken from, say, the bibliography to this current book in order to compose their own academic work on cultural theory. Clearly, their resulting text would diverge from this one, even while using exactly the same legitimating sources (and no others). This imagined example demonstrates that the intertextual matrix of Theory confers value, and constructs a sense of order, while also allowing for a practically infinite number of individual acts of Theory, just as the system of language, or what Ferdinand de Saussure dubs 'la langue', allows for a practical infinity of speech acts (Saussure 1983:14). Indeed, it could be suggested that the argumentative moves made by structuralist de Saussure actually project Theory's value system into other arenas of life. Saussure's description of language *per se* could just as well be a description of Theory's intertextual matrix:

> It is . . . external to the individual who by himself is powerless either to create it or to modify it. It exists only in virtue of a kind of contract agreed between the members of a community. On the other hand, the individual needs an apprenticeship in order to acquaint himself with its workings . . . he assimilates it only gradually (1983:14).

Similarly, French theorist Roland Barthes who infamously declared the relative insignificance or death of the author in literary theory, did so in favour of analysing literature as a 'tissue of signs' drawn from an 'immense dictionary . . . that can know no halt' (1977:147). Akin to de Saussure's definition of language as a dispersed and relational system without terms carrying internal value, Barthes's reading of literature makes it resemble Theory's rampant intertextuality. Theory's fetishisation of a matrix of preceding works which must frame any individual act of Theory is mirrored in Saussure's theories of language and Barthes' theories of literature. Theory, we might say, carries a fundamentally structuralist bent, even when it argues against the theories of Saussure and Barthes by naming and citing them.

All of this suggests that Theory is a highly self-referential practice, whereas we might expect it to reflect a reality in place of chasing its own intertextual tail. However, this reality versus intertextuality opposition, whereby Theory is castigated for its Ivory Tower retreat from the real, and supposedly needs to be forcibly dragged back to reality, is somewhat spurious. Theory is always at one and same time self-referential, citing a preceding intertexual matrix, and referential or directed outwards at an object of study. It is this simultaneity which causes George Ritzer to conclude that there can be no clear separation between metatheory and theory:

> a metatheorist is one who studies . . . theories of the . . . world, while a theorist is one who studies the . . . world more directly in order to create (or apply) . . . theory. However, despite this seemingly neat distinction between metatheorist and theorist, the categories overlap . . . For example, . . . those we consider metatheorists also study the . . . world and . . . those classified as theorists also study theoretical works (2001:14).

It is difficult to sustain the idea that Theory is a distinct thing meaningfully set apart from the world. Otherwise when students read books of cultural theory taken from their university libraries they would be entering non-worlds for the duration of any such reading, academic bookshops and libraries could only be non-worldly fantasies, and this very book you are holding or looking at could not exist as part of the world. The pernicious common-sense opposition between theory and the real world generates all manner of absurdities, and it also participates in dematerialising Theory – treating it as a set of pure concepts or ideas rather than as a set of material products which circulate in the real world, at best persuading real people of the value of new ways of thinking and behaving, or at worst creating headaches for hard-pressed real students.

Ritzer's argument calls to attention the fact that Theory is always already 'meta-'; it is always situated in relation to preceding Theory as an intertextual matrix, even while it seeks to say something about the world, or about theory in the world. What could then be termed the 'duality of reference' possessed by Theory – it is inextricably self-referential and referential – means theoretical work can never simply 'reflect' the world (Smith 2001:4). Theory is not clearly 'constative' in J. L. Austin's (1976:3–5) terms: it does not act as a description that can be judged as true or false. Instead, Theory

> is more than a description of, or generalization about, the . . . world. Rather, it consists of abstract and systematically ordered understandings and models that can be used to account for what goes on in the world (Smith 2001:4).

This sense of systematically abstracting and modelling the world is also captured in John Shotter's definition of academic discourses:

> we can define an academic discourse as a rational body of speech or writing, a set of *ordered* statements, that provides a systematic way of representing, for the purposes of disciplined, academic inquiry, a particular kind of knowledge about an entity (Shotter 1993:139).

And Thomas McLaughlin's study of vernacular theory, which aims to critique academic theory's construction of lay theory as a degraded Other, continues to emphasize the distinctive rigour and systematics of academic Theory (1996:6 and 59). Given such apparent agreement over Theory's status as rigorous and systematic – again resonating with an emphasis on such theory as written and occurring in relation to an intertextual matrix of sources – it can be suggested that one of the associated values of Theory is that it works to transform reality rather than simply describing it. As a material form and force in the world rather than a set of ideas floating magically in the ether, Theory works in and on the real, sometimes provoking us to think in new ways about our experiences, sometimes challenging inequities and injustices, while at the same time making us feel that we belong in the Theory club or causing us to feel excluded from this professionalized group.

Theory's transformative work partly occurs through the new words, or neologisms, that it coins. In an excellent analysis of jargon and what is dismissed or attacked under this banner, Marjorie Garber discusses the 'jargon effect', saying that:

> The jargon effect is a sign that something intrinsic to the discipline is happening at two different points along the critical continuum. First, among theorists and scholars who coin new terms or formulations so as to make headway on difficult problems within the discipline. And second, among apprentices to the discipline (Garber 2001:116).

Against charges of jargon, which inevitably work to construct academic writers and their group as Other to the accuser ('What's the point? I can't understand what they're saying.'), academic jargon is for Garber always partly performative, being 'language in action, a sign that something is happening in language' (2001:118). This language action may operate to exclude the uninitiated, but such an effect is not inevitable. Some of the greatest instigators of systems of jargon, such as Sigmund Freud and Karl Marx, created specialized terms which now have an everyday currency, more than a hundred years after they wrote for more or less specialist readerships (Garber 2001:116–7). Is referring to somebody's 'ego' a piece of jargon? Clearly the quality of jargon doesn't inhere in words. Rather, it accrues through their social circulation (or lack thereof): words that more clearly belong to specific specialized groups are liable to be attacked as jargon, but yesterday's jargon can be today's plain speaking.

Garber identifies the types of terms that are most likely to be dismissed as academic jargon by those in other social groups (and other professions such as journalism, see Barker with Petley 2001). These terms include:

> Nouns that are turned into verbs, sometimes but not always via the much despised -ize suffix (e.g. problematize) and adjectives that become nouns (e.g. the ethical, the other, the abject, the Imaginary, the Symbolic, and the Real). Also on the hit list: proper names that become adjectives (Adornian, Althusserian, Foucauldian, Barthesian . . .) as if they referred to adherents of a sect. Freudian and Marxist have long been hurled about as labels . . . But do we object to Jeffersonian? [Or Thatcherite, Blairite etc? – MH] . . . Jargon, as always, is in the ear of the listener (Garber 2001:109–110).

Jargon is hence a moveable feast: it depends on the standpoint of the accuser, and thus upon the social group they feel allegiance to, or the profession they are accredited within. And professions always construct themselves and their valued identities against ranges of Others, such that '*academic* is one of the harshest things you can say about a book written for . . . mainstream audiences, while *journalistic* is the kiss of death for scholarly writing' (Garber 2001:111).

However, attacks on Theory as jargon do not only work in this way. It is not only the case that academics defend their professionalized, specialized words, whilst non-academics, especially those working in other professions, demand 'plain-speaking' (Murdock 1994). For academics too tend to attack certain theories as excessively jargon-heavy. Indeed, Theodor Adorno wrote a book entitled *The Jargon of Authenticity* which attacked a specific type of existentialist philosophy, labelling its followers as 'anti-intellectual intellectuals' (cited in Garber 2001:135). It is this phenomenon of Theory that I want to consider next. As McQuillan *et al* (1999:ix) have observed, '[r]elegating resistance [to "theory"] to an external reactionary force is . . . a profoundly comforting strategy [and yet] the death of Theory is [also] a persistent theme *in* Theory'.

Valuing and devaluing: Theory's Others inside the academy

The struggle to define academic 'Theory' as legitimate, valued and morally good, in the face of non-academic attacks, is complicated by internecine, internal struggles regarding which theories should be valued over others. Peter Brooker captures this level of professionalized disagreement when he says:

> 'Theory' entered into literary and cultural studies and allied areas in a new way in the 1970s and in some quarters has continued in an abstract and indulgent vein that many find abstruse and only fleetingly relevant to . . . day-to-day concerns. Yet . . . this is not true of all theory . . . There is bad use of theory (hermetic, intimidating, indifferent to readers and the world at large) and a good use (. . . tracking debates and changing usage, questioning the coherence and consistency of concepts, thinking through their implications for analysis) (Brooker 2003:vii).

Brooker's moral dualism here – his construction of good academic theory versus bad Theory – recalls the moralizing tone of academics' frequent dismissals of conspiracy and lay theory as degraded, much as it resonates with non-academic attacks on academic jargon. This pushes us to consider how attempts at valuing and devaluing Theory have a 'fractal' quality. That is, Theory as good or bad is first defined and defended across the lines of professional and social group identities, which is where this chapter came in. However, moving down a level of analysis, and into the academic social group alone, cultural theory breaks down yet again into new sets of good and bad oppositions. The good/bad theory dualism, and its moralizing language, thus crops up in academic versus non-academic discussion, and (nested within this) recurs within academic debate. It seems that academics mobilize the common sense of anti-academic social groups in order to lambast their own academic rivals. The commonsensical, conservative notion that academic theory exists within an ivory tower cut off from the real world is thus, perhaps rather bizarrely, also an accusation levelled by academics against other academics' work (see, for example, Philo and Miller 2001). Note that the alleged indifference and hermetic quality of bad theory can never be definitively demonstrated, and that the academic attacker almost always uses as much specialized language as the approach they are criticising. Again, 'jargon is in the ear of the listener'. And again, such accusations work to define in-groups and out-groups, this time within the academy. These factions tend to be defined either by discipline, with sociologists attacking literary theorists, or by theoretical affiliation, with Freudian film theorists attacking Deleuzian film theorists (followers of philosopher Gilles Deleuze) for their indifference to reality or their excessive jargon (see Bordwell 1996:19).

This process of recomposing distinctions, such as between good or bad theory, at ever-decreasing levels of social grouping nested within each other has been analysed by Andrew Abbott. He argues that many social structures, but especially professions, have a 'property of self-similarity' (2001:xv). By this, he means that these structures are organised via fractal distinction which 'repeats a pattern within itself, as geometric fractals do' (2001:9; see Hills 2004). One example of this is the distinction between qualitative researchers (trying to capture the quality of things) and quantitative researchers (trying to count things defined as units). Abbott argues that if you pitted quantitative against qualitative, and then moved down a level of analysis to consider each group, you would find a version of the same distinction replayed within supposedly unitary groups of qualitative or quantitative researchers (Abbott 2001:11). Abbott uncovers a number of other fractal distinctions in social science (2001:13 and 18), arguing that these operate over time within academic disciplines. There are winners and losers as the supporters of one side of a fractal distinction move into the professional ascendant before their group then splits again into a recomposed version of the opposition it had supposedly resolved. This means that certain key distinctions, such as whether one theorizes an active or passive media audience, for instance, can be used by professional scholars in the discipline concerned (for example, media studies) to

> know roughly where they stand relative to one another and relative to the principal . . . communities in the discipline. The single dichotomy . . . encapsulates a whole proliferating system of relations . . . In this lies the great power of these simple contrasts (Abbott 2001:11–2).

Two academics discussing their theoretical assumptions regarding media audiences might, therefore, agree that audiences are active (that they make their own meanings from media texts). But by then displaying a fractal distinction, and moving down a level or 'frame of reference' (Abbott 2001:12), theorist A could go on to argue that this activity is constrained by the audiences' social position – they are not entirely active, but are also somewhat passively put in their place by social structure. By contrast, theorist B might adopt a more celebratory position regarding audience activity, viewing this as virtually unfettered. Indeed, just such an example of fractal distinction framed much debate in media studies in the 1980s and 90s (see, for example, Morley 1992 and Fiske 1987). The distinction between active and passive would thus be replayed within what at first looks like a position of agreement at the active pole, and where both theorists begin by rejecting earlier theoretical assumptions regarding audience passivity.

The good theory/bad theory binary can be added to Abbott's set of fractal distinctions. Rival theorists outside one's disciplinary community can be depicted as out of touch with reality and as using too much jargon, but so too can those within one's disciplinary community but positioned in alternative factions. So it is that Greg Philo and David Miller, media studies scholars writing from the vantage point of critical Marxism, attack other theorists in media studies for their 'obfuscation and abstraction' (2001:76). Philo and Miller suggest that 'theoretical dead-ends' have been pursued (2001:33). Bad theory has been used as a magic charm or a kind of 'waffle-iron . . . to be banged on top of the material' studied (Hoggart cited in Milner and Browitt 2002:12). 'Cookie-cutter' Theory thus allegedly becomes detached from real social inequalities such as the exploitation of third-world workers by major multinational corporations, or economic imbalances in wealth that are structured by social class.

When professional academics claim that other professionally produced theory in their discipline has become excessively abstracted and disconnected from reality, then this indicates an internal struggle over status and legitimation. Moral terms such as 'bad' theory are useful in these exchanges because they can present the accuser in a positive light, as somebody who speaks on behalf of oppressed others (a public oppressed by the free market), not pursuing professionalized self-interest but acting altruistically. Bad theory is recurrently depicted as having a material self-interest (Philo and Miller 2001:48), whereas the good theory espoused in its place is depicted as magically free of such investments, a sleight of hand achieved by steering debate on to moral terrain. Failing to treat Theory as carrying a duality of reference – always being self-referential and referential, always being about the world in certain ways – Philo and Miller assume that their work is purely and heroically referential, while their opponents' work is purely self-referential and unreal. Furthermore, they do not apply the same critique of self-interest to their own work that they level at others' work. In Nick Couldry's terms, this makes Philo and Miller's (2001) theory non-accountable, since in accountable theory 'the language and theoretical framework with which we analyse others should always be consistent with . . . the language and theoretical framework with which we analyse ourselves' (Couldry 2000:126).

It is not only in social science and media studies that one can observe fractal distinctions relating to good or bad theory, with one disciplinary fraction rejecting another for its overly-abstracted Theory. A similar split has occurred in film theory, with a group of writers seeking to reinvent the study of film (Barker with Austin 2000; Bordwell and Carroll 1996; Gledhill and Williams 2000). These interventions have been premised largely on the idea that prior Theory is dangerously 'top-down', that is, it is imposed on a range of films, and 'spins out into mere appeal to authority. The pronouncements of Lacan, Althusser, Baudrillard . . . are often simply taken on faith' (Bordwell 1996:21). Theory is morally castigated as bad for failing to live up to the ideal of coherence expected of academic theory:

> Top-down theorizing of 1975 Theory drew from widely diverse intellectual traditions – not only the triumvirate of Marx, Freud and Saussure, but also . . .

> a host of others. Far from being a coherent system, this Grand Theory was a patchwork of ideas, any of which might be altered or removed . . . The result was what Jonathan Rée has dubbed the *nouveau mélange*. (Bordwell 1996:21).

David Bordwell thereby argues for 'Post-Theory', and for the need to go beyond top-down applications of Grand Theory. However, much like Philo and Miller (2001) in media studies, Bordwell (1996) and Carroll dismiss Theory for its vested interests, whether legitimating the study of film in the academy or spurring the demand for film courses (Carroll 1996:37), but fail to position their own interventions as having any self-interest. Instead, one gets the impression that Bordwell and Carroll are simply and morally interested in cutting through 'theoretical verbiage' (Barker with Austin 2000:15). And yet, Bordwell and Carroll rely on a specific theoretical framework (cognitivism) which is actually no less characterized by jargon than its Grand Theory predecessors, and which continues to frame film study through legitimating and limiting assumptions (see Hills 2005). Yet again, the scholarly moral dualism of good versus bad theory works to devalue academic opponents' theory and falsely construct one's own assumptions – whether these are Marxist or cognitivist – as innocent, pure reflections of the real.

The ability to position somebody else's theory as degraded, and as not meriting the term, allows academics to elevate themselves as a professional elite in comparison with their amateur, non-expert Others, as well as in relation to rival knowledge professions like journalism. But the allegation that a rival academic theory is bad – abstruse, jargon-heavy, abstract, out-of-touch-with-the-real, and a matter of faith rather than reason – also allows scholars to devalue competing theories within their own professional, disciplinary domains. It allows academics to perform their identities as properly rational in contrast to allegedly irrational tendencies in their field. One's own scholarly Theory is always rationalist and realist, in marked contrast to that of scholarly Others whose 'contrived narratives of wishful theory insulate their adherents from social reality' (Dollimore 2001:39). Bad theory is condemned as 'intellectual fashion' that is 'tenuously connected with the real' (2001:39), or it is 'a sort of "acting out", an indulgence of the irrational under the guise of the rational' (Craib 1998:141). Attacking bad theory means bidding for scholarly rationality and legitimation within the academy. It is almost always part of a power struggle between different factions of theorists.

In this chapter, I have suggested that we can illuminate what theory is by analysing its range of Others – what it has been defined against. I have pointed out that what is often referred to as Theory (with a capital T) actually demarcates an historically specific type of literary, social and cultural theory – structuralism, culturalism and post-structuralism – which is linked to generational and power shifts in the humanities. Theory has been attacked for its jargon, for turning away from reality, and for serving the material self-interests of professionalized academics. But it has been criticized in these ways along lines of cultural difference – these criticisms are the evidence of one social and cultural group attacking another, such as journalists dissociating themselves from the academy and boosting their professional self-image as serving the public interest. Theory has also been attacked by professional theorists wishing to occupy positions of moral force within academic debate and so invoking a return to reality. Various scholars have thus declared the era of Theory (1970s grand theory) to be over, exploring spaces and possibilities of post-theory by basically proposing their own just-as-theoretical alternatives.

Having traced a range of (de)valuations of Theory, both without and within academia, it is possible to build up an idealized image of what a theory of culture should be:

- It should be rational, coherent, systematic and abstract knowledge that works to explicate or illuminate aspects of the cultural world.

- It should provoke new ways of thinking about ourselves, our society and our culture(s) by interrupting or challenging common-sense ideas.

- It should use neologisms where necessary to work around difficulties in disciplinary debates or to conceptualise the social and cultural world in productive ways.

- It should avoid being used for subjective ends, either as wish-fulfilment or in pursuit of imagined power.

- It should refer to and cite canonical scholarly works, thus displaying a duality of reference by recognising disciplinary debates and referring outwards to social and cultural groups and issues beyond academia.

- It should position itself in relation to the intertextual matrix of previous related academic texts, thereby displaying its indebtedness to academic knowledge as well as its difference from, or addition to, this knowledge.

Bad theory supposedly fails to live up to these norms, but any such moralizing accusation is a way of doing something with theory – legitimating one theory by positioning the accuser as a legitimate and rational scholar in contrast to their devalued competitors. Such accusations usually occur where scholars are attempting to supplant one dominant theoretical perspective with another, emerging at moments of crisis in a discipline, where the legitimacy of a prior theoretical framework is called into question. The proposed new theory usually possesses all the faults attributed to what it is supposedly superseding, given that academic separations of good and bad theory fail to recognize that all academic theory displays a duality of reference. That is, all scholarly theoretical frameworks are simultaneously self-referential and referential. Other social groups may not use Theory in the way academia does, but this is a matter of cultural distinction, with different social groups displaying different communal practices of quotation and citation and different communal notions of what should count as proper knowledge. Neither academic jargon nor plain speaking have any monopoly on truth or on claims to represent the real; instead we should seek to critically evaluate both for their assumptions and limits, even if this activity requires a greater investment of time and labour in relation to Theory.

This suggests that how Theory should be defined is never a simply formal question. Theory is not just a matter of pure conceptuality, logic or ideas to be neutrally and perfectly captured in language. Academic theorizing is, rather, a specific set of 'routines and practices' (Bordwell 1989), and thus a specific way of working on and with theory's intertextual matrix. In Jeffrey Sconce's terms, we could say that there is a 'culture of theory' (2003:186) in contemporary university departments of culture, media, literature and philosophy, if not in the humanities more generally. This 'theoretical culture' (Craib 1998:141) is, like the definition of culture sketched out in Chapter One, a form of textualized agency. That is, Theory does things with academic-theoretical texts, distinguishing itself by virtue of working on these texts in particular ways (directly quoting sources, compiling bibliographies, and combining strands of thought into a synthesising, creative expression).

By sifting definitions of 'culture' (in the previous chapter) and 'theory' we therefore arrive at a position where the two terms seemingly cannot be separated out. Although culture is taken to be the object of specific theories, Theory itself occurs within a distinguishable 'theory culture' (Sconce 2003:187; see also Hopper 1995; Lewis 2002:3), much in the manner that fan cultures have their own fan-cultural norms of reading, interpreting and valuing texts (see Hills 2002, 2005 and Chapter Seven here). By making the '-cultural' suffix of theory-*cultural* norms invisible or trivial, academics elevate one type of cultural practice into an unmarked and supposedly transcendent form of idealized thought, disconnected from its material conditions of possibility and its interpretive communities (Fish 1980). Pretending that theoretical issues can be definitively bracketed off from the matter of 'theoretical issues as *cultural* phenomena' (Bennington 1999:105) does nothing less than falsely divorce theory from its generative theory culture, magically converting it into a realm of pure ideas, once again spuriously idealising the professionalized, specialized academic as a detached, modernist hero of deep thought. Arriving at the notion that cultural theory always operates as part of a theory culture is, of course, not to invalidate this Theory. But such an approach does indicate that merely recapping the thoughts of previous thinkers on culture – as do a range of introductions to cultural theory and cultural studies (Eagleton 2000; Jenks 1993; Lewis 2002; Smith 2001; Tudor 1999) – somewhat misses the essential duality of reference of cultural theory, treating it more as a reflection of what culture is and less as a series of internal, scholarly debates and ways of doing things with texts.

Two of the more obvious things to be done with cultural theory's texts, in terms of the practices of theory culture, are reading and writing. Linda Brodkey has analysed the social practice of scholarship, noting that 'the academic community is literally a community of readers who write and writers who read' (1987:5). Although this may suggest that reading and writing are inseparable components of theory culture, in Part Two I want to analytically separate them, considering the range of activities captured under these seemingly discrete verbs. What does it mean to read cultural theory, and how can this activity be most successfully carried out? I will argue that reading theory is about much more than understanding or deciphering marks on a page. Producing readings of cultural theory can instead be a creative articulation of any given reader's concerns and cultural identities, as they challenge and refine prior Theory. And, insofar as writing can be analytically detached from reading, in Chapter Five I will also consider issues raised by the mediation of cultural theory: who is it written for? What norms and conventions govern its 'written mode' (Branston 2000:27)? *How can one best write and produce theory under conditions of assessment/evaluation?* Basically, the next three chapters will follow cultural theory/studies' classic emphasis on questions of cultural production and consumption (Marshall 2004). However, they will not deal with the consumption and production of novels, films or TV series, but rather with how cultural theory itself is consumed and produced.

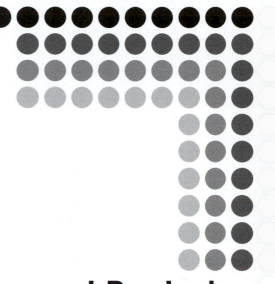

PART 2

Consuming and Producing Cultural Theory

chapter three

Reading Cultural Theory

Just as 'the text' has been central to work in cultural theory/studies, so too has reading been central to cultural theorizing and to theory culture. It is common to encounter introductions to the area which compile 'required readings' (Katz *et al* 2003:1), usually in chunky volumes themselves entitled 'Readers'. One introduction to cultural studies presents itself as 'a book of readings . . . which revisit . . . key texts in the emergence of cultural studies . . . and we think students should visit them' (Barker and Beezer 1992:5). In this case, readings are the things themselves – the collection of key readings – *and* what is done to them by later scholars, who then present their newly produced readings of these key readings for student consumption. In this chapter and the next I want to consider how students can best make their way through cultural theory's sometimes dizzying world of readings, before then moving on in Chapter Five to consider the writing of cultural theory, whether for an undergraduate essay or for a commercially published academic book like this one. Of course, it could be said that my separation of reading and writing is itself overly clear-cut. For, as what has been called 'reader-response' work in literary theory has argued, we can consider 'how far the reader reads and how far . . . s/he rather rewrites the elements of an "originary" text in the moment of reading' (McCracken-Flesher 1994:181; for more on reader-response theory see Tompkins 1980). Readers may rewrite texts metaphorically, by making sense of them, or literally by subsequently producing their own texts (Fiske 1992). And writers may reread, since their own textual productions 'enact . . . a reading' (McCracken-Flesher 1994:181) of prior works. Despite potential blurrings of reading and writing, in this part of *How To Do Things . . .* I will nevertheless treat these as analytically distinguishable moments.

In the following section, I will consider how reading cultural theory actually tends to mean reading in certain ways. Rereading, close reading and analytical reading are all characteristic of theory culture's textualized agency, by which I mean its way of doing things with academic texts construed as 'wholes'. These modes of reading can be contrasted with instrumental reading, where parts of a text are skimmed for specific material. In what follows, I will therefore argue that how cultural theory is expected to be consumed, within the routines and practices of theory culture, significantly differs from how non-fictional, informational matter is expected to be consumed outside the academy. Having made this argument, I will then go on to examine two key cultural theories of reading (Hall 1980; de Certeau 1988), considering how these theories do things such as performing rhetorical and logical balancing acts which allow them to appeal across disciplinary 'fractal distinctions' (see the previous Chapter). Such theories can thus be used to argue for active or passive readers, never definitively resolving theoretical debate in one direction.

Prescribing, analysing and romancing

Cultural theory's emphasis on reading occasionally surfaces as a signal of tensions between schools of thought, with one theorist accusing another of misreading their work (as in the exchange between Jacques Derrida and John Searle; see Derrida 1988). These types of disagreement can involve the to-and-fro 'querying [of his] . . . reading of my reading of his reading of my reading . . .!' (Morley 1996:300). Despite noting the 'potential absurdities' of this situation, it is a scenario which David Morley nevertheless pursues in order to encourage 'people to go back and read (or re-read . . . even . . .) the history of audience research' (1996:304). This 'Media Dialogue: Reading the Readings of the Readings' is, of course, also centrally concerned with who is more authoritatively able to make assertions about the historical narrative of audience research – David Morley or his opponent in the dialogue, James Curran (Morley 1996:301–2), just as the Derrida-Searle exchange concerned who was more authoritatively able to outline and patrol the possibilities of something called 'speech act theory'. Authority and status are always at stake in readings of readings of readings, which become challenges over what was really meant. These exchanges are the tennis rallies of cultural theory, if you like, as rivals whip point-scoring arguments backwards and forwards. They can become quite a spectator sport for non-participating scholars, since they symbolically demarcate rival arguments and positions while testing the mettle of competing disciplinary factions.

Another type of scholarly reading is the prescribed rereading of prior theoretical sources. Not usually being part of an ongoing and direct debate between theorists, rereading tends to canonise particular books or papers as 'artefacts that are set aside as relatively durable objects by members of a community of inquiry' (Katz *et al* 2003:2; see also Galef 1998:29). By establishing canons of books that become durable objects encountered time and time again by new generations of students, scholarly modes of reading hence tend to prioritise the notion of rereading. This is something that theory culture prescribes as a norm: many different people are directed to read the same key texts which are thus reread despite being read for a first time at the level of individual biography. And rereading is also something expected of the individual reader, who is unlikely to read key texts only once:

> Rereading, an operation contrary to the commercial and ideological habits of our society, which would have us 'throw away' the story once it has been consumed ('devoured') . . . [and] buy another book, and which is tolerated only in certain categories of readers (children, old people, and professors) . . . is here suggested at the outset (Barthes 1974:15–6).

Or, in David Galef's terms: 'As teachers and students, we are so involved in the study of texts that we fail to realize the fundamental peculiarity of what we do; that is, while most people simply read a document, we go over and over it' (1998:17). Now, this peculiarity may be somewhat overstated; it is not as if contemporary commercial operations and the habits of our society are entirely opposed to rereading. Indeed, the rise of sell-through videos and DVDs seems to presuppose at the very least a potential mass-market desire to read favoured audio-visual texts more than once. And media fans certainly invest time and energy in rereading beloved texts over and over again (Jenkins 1992:67–8), just as academics do. In fact, fan and academic reading practices repeatedly resemble one another (see Chapter Seven). As well as the matter of rereading, there is also a tendency for fans and scholars to carry out close readings. This type of reading assumes

> that people should consume texts . . . as complete wholes . . . [and that] we should never attempt interpretations of texts unless we draw on information about every element of the text – 'the total system'. *This 'close reading' approach . . . is a prescriptive one,* rather than a descriptive one. [It] is only one, very limited approach: what we might call the scholarly mode of engagement, the province of academics and fans (McKee 2003a:75, my italics).

But while academics and fans view the text as a symbolically bounded and valued entity, following industrial and cultural processes of textualization, many other consumers may not act as close readers at all: 'we catch bits of songs on the radio, flick in and out of television programmes, read some bits of some articles in magazines, miss bits of films' (McKee 2003a:75). In an article concerning the differences between fans and anti-fans (people who strongly dislike certain texts), Jonathan Gray similarly distinguishes 'close' from 'distant' readers (2003:70–1). The former are fans or academics, while the latter appear to be almost everyone else!

Theory culture's prescriptive close readings and rereadings thus distinctively favour approaching texts as detailed wholes, respecting the symbolic boundaries of texts as units or total systems of meaning. Peter Ekegren goes so far as to refer to this as 'the fallacy of the holy whole' (1999:116). Rather than dismissing it as a fallacy, McKee (2003a:75) notes simply that it is one way of reading among others, albeit one presupposed and enforced as a theory-cultural norm. This general procedure and practice of theory culture works to powerfully oppose the notion of skimming texts for a specific quote, or dipping into an introduction or a conclusion, or analysing one scene in a film without having seen the whole text. Frank Furedi's tirade against the alleged dumbing down of contemporary UK universities begins, for instance, with his outraged observation that 'in many cases, students . . . [can] . . . spend an entire year at university *without reading a whole book*' (2004:1, my italics). Furedi's gripe here perfectly encapsulates the value system of what McKee terms 'scholarly' reading: whole books should be read. Otherwise, students fail to accord with the prescribed norms of scholarly close reading and rereading.

Whole books, or whole journal articles or papers therefore constitute the gold-standard of academic attention within theory culture. And although (post-)structuralist theories might be assumed to move beyond this position, they too construct a canon of Theory books that need to be properly read as whole expressions of their authors' detailed and sophisticated arguments, whether this is the post-structuralism of Jacques Derrida or John Hartley (McKee 2003a). To offer one further example, a recent issue of the *European Journal of Cultural Studies* (*EJCS*, Volume 7, Number 2, 2004) features a section entitled 'Atlantic Crossings: Rereading North American Cultural Studies'. In what shouldn't now come as a surprise, this section boasts rereadings of five whole books: *The Souls of Black Folk* (Du Bois 1903), *Make Room for TV* (Spigel 1992), *Reading the Romance* (Radway 1984, 1987, 1991), *Writing Culture* (Clifford and Marcus (eds) 1986), and *We Gotta Get Out of This Place* (Grossberg 1992a). The journal's editors offer no substantive or ultimately convincing defence of their selection of these particular books, noting instead that 'much of the pleasure we take in any field of knowledge is contained in its great books and articles' (Hermes, Gray and Alasuutari 2004:131). This observation resonates with the notion that cultural theory is constituted through an intertextual matrix, though its link between pleasure and theory may not always be shared by cultural theory's student readers. What such an observation brings home, however, is that these journal editors are preaching to the converted: they are writing of the pleasures of a field of knowledge for professionalized readers who are assumed to traverse that very field of whole texts.

These *EJCS* rereadings are not just testaments to, and reconstructions of, the canonical value of their chosen books. They are also commentaries on the books concerned, and explanations of their importance to theory culture as nodal points within theory's intertextual matrix. Janice Radway's *Reading the Romance*, the third of the *EJCS* 'famous five', is discussed by Helen Wood in the following terms:

> Radway's work is marked as a key text in a seismic shift in thinking on culture on both sides of the Atlantic, from a ' "literary-moral" definition of culture to an anthropological one' (Radway 1991:3). *Reading the Romance* therefore helped guide the crossing of borders for cultural studies, but it was not a comfortable process. In so doing, the book returns as a key text on our reading lists because of the chords that it continues to strike with the tensions that cultural studies has fought (Wood 2004:148).

Reading the Romance is itself a study of how non-academic fans of the romance genre make use of popular romantic fiction in their everyday lives. It therefore dignifies the study of popular romances, rather than viewing Harlequin or Mills and Boon novels as junk to be denigrated. Making this move, Radway's work does indeed link into the foundational moves of cultural studies with its view that culture is ordinary (see Chapter One) rather than the capital-C Culture of great works of art. However, Wood's commentary on the academic appropriation and use of *Reading the Romance* points out that Radway was actually writing in ignorance of the cultural studies of Raymond Williams and was addressing US literary scholars rather than cultural theorists (Wood 2004:147–8).

This indicates that academic rereading is always a certain type of textualized agency: it brings new intertexts to the moment of (re)reading, actively producing connections between key texts and others in the intertextual matrix of cultural theory. Hence, Radway's work, which involved studying real readers of romance rather than speculating on how people made sense of such texts (Modleski 1986:xii), is linked in its subsequent academic readings and rereadings to the work of the Birmingham School, becoming a symbol or a metonym – one part standing in for the whole – for the very project of cultural studies. As Matei Calinescu notes in

Rereading, 'we return to . . . texts with new . . . unexpected intertexts . . . rereading is always intertextual' (1993: 55–6). Unlike fan rereadings, which may also be close readings respecting the boundaries of whole texts, scholarly rereadings are about placing whole texts in relation to intertextual patterns of affiliation and rupture. Such rereadings are about making connections, they are about networking texts, if you like, into schools of thought and into symbols for historical narratives of scholarship. Key texts are those that herald a seismic shift in paradigms of thought. These texts can be used to demarcate boundaries between how cultural theory was in the past, and what it then changed into. In such accounts, which are effectively narrative histories of cultural studies as a genre, cultural theory/studies therefore becomes

> a central protagonist whose fortunes organize the narrative. Narrative histories
> of a genre therefore usually become the story of something . . . that exists above
> and beyond the individual [instance], an essence which is unfolding before us,
> and is either heading towards perfect realization . . . or failure and
> corruption . . . It is for this reason that narrative histories also tend to
> concentrate on classic moments (Jancovich 2002:9).

Such classic moments are indicated by those texts symbolically positioned in the narrative as bringing about generic transformation. Jancovich's account actually concerns film history, and the way that cinephiles (that is, lovers of film) value and elevate specific films as having been especially transformative in film history. But this process of evaluation and elevation is shared by the academic as cultural-theory-phile. They also hold up key texts as exemplars of specific ways of doing cultural theory/studies (Wood 2004:150; Purdie 1992:149). Rereading thus clusters around the classic moments of cultural theory/studies (Barker and Beezer 1992; Kim 2004). It is these metonymic texts that are most repeatedly reread for students in textbook commentaries on cultural theory/studies: 'Textbook summaries of *Reading the Romance* often position it with developments in cultural studies that have since been criticized for celebrating the . . . resistance of cultural consumers' (Wood 2004:148; see also, for example, Morley 1992). As I noted in the introduction, these textbook summaries do not simply tell it how it is. They too do things with cultural theory, producing parallels and links between different whole books, and shaping narratives of cultural theory/studies.

Crucially, however, textbook summaries do something else with cultural theory. Their rereadings convert the complexities, nuances and symbolic excesses of original whole books into a type of pre-reading for apprentice theorists. Textbooks offer to cut out the time-consuming labour of approaching cultural theory as an intertextual matrix composed through specialized languages. These textbook rereadings are simultaneously pre-readings that work to shape the expectations of readers, or which function in place of any encounter between whole book and reader. Some student readers (and some academics) may therefore become more or less distant readers, forming an image of the text concerned, such as *Reading the Romance*, that they assume is accurate without ever actually reading the text itself (Jonathan Gray 2003:77). These cultural theory readers are akin to movie-goers who always leave after the trailers, or TV viewers who only watch the 'coming up' adverts. And while such activity would, I suggest, seem very aberrant indeed in these media contexts, it may be rather less unusual in the context of cultural theory's mediation. It is likely to be the case that many professional academics have not read specific texts that they nevertheless recognise as key works, being familiar with these totemic sources only via repeated commentaries and textbook rereadings.

We might assume that professional academics lapse into distant readings of cultural theory, rather than ideal close readings, because of time pressures. Is the same true of student readers? Time is undoubtedly at a premium for both students and scholars. However, it is also worth considering a further difference between reading the romance (or other popular texts) and reading *Reading the Romance* (or other cultural theory) in order to then offer another explanation of students' distant readings:

> In contrast to the typically engrossing reading experience of the romance novel, it is difficult to go through *Reading the Romance* at one stretch. The text contains too many fragments which compel its reader to stop, to reread, to put the book aside in order to gauge and digest the assertions made – in short, to adopt an *analytical* position vis-à-vis the text. Contrary to what happens, as Radway sees it, in the case of romance novels, the value and pleasure of this reading experience does not primarily lie in its creation of a general sense of emotional well-being and visceral contentment . . . Rather, *Reading the Romance* has left me, as one of its enthusiastic readers, with a feeling of tension (Ang 1996:98).

Ien Ang reminds us that Radway's cultural theory of romance-reading 'does not exactly read like a romance' (1996:98). Nor should it, given that it 'belongs to a completely different genre than the genre it is trying to understand' (1996:99). Ang's observations are useful, though, as a reminder that cultural theory is generally expected to be read, within theory culture, in a specific way. Not only are close reading and rereading important, so too is analytical reading, with all of its tension-generating, putting aside, reflecting upon and struggling with. Although Ang does not fully explain what might be meant by the term 'analytical reading', we can recover a fuller sense of this by examining how she reads *Reading the Romance*.

Firstly, Ang contrasts analytical to therapeutic concerns (1996:98–9): analysis is set up as rigorous cognitive work which can tolerate frustration and difficulty, while therapy is in Ang's use of the term concerned with releasing tension and so acting as a form of pleasurable escape from difficulty. Analysis confronts us with the problems of our world, while therapy allows us to hide from these problems. Ang then goes on to allege that rather than being able to fully contrast all academic work (as analytical) to all romance reading (as therapeutic), there may also be comforting material, or a 'therapeutic momentum' in much cultural theory (1996:99). This is then discerned in Radway's work: 'what is therapeutic (for feminism) about *Reading the Romance* is its construction of romance readers as embryonic feminists' (Ang 1996:103). This is so because having defined two groups as an 'us' (academic feminists who are not romance fans) and 'them' (romance fans who are not academic feminists), Janice Radway then concludes that academic feminism can help romance readers (Ang 1996:102). These readers can be saved from their compensatory and escapist romance-reading by the consciousness-raising of feminism, 'as if feminism automatically possessed the relevant and effective formulas for all women to change their lives and acquire happiness' (1996:103).

Carrying out her own 'analytical reading' Ang examines the limits and assumptions of Radway's work (see also Chapter Four). She demonstrates that one limiting factor is that Radway approaches her encounters with romance readers as a 'realist', that is, she assumes that a community of romance readers precedes her own study: all she is doing, as a scholar, is reflecting the reality of this community. Against such a realist position, which assumes that the real is out there just waiting to be academically mapped, Ang points out that Radway's own work, which involved getting romance readers together and asking them questions about their reading activities, 'helps to construct the culture it seeks to describe and understand' (1996:101). Ang thus reads *Reading the Romance* analytically by highlighting its assumptions: Radway assumes a community of readers, and assumes that feminism has all the answers for this community. To observe this is to realise that 'any reading of a text, including an academic reading, is . . . embedded in a particular social context and . . . agenda . . .' (Saukko 2003:112).

The analytical reading experience, which refuses to fall back into the self-comforting position of therapeutic reading, is typically a fraught one. It casts the reader into a state of unease (see Hills 2005:145–60). As Stuart Hall has suggested with reference to the struggles of cultural theory: 'the only theory worth having is that which you have to fight off, not that which you speak with profound fluency' (1992:280). By issuing such a challenge, reading cultural theory opposes itself to reading for pleasure wherein 'pleasure reading is playful: it is free activity standing outside ordinary life; it absorbs the player completely, is unproductive' (Nell 1988:2). Although we may occasionally find ourselves lost in a book of cultural theory, this is unlikely to indicate the immersive, playful sense of self-loss indicated by Victor Nell's term 'ludic reading' (1988:2), which is what we might hope to experience when reading a romance. The very different sense of getting lost in theory is, instead, often a matter of not yet understanding:

> The illumination that comes to us when we truly understand something which was earlier a deep puzzle to us is like coming out of a dark, twisting path in the woods where we are anxiously lost, into the wide space and bright light of a clearing which leads us out into the open. The relief of such a moment and the exhilarated surge of the sense of freedom and happy self-possession which goes with it is at the heart of education. It is for this that we use a theory (Inglis 1990:175).

If reading cultural theory can be a bit of a pain as well as considerably time-consuming and a challenge to our sense of self-possession (as we get lost in theory's dark woods before finding illumination), then student readers' distant readings of cultural theory via textbook pre-readings may be eminently sensible and rational responses to this situation. Not having fully internalized the value system of theory culture, students are likely to find reading cultural theory an unhappy experience. To submit to being lost in the dark requires the trust that wide, open spaces can be safely found again. Although it is not often remarked upon, reading cultural theory effectively may presuppose a specific emotional stance of trust, and an ability to tolerate states of confusion.

Cultural theory uses its own specialized terms and refers readers to an extended intertextual matrix of prior texts, but beyond these difficulties, Theory also presupposes a particular mode of reading, as Ang (1996) intimates. Consuming theory is not generally assumed to be a kind of 'efferent' reading, in which 'the reader's attention is focused on what he will take away from the transaction' (Louise Rosenblatt, cited in Donoghue 1998:13). Denis Donoghue points out that if

> you are reading the directions on a bottle of medicine, an efferent reading is enough. It is enough, too, if you are flicking the pages of a newspaper in search of information. Efferent reading is often called Practical English or Business English (Donoghue 1998:13).

'Efferent', meaning carrying from a part of the body, especially the brain, captures a sense of how Practical English's clarity just seems to naturally carry from someone's brain out into the world, ready to be read (by English speakers). So-called 'efferent' reading is strikingly instrumental: the reader knows what they are looking for and searches through a text for a specific bit of information. Theory rarely offers itself up to this degree of instrumentality, yet efferent reading is what most of us do most of the time, at least when we are encountering non-fictional material. And since theory is not fiction, and since it refers informationally to the world, we might assume that efferent reading is the appropriate response. After all, such reading is rapid, practical and to the point. It achieves results.

But approaching cultural theory in such a common sense way can only produce disappointment and dismay. Cultural theory is not meant for efferent reading; it calls for 'a distinct kind of reading, requiring an initially different stance' (Donoghue 1998:13). Analytical reading (which I will return to in Chapter Four) is inherently risky rather than instrumental: we cannot say from the outset what its results will be, nor can we set targets for such reading. We cannot entirely standardize analytical reading so that every reader produces exactly the same outcomes, whereas we may expect efferent readers to find the same bit of information. There is thus a powerful clash between how cultural theory is expected to be read within theory culture and how readers external to this culture (new students) may expect to read non-fictional, informational material. Managing this disjunction has become the mediating role of hand-outs and textbooks. Hand-outs predigest theoretical material for students by focusing on specific bits of theory, and specific explanatory examples. Rather than supporting analytical and close readings, these theory primers are more amenable to the standardisations of instrumental and efferent reading, for example, 'what do I need to know to pass the module assignment?' (Evans 2004:71–2; Furedi 2004). Hand-outs and textbooks typically reduce or minimise the need to engage analytically with cultural theory, and to self-transformatively wrestle with it. They move cultural theory closer to the domain of Practical English in which specific outcomes can be anticipated:

> In British universities all teaching is judged (by a sort of spectral, invisible or scarcely visible body of authorities) in terms of 'learning outcomes'. As a teacher one is obliged to act and feel like a sort of automaton, someone concerned with 'delivering a unit' (rather than teaching a course), the 'outcome' of which should be specifiable in advance. Teaching is becoming mechanized . . . It is not only the teacher who becomes an automaton, but also the student, for he or she too is

obliged to live up to the 'learning outcomes' set down in advance, in other words in a sense not to *live* at all, merely to 'receive delivery' (Royle 2003:54).

What these institutional shifts achieve, when allied with the increased use of hand-outs and introductory textbooks, is the uneasy installation within theory culture of those common sense values and expectations of efferent reading. It may well be, then, that cultural theorists are hardly masters in their own not-so-ivory towers, as theory culture's ideals of analytical, close (re)readings come increasingly under threat. Although efferent reading appears more natural and easier for students, it is just as much a constructed mode of reading as analytical reading. And the seeming gains of efferent reading are actually profound losses in relation to reading cultural theory because efferent reading partakes of a 'modern myth of transparency':

> The modern ideal of transparency . . . has certainly been one of the factors that favored the writing and reading of clear, unmysterious, largely self-explanatory texts, be they for entertainment, as in the case of the modern popular genres and subgenres of fiction, or for instruction and intellectual enlightenment. This same longing for transparency explains the proliferation of explanatory texts – commentaries on more difficult primary . . . texts and even commentaries on commentaries – which many students . . . prefer to read in place of the more difficult primary texts (Calinescu 1993:265).

Although evading difficulty, efferent reading places the reader within a calculus of standardized, predicted and repeatable responses. This is a routinized transmission model through and through, in which the impact of cultural theory on new generations of students is dulled to a 'McDonaldized' (Ritzer 1998) repetition of the pre-programmed and the already-said. In such a context, pre-readings of cultural theory are likely to be learnt by rote and repeated back to university teachers. The risk, pain and difficulty of analytical reading are defused, and a sameness of reading is safely installed, but at the cost of reducing those moments of creative analysis which wrestling with difficult cultural theory can produce. To be sure, difficulty for difficulty's sake is hardly a good thing, but the mysterious nature of cultural theory's non-forecloseable and intertextual matrix, and its ability to inspire and sustain an almost infinite number of pathways and navigations, are both potentially forfeited to an encroaching value system of transparency and efferent reading.

And yet, analytical reading might not after all be so fully opposable to reading the romance. Ien Ang concedes that the opposition 'invites a somewhat oversimplified view of the relationship' (1996:98) between readers of cultural theory and readers of popular fiction. In *Feminism and the Politics of Reading*, Lynne Pearce theorizes 'reading *as* romance', discussing how the process of reading opens us to a 'textual Other' (1997:17–20), which can be a character or a quality in the given text, or even an act of interpretation of that text projected on to someone else. Pearce makes the emotional experience of reading central to her theory, arguing that reading has generally been treated as cognitive rather than being thought of as involving a 'relationship' to the text which carries a 'full emotional range' (1997:19). While self-consciously utilising languages of romance to make the emotionality of reading visible, Pearce also challenges the reading practices and protocols of professional readers, such as academics and journalists, for the ways in which these groups frequently minimize their own emotions within prescribed processes and modes of reading. Academics hence hide or prohibit their emotional relationships to texts, which can be theory books as much as popular fictions:

> The 'special relationship' [of an individual self to a text when reading] is frequently disrupted by the intrusion of the extratextual others (the interpretive community, the public and private audience) of our readings. . . . [O]ur emotional involvement in the reading process remains largely unacknowledged by professional readers and critics. Because of the taboo of presenting one's reading as an 'experience' of the authentic-realist kind . . . very few of today's academically trained readers are likely to be self-reflexive about their 'relationship' to the text (Pearce 1997:215).

Pearce suggests that academic readers are trained, via their participation in the various factional communities of theory culture, such as feminism and post-structuralism, to mask their feelings of devotion and frustration in the reading relationship. There is thus a tension between 'making a reading' and the 'reading process' (1997:220). While the latter is felt to be emotionally real, embodied and beyond the self-control or volition of the reader – the self being opened to the text – the former is, as a matter of disciplinary identity and opposition to 'authentic-realist' experience, rationalized and tailored to norms of analytical scholarly reading. Rereadings presented in textbooks and elsewhere are, then, interpretations which make-over the actual experience of reading, placing this into the appropriate discourses and evaluations of the properly trained academic community (see Mills 1994; Bordwell 1989). Note that Pearce does not wholly reduce trained academics' readings of theory and popular fiction to matters of their training and academic-institutional or disciplinary identities (as Bordwell 1989 does). The romance of reading is obstinate and refuses to be dispelled in this case by the normative pressures of proper academic interpretation. Pearce therefore holds on to the possibility that 'textual Others' can transform us, just as our other romantic relationships have the potential to remake us and remake our worlds.

As a language for thinking about the reading experience, romance may have certain limits: what, for example of the reading experience that is broken off and discontinued because it is simply felt to be too frustrating? Despite this, it is helpful insofar as it indicates again that scholarly modes of reading are not reducible to efferent, instrumental readings. Although the academic readers studied by Pearce produce readings of films and fictions that fit into the already-said of their scholarly interpretive communities, reading-as-romance suggests that their reading relationships will always exist in excess of these frameworks. Approaching theory-reading as romance means remaining open to the theoretical text, perhaps finding a new way of thinking or a new sense of self through the transformative potential of such reading relationships. After all, professional academics in cultural theory/studies were all students themselves once, and all could probably recount the visceral, embodied (or authentic-realist) impact that a now-favoured theory had on them, even if such self-reflexivity tends to be pushed out of academic self-accounts.

Thus far, I've argued that students and professional scholars may not always share a commitment to the prescribed norms and value-system of close reading. Students may favour instrumental, efferent reading over wrestling with analytical readings of texts which refer them to a universe of debates and terminologies in Theory's intertextual matrix. To an extent, I have argued for the value of analytical over efferent reading, but I have also begun to suggest that there may be shared limits to efferent and analytical reading: both trained academics and new students tend to exclude their reading relationships when they turn to established interpretive frameworks (as many scholars do) or appeal to textual transparency (as many students do).

However, types of scholarly reading that I have touched on here are all 'tutored' readings (Bennett and Woollacott 1987) produced by professional academics, whether they are close readings or textbook commentaries that partly move away from modes of analytical reading and towards efferent reading. But those beyond the terrain, training and textualized agency of the academy have also been addressed in cultural theory as readers both literal and metaphorical. Non-academics too ' "read" their own environments' (Ang 2005:482) in an enlarged sense of the word where reading is equated with any act of decoding meaning. And in a further stretching of the terms of literary theory into cultural theory/studies, consumers of film and TV are also said to be 'readers' of these 'texts' (Jenkins 1992; Lehtonen 2000). Readers in the more usual sense of those scanning words on a page have, of course, also been analysed from childhood through to adulthood (Cherland 1994; Hermes 1995; Radway 1987, 1991).

Cultural theory most certainly doesn't lack theories of reading, and it is two of the more influential such theories that I will examine in the following section, addressing work by Stuart Hall and Michel de Certeau. Having considered these theories, I will move on (in Chapter Four) to suggest that what cultural theory does lack is empirical work on the reading of cultural theory itself. Reading is most often carried out in a taken-for-granted way within theory culture, given that types of reading and rereading are its primary modes of textualized agency. At the same time, reading has been incessantly and recurrently theorized as a practice carried out by empirical, non-academic Others (e.g. romance-readers, as we saw above). But the actual activity of reading cultural theory, an activity which academics assume professional authority and expertise over (and which students are expected to do), has remained a mysteriously blank page within the annals of cultural theory/studies. Before returning in the next chapter to this striking absence, though, I will first introduce a few key texts in cultural theories of reading, arguing that they share a particular quality – that of balancing opposed theoretical assumptions over readers' activity/passivity or empowerment/disempowerment.

Decoding, see-sawing and poaching

Stuart Hall's essay 'Encoding/decoding' (1980) is contained in the edited collection *Culture, Media, Language,* a longer version having first been published as a CCCS (Centre for Contemporary Cultural Studies, Birmingham) stencilled paper in 1973. The influence of this eleven-page essay can hardly be understated in cultural studies/theory (see Davis 2004; Gilroy *et al* 2000; Morley and Chen 1996; Procter 2004; Rojek 2003). Indeed, Gurevitch and Scannell (2003:231–2) suggest that the canonical status of this essay inheres partly in its productivity: it inspired, framed and generated much later work. Major studies by David Morley (1992), Justin Lewis (1991) and Jhally and Lewis (1992) followed in the wake of

Hall's work. Looking back on this phase of theoretical ferment, Gurevitch and Scannell suggest that a certain fate has befallen 'Encoding/decoding':

> The canonized text no longer lives within a set of concerns and commitments. It is no longer something to be thought with or about, engaged with and argued over, confronted or challenged. It becomes something to be ritually invoked (2003:232).

This may be a step too far, since the 'Encoding/decoding' model has yet to definitively lapse into an historical mode, becoming a text explored only for its value as an expression of how cultural theorists used to think. Rereadings, uses and returns to the model continue, as in Kim (2004), Lewis (2001:31–3 on 're-encoding') and Gray (forthcoming on 're-decoding'). Undoubtedly an 'ur-text' (founding model) of post-1970s media and cultural studies (see the interview comments in Hall 1994:255), 'Encoding/decoding' is significant for the way in which it separates out two moments in the existence of a mediated text. Hall's model suggests that a text is first encoded or constructed (usually by media professionals). This process of making meaning draws on conventions of language, genre and professionalism, which Hall terms 'frameworks of knowledge, relations of production and technical infrastructure' (1980:130). Then, in a second moment a different set of 'meaning structures' operate on the text (1980:130). These are the codes through which readers encounter and decode the text – forms of meaning-making that are linked, strongly or weakly, to the reader's social and cultural identity, for example, their gender, class, ethnicity and so on (see Kim 2004). Audience members do not merely receive the text, but actively read it via potentially different codes of meaning to those used by the text's creators (see Davis 2004:62). Hall's work therefore attacks any linear or sender-receiver model of communication. The text is not merely a fixed unit that is sent and arrives unchanged at its destination; nor is it a fixed unit subjected to distortion, noise, or any other form of interference with its supposedly true message. Instead, Hall theorizes that 'the decoding process may be independent of the encoded meaning, with a life and power of its own' (Gurevitch and Scannell 2003:239). As Andy Ruddock has noted, 'encoding/decoding implied that the only way to assess the impact of a text was to look at the audience' (2001:125), as it is only through its decoding that a text eventually takes on meaning. This does not, however, open the floodgates to a situation where a text can mean anything at all:

> Since there is no necessary correspondence between encoding and decoding, the former can attempt to 'pre-fer' but cannot prescribe or guarantee the latter, which has its own conditions of existence. Unless they are wildly aberrant, encoding will have the effect of constructing some of the limits and parameters within which decodings will operate. If there were no limits, audiences could simply read whatever they liked into any message. No doubt some total misunderstandings of this kind do exist. But the vast range must contain *some* reciprocity between encoding and decoding moments (Hall 1980:135–6).

The encoding/decoding model therefore de-couples its two moments only to reinstate a link between them that doesn't work automatically or naturally, but rather occurs through the action of cultural power. This means that although texts can't assume or prescribe how they will be read, they will nevertheless tend to be structured to convey preferred readings that have an ideological force – that is, possible readings will be restricted in line with the interests of cultural norms and powerful elites. Ruddock's example of this process (2001:125–6) concerns screening the Tom Cruise-Jerry Bruckheimer film *Top Gun* to students. While students interpreted the film as shamelessly pursuing a 'USA #1' ethos, almost to the extent of it becoming self-parody, they nevertheless decoded the text in terms of its assumed notion of US military and cultural dominance. Their responses were structured in relation to this preferred reading. Of course, some texts may be structured in a way that opposes the interests of power elites and cultural norms: satire often works in this way, aiming to point up the shortcomings and limits to ways of seeing the world that are associated with certain politics. In this case, preferred readings would themselves work to challenge forms of cultural power, such as preferred readings of the UK satire *Brass Eye* (see Mills 2004) which mocked mainstream TV news and current affairs shows for their sensationalist, scare-mongering coverage, while also satirizing the use of celebrities in consciousness-raising media campaigns.

The encoding/decoding model sets out three 'hypothetical' (Hall 1980:136) types of reading that can occur in relation to preferred meanings. Although Hall is careful to note that these categories 'need to be tested and refined' (1980:136), almost all subsequent work proceeds as if they are actual and exhaustive categories to be applied. Hall's hypothetical reading positions are 'derived from [the work of Frank] Parkin' (Morley 1992:126; see Parkin 1971) and amount to an extremely conventional piece of philosophizing whereby all possible textual responses are carved up into a tripartite logical system. Two opposed options (thesis and antithesis) are supplemented by a mediating middle way (or synthesis):

- *Thesis:* Audience readings may be aligned with the 'dominant' position (1980:136). These readings would entirely accept the preferred meaning of a text – viewing *Top Gun* as a celebration of ideal masculinity and US military potency, or laughing along with *Brass Eye*'s belittling of TV news as dumbed down, formulaic, vacuous and clichéd.

- *Antithesis:* In complete contrast, readers may 'decode the message in a *globally* contrary way' (1980:137–8). Here, readers reject the framework within which a message is framed and respond via a totally different set of codes. This is termed an 'oppositional' reading (1980:138), for obvious reasons. Reading *Top Gun* as ludicrous US military-industrial propaganda that is laughable in all respects would be an oppositional reading, as would reading *Brass Eye* as wholly offensive, and as an unremitting affront to the good sense of usual news broadcasts.

- *Synthesis:* Alternatively, readers may adopt a 'negotiated' position (1980:137) between the two extremes given above. This would mean partly reading in line with the preferred meaning but also introducing some oppositional elements. Interpreting *Top Gun* as a ridiculously inflated version of US military might, but still accepting its codings of masculinity and romance would be a negotiated reading: aspects of the text are accepted and others are rejected. Or, laughing at certain elements of *Brass Eye* (its exaggerated, absurd computer graphics), but being offended by its take on paedophiles ('they shouldn't make jokes about this!') would be another negotiated reading.

The encoding/decoding model therefore relies on the presence of preferred readings. As Hall notes in one scholarly interview: 'I want to get a notion of power and structuring in the encoding moment which, nevertheless, does not wipe out all . . . other possible meanings' (1994:262). He argues that reading is an active process, but goes on to indicate that this is nevertheless a fundamentally restricted and limited activity, a shift which leads critics such as Andrew Tudor to conclude that the encoding/decoding model is 'at heart committed to a top-down view' (1999:130) of meaning. Although not strongly determining readers' responses, texts are still ultimately determining forces. Hall rejects the idea that a preferred reading may be the analyst's imposition or projection, asserting that such readings can be recovered by examining texts as 'as neutrally as you can get . . . [in] a sort of necessary objectivity' which is still not a final or pure objectivity (Hall 1994:266).

This (limited) claim to objectivity indicates one difficulty with Hall's position. It ultimately appears to grant a 'zero-degree' or code-free/code-neutral reading to cultural theory/studies' academics – something which is denied to all other readers. Furthermore, encoding/decoding relies on a certain philosophical or logical division into only three reading categories that are imposed by overtly political considerations (Wren-Lewis 1983:187–8; see Morley 1992:126; Tulloch 2000:189; Ann Gray 2003:132). We could adopt a different philosophical image (Le Doeuff 1989) – that of the continuum rather than the category – and suggest that readers may be positioned along a finely graded continuum ranging from dominant to oppositional, rather than being herded into three categories. My point is not so much to correct the encoding/decoding model as to highlight its own constructedness, and the way in which a certain hypothesis has been seemingly shuttled over into the empirical or the real by cultural theorists. Encoding/decoding has perhaps partly gained its strength precisely through the very rhetoric of its neatly tripartite schema. It promises a clearly defined and exhaustive model of differential readings which escapes being an either/or, instead replaying deep-rooted habits of philosophical thought which tend to prioritize thesis-antithesis-synthesis structures. More substantively, encoding/decoding has also been highly influential thanks to its move towards theorizing reading as active, and as not fully determined by the text. At the same time, Hall's model preserved a notion of media texts as culturally powerful and systematically limited representations of the world. The encoding/decoding model can hence be imagined and visualized as a kind of delicately balanced 'see-saw model', offering cultural theorists a way of keeping celebration and critique of readings in the air, without definitively tipping to the ground on either side. It celebrated audience decodings as active constructions, but these decodings were only ever active in the shadow of constraining ideological forces requiring critique.

See-saw models, and their careful balancing acts, appear to carry a significant appeal in cultural theory and theory culture. The second influential model of reading in cultural theory/studies that I want to introduce also has aspects of this see-saw quality. This is French theorist Michel de Certeau's theorization of reading in *The Practice of Everyday Life* (1988), 'the core [de] Certeau work for cultural studies' (Driscoll 2001:382). Like Stuart Hall, de Certeau has become the object of book-length commentaries (Ahearne 1995), with one such book making a case for the pre-eminence of de Certeau's work via its stark title, simply being called *Michel de Certeau: Cultural Theorist* (Buchanan 2000a).

De Certeau's work entered cultural studies partly through its application in the work of 'populariser' John Fiske (Hartley 2003:165). Fiske's *Understanding Popular Culture* promotes de Certeau as a theorist of the everyday, noting that unlike many of his rivals, de Certeau's 'distinctive contribution . . . is his insistence on the power of the subordinate' (1989:34). Fiske utilises de Certeau's work to make a case for the 'productivity of consumption', suggesting that 'consumption is a tactical raid upon the system' (1989:35), even if this monolithic system isn't always clearly identified or identifiable in Fiske's work. Such a reading of de Certeau (Fiske 1989:35–40) draws on his concepts of 'tactics' and 'la perruque'. Firstly, tactics are opposed by de Certeau to 'strategy':

> I call a *strategy* the calculation that becomes possible as soon as a subject with will and power . . . can be isolated. It postulates a *place* from which relations with an exteriority composed of targets or threats . . . can be managed . . . [E]very 'strategic' rationalization seeks first of all to distinguish its 'own' place (de Certeau 1988:35–6).

In contrast, de Certeau defines a tactic as 'a calculated action determined by the absence of a proper locus' (1988:37). Tactics have no proper place of their own, they play across the territory of a foreign power. A tactic 'is an art of the weak' (1988:37), a way of fleetingly traversing strategy's proper places. De Certeau creates an analytical splitting of space and time through his account of strategy versus tactics: 'Tactics, he argues, abandon space for time, for a clever, tricky, essentially opportunistic use of time which exploits the transformative possibilities of particular moments' (Bennett 1998:186).

Strategy is always organized by 'the postulation of power' whilst a tactic is 'determined by the *absence of power*' (de Certeau 1988:38). And yet the powerless are artful, creative and active. They do not merely accept the cultural order imposed on them, but instead practice ruses and trickery to turn forms of authority against themselves, to pull a fast one and to get away with fooling those in power. La perruque, or the wig, is one of de Certeau's examples of this trickery. It 'may be as simple as a secretary writing a love letter on company time, or . . . a cabinetmaker's "borrowing" a lathe to make a piece of furniture for his living room' (1988:25). Or it could involve an office worker surfing the web when they are supposed to be writing a report. Fiske provides the instance of youth consumers who, as 'shopping mall guerillas' (1989:37) congregate in shopping centres, drink alcohol disguised in 'soda cans', and act as consumers of the place and its images rather than the commodities for sale, thereby asserting their distinctive social identities (1989:38). These are productive arts of making do, evading the authority of the mall's security guards and tactically using the 'proper place' of the shopping centre.

Fiske has been repeatedly criticized for using de Certeau's work to romanticize and celebrate the activities of subordinate, disempowered groups (see Garnham 2000:125; McGuigan 1992:72; Morley 1992:273–4). However, Fiske's invocation of de Certeau relates not only to generalized consumption as tactical, but also deals with 'tactical reading'. Cranny-Francis *et al* (2003) define this as follows:

> For some readers, the text is less a focus than a point of trajectory; meanings generated by a reading are extrapolated beyond the text into

> a reading/meaning-making practice which states and reinforces the attitudes and values of that reader. [I]t is . . . a reading which, at some level, empowers the reader. It is not necessarily a socially critical reading, and it is not necessarily a reading which accords with mainstream reading practice (2003: 129–30).

Tactical reading, then, is a version of de Certeau's more general thesis that consumers use products imposed on them in creative and guileful ways, but that these uses nevertheless indicate a certain lack of strategic power (Bennett 1998:181). De Certeau argues that 'reading is only one aspect of consumption, but a fundamental one' (1988:167). Here, it is the text which becomes the territory of a foreign power, since its tactical readers have no ability to determine what goes into this text. Instead, all they can do is twist its meanings, or read selectively, in line with their own interests (Chartier 1995:90). De Certeau explains this rather poetically by suggesting that 'readers are travellers; they move across lands belonging to someone else, like nomads poaching their way across fields they did not write' (1988:174). However active such readers may be, they are nevertheless condemned to poach meanings from the authorities of official textual production. And however empowered such readers may subjectively feel, reinforcing their pre-existent values and attitudes through a calculated reading, they remain ultimately disempowered and marginalized. Their readings are, in the end, tactical.

Following on from his mentor, John Fiske, Henry Jenkins (1992) has probably done the most to develop notions of tactical reading, or textual poaching as it has been termed (Cranny-Francis *et al* 2003:130). Jenkins describes fans of TV shows as near-perfect examples of de Certeau's tactical readers:

> Like the poachers of old, fans operate from a position of cultural marginality and social weakness. Like other popular readers, fans lack direct access to the means of commercial cultural production and have only the most limited resources with which to influence entertainment industry's decisions. Fans must beg . . . the networks to keep their favourite shows on air, must lobby producers . . . (1992:26–7).

At the very moment that he links this idea to fandom, however, Jenkins also relates it to academia:

> de Certeau's notion of 'poaching' is a theory of appropriation, not of 'misreading'. . . . A conception of 'misreading' . . . implies that there are proper strategies of reading (i.e., those taught by the academy) which if followed produce legitimate meanings and that there are improper strategies (i.e., those of popular interpretation) which . . . produce less worthy results (1992:33).

Jenkins argues that de Certeau's account challenges the authority of academics, within a 'scriptural economy', to police and patrol 'proper' readings and meanings (1992:25). De Certeau appears to accord equal respect to tactical and strategic readings (1988:169). Despite this, it remains the case that just as fans are typically cut adrift from the commercial means of production of official media texts, so too are student readers of cultural theory typically cut adrift from the commercial means of production of Theory (Striphas 2002). The fan poaching from a media text is thus akin to the student poaching from commercially published cultural theory. The student reader seemingly does not read from a position of accredited, strategic academic expertise. But they may still read in such a way as to feel a sense of empowerment, approaching academic texts as foreign territory to poach selected meanings from, possibly even using theory as a vehicle to articulate their prior attitudes and values. The reader who instrumentally skims a scholarly tome rather than tackling it as a whole book, or who reads only end-of-chapter summaries, is arguably reading tactically and getting one over on textual authority. We can therefore suggest that de Certeau's strategy versus tactics opposition might make sense not only of popular reading but also of students' theory-reading. De Certeau's work (1988), much like Stuart Hall's encoding/decoding model, has allowed critics to celebrate the active nature of reading, but students' tactical readings have not been similarly celebrated, further suggesting that theory culture generally remains wedded to notions of proper and prescriptive (strategic) theory-reading, as I argued earlier in this chapter.

Again resembling Hall's model, where preferred meanings are inherently culturally powerful, de Certeau simultaneously installs a fixed narrative of power. This time around, strategies possess power and tactics don't:

> Nowhere in [de Certeau's] work is there anything other than a polar model of domination, according to which sovereign power is exercised by a ruling class (or, more often by an elite . . .) over a mass of oppressed popular subjects who lack all power. It is true that these subject groups exercise an art of the weak which . . . deflects the power of the dominant order, but the flow of power is nevertheless all in the one direction and from a singular source (Frow 1995:55).

We might argue that Stuart Hall's model of reading has a more complex sense of power, though it tends to fall back towards viewing this as held in the moment of encoding, just as de Certeau's poaching metaphor still fixes power in the making of the text rather than in its readings. Jenkins (1992:34) distinguishes de Certeau's model of reading from Hall's by arguing that 'Hall's model, at least as it has been applied, suggests that popular [readings] are . . . classifiable, while de Certeau's model emphasizes the . . . fluidity of popular interpretation' (1992:34). But this is only true if we ignore the key classification carried in de Certeau's model of reading as either strategic or tactical. Also comparing the work of Hall and de Certeau, Rick Altman concludes that both models of reading are marked by a 'fundamental conservatism' (1999:211), insofar as both tend to assume that power is legibly fixed in placed and conserved. The powerful remain so, as do the powerless:

> As Hall and his followers model the situation, even the most oppositional reading is still just an act of decoding, ultimately dependent on a prior act of encoding. While the connections between encoding and decoding are carefully traced, no clear path leads from decoding to subsequent encoding, . . . from the margins of a current society to the centre of a reconfigured society. Similarly, de Certeau assumes that the map has been drawn by others, and that no nomadic [poaching] activity can ever alter it (1999:212).

I would suggest that this conservatism serves a specific function in the theories of Hall and de Certeau. Rather than indicating that cultural studies/theory does not believe in any possibility of the world (or society) ever changing, this pessimism may act, instead, as a kind of cultural-theoretical call to arms. Altman's criticism is that such theories are not good constative descriptions of the world: social change does occur over long periods of time. But Altman fails to consider that cultural theory may also be performative, seeking to act on readers in a text–reader relationship, even aiming to so affect its readers that they may go on to challenge the social order in whatever way possible, changing the world rather than reading it – or changing it by reading it differently. Whether displaying conservatism or an incitement to activism, Hall's and de Certeau's models work to make reading classifiable. They are what I've called 'see-saw models', seeking to keep up in the air notions of reading as active and reading as ultimately secondary or disempowered. And although this may help explain their shared appeal as theories of reading, it also means that cultural theory needs to consider ways of thinking about reading that tell different stories rather than this curious mono-tale of 'readers are active/readers are powerless' that allows cultural theory's consumers to view the readerly glass as half-full or half-empty.

In this chapter, I have considered how doing things with cultural theory involves prescribing specific modes of reading. Whatever else the theorist does, and whatever they study, their work will metaphorically read the world and literally read previous texts of theory – which are, of course, themselves in and of the world. I have examined the practices of instrumental or efferent reading, suggesting that reading cultural theory is unlikely to fit with these expectations: its consumers are called upon to read analytically. And I have contrasted close and distant reading, highlighting how scholarly readers treat close reading as an ideal. Reading only textbook commentaries, rather than theory in the original, deviates from this norm and becomes a sort of devalued and distant reading. Reading both commentaries and originals, on the other hand, allows textbook pre-readings, such as my commentaries on Stuart Hall and Michel de Certeau, and analytical readings to interact, sharpening our sense of cultural theory's intertextual matrix.

I have also argued that we can usefully think of reading as romance (following Pearce 1997). We have affective relationships with texts which exceed either instrumental or efferent or strictly analytical reading positions (for more on this, see Chapter Seven). We therefore also need to hold on to the affective dynamics of how we read cultural theory (Craib 1998), and the private aspects of reading which may not always be easily placed within the frameworks of academic interpretive communities (Fish 1980). Finally, I introduced key theories of reading put forward by Stuart Hall (1980) and Michel de Certeau (1988), considering the structural similarities of these see-saw models.

Although de Certeau views reading as 'poaching, ruse, metaphor, invention, self-pluralization, adaptation, insinuation' (cited in Frow 1995:57), he also suggests that it is extremely difficult to research the act of reading itself as it 'lacks . . . traces' (de Certeau 1988:170). However, in the next chapter, I will consider how we might analyse the traces of cultural theory's student readers, remembering that reading and writing may not always be clearly separable. Some readings may leave their mark, quite literally, as we do not 'simply read the piece of . . . theory . . . but [also] . . . take notes' (Miles 2001:13). In Chapter Four,

I will not treat how people read cultural theory as something which can be separated off from cultural theories of reading. Instead, I will apply and revise de Certeau's work to make sense of readings of cultural theory. I will do something with cultural theory, in other words, turning it back on itself as an object, and carrying out 'cultural studies of cultural studies' (Hall 2002:111). This move cannot be dismissed as theoretical self-referentiality. For, if contemporary academia 'needs urgent . . . investigation . . . as a form of social life' (Evans 2004:ix) then what has been termed 'accountable theory' (Couldry 2000:126) should be of great value here. Accountable theory means quite simply that theories used to account for social and cultural 'Others' should also be used to account for cultural selves: here, what students of cultural theory do when they read Theory. To assume that academia does not require auto-cultural studies because changing the world out there must take moral and intellectual priority is an act of considerable hubris. It falsely implies that studying one's own culture, theory culture, is inherently of lesser consequence than studying Others' cultures. Academic, 'read thy self' (Hartley 1999:487 and 507).

chapter four

Using Cultural Theory

Relying on cultural theorist Michel de Certeau's (1988) distinction between strategies and tactics, I suggested in the previous chapter that cultural theory is typically approached as something to be read correctly. This implies that academics have strategic power within the institution of the academy; marking undergraduate work and assessing postgraduate work are both concerned with evaluating readings of cultural theory as correct. In this chapter, I want to shift my focus from considering prescriptive modes of reading that characterise theory culture to addressing *how actual readers use cultural theory*. In the first section I will suggest that readers of theory act as poachers, just as cultural studies work has suggested of media fans: 'students are also members of educational "audiences" – and they may often be much more "active" and "resisting" than their teachers might wish' (Buckingham 1993:213). Examining cultural theory's active use, this chapter has a number of aims. By introducing the topic of 'theory poachers' I will partly challenge de Certeau's separation of strategy and tactics, as well as presenting a brief case study of students' actual reading activities. I will then conclude with a section entitled 'Succeeding: Using cultural theory as a strategic-tactical reader'. This includes guidance on how apprentice theorists can most effectively use and challenge material from cultural theory without slavishly reproducing established viewpoints. Firstly, though, I want to consider how the process of teaching and learning cultural theory appears to be a matter of disciplining students' resistive readings into correct ones.

Disciplining and innovating

Professional academic David Harris has observed that 'students rarely . . . read . . . pieces [of cultural theory] in the way I think they should read them' (1992:4). In part, this resistance occurs within an opposition to the practices of theory culture. Students assume that they already know (common-sensically as fans, or as members of subcultures) about their cultural objects and so do not need cultural theory:

> The reception of . . . texts and readings in my own courses is interesting in that students often behaved completely contrary to my expectations when I taught. I expected them to be enthusiastic about politics, or at least about the content: in

> cultural studies, it was their cultures I was talking about . . . However, those
> closest to the activities in question found it hard to take the contributions
> seriously: when we read Willis's descriptions of bikers . . . or Hebdige's account
> of punk . . . they sniggered (Harris 1992:5).

Perhaps Harris should not have been surprised. His assumption that students would read in a certain way involved projecting on to them the values of theory culture as an 'interpretive community' (Fish 1980). Yet, over time, the most successful students actually do internalize values and practices of theory culture: they carry out close readings of whole books, and read analytically (see Chapter Three). Harris mistakenly assumes that these students are already securely within the 'culture of theory'. He also reports that others among his student audience 'realised with relief that "[theory] . . . can explain everything". Some of the instrumental ones wrote it all down with no comment, went away and produced "correct" assignments' (1992:5). However, this docile learning by rote of a correct response is again problematic for cultural studies/theory. It implies a situation where the writer alone is, according to John Hartley, understood to be a knowing subject, and the reader on the other hand is subjected in a more direct way – being subject to examination. Hartley goes on to say that the use of cultural studies to them is not emancipation but certification (2003:150).

The paradox which cultural theory finds itself in runs as follows: we (writers and teachers) want you (students and readers) to actively make meaning and produce new readings but at the same time we also want you to passively (re)produce meanings and readings that we can recognize as correct:

> [T]he popular text . . . [can] . . . be pedagogically organised as a vehicle for
> inducting students into resistive readings which, with the assistance of the
> cultural studies teacher, can be corrected, revised and even assessed. It is,
> however, difficult to see how this amounts to anything but *a form of licensed
> poaching performed under the watchful, tutelary eye of gamekeepers in the
> employ of the literary apparatus* [that is, the academy – MH] (Bennett
> 1998:184, my italics).

Literary theorist Robert Scholes has argued in a related context that 'our job is not to produce "readings" for our students but to give them the tools to produce their own' (1985:24). The 'ultimate hell' for Scholes is the notion of a lecturer performing a brilliant reading of a theory that students compliantly reproduce for the purposes of assessment. As Scholes notes, academically correct readings can still be innovative and creative rather than slavish. The expert readings of theory and culture produced by trained academics, and by trained students, can possess substantive novelty, amounting to accredited poachings or appropriations from previous theory. Some readings are more correct than others. Some use theory as a mantra to be repeated, while others set out new terms of debate (Derrida 2003:9–10; Eagleton 2003:2; Sconce 2003:189). And between readings that work as applications (repetition of cultural theory) and those that work as inventions (pioneering new frameworks) there exists a wide spectrum of admixtures, of readings that refine and critique previous theories through application and through the staged clashing of rival theoretical voices. The issue here is how to produce readings that are strategically correct within the realm of proper theorizing and yet are tactical poachings from theory at the same time:

> How is the . . . [cultural theorist] . . . to give the . . . [reading] . . . sufficient novelty? The institution discourages critics from replicating one another's readings (although students may be permitted to do so as a learning exercise). The . . . [reader] . . . is expected either to (a) initiate a new critical theory or method; (b) revise or refine an existing theory or method; (c) "apply" an existing theory or method to a fresh instance; or if the . . . [object of study] . . . is familiar, point out significant aspects which previous commentators have ignored or minimized (Bordwell 1989:30).

The distinction between strategic readings of cultural theory that are correct and tactical readings that are instrumental or resistive is therefore overly simplistic. Within the proper place of cultural theory there are possibilities for cultural theory's regeneration. What can be termed 'strategic-tactical theory poaching' takes place. *Contra* de Certeau's splitting of strategy (space) and tactics (time), tactics can also operate fully and directly within the proper place of the strategic. These internalized tactics indicate that the strategic proper place can be internally divided by attacks on its authority rather than being wholly free of poaching's arts and ruses. Strategic-tactical appropriations tend to prefigure academic transformations from one paradigm to another (Kuhn 1970), as previous authorities are reread and recontextualized. These moments of transformation suggest that strategic forms of power can be subjected to their own processes of internal trickery; strategy confronts not only an 'exteriority' of tactics but also a rogue 'interiority' of strategic-tactics.

In an attempt to contain the generalized possibility of strategic-tactical reading, distinctions between different types of proper theory-reading are often upheld within theory culture. The creativity of strategic-tactical reading is contained via the notion that only certain theorists create and pioneer new theoretical frameworks, while others just apply theory. The former are what Michel Foucault calls 'transdiscursive' authors or 'initiators of discursive practices'. These great individuals do more than simply produce readings, they produce the terrain within which later readings and 'new books and authors can proliferate' (1979:24–5). Foucault's examples are Sigmund Freud and Karl Marx. This hierarchy of trandiscursive pioneers versus acolytes is typically mapped on to the distinction between professional academics (authorised to do things creatively with theory) and students who are only authorized to apply theory. But the problematic figure of the student who is too unruly or too docile in their use of cultural theory (Harris 1992) belies the possibility that students may nevertheless, as theory poachers themselves, creatively transform cultural theory in their readings and rereadings, thereby operating between the realms of pure theory-repetition and pure theory-creation, and within a more generalised terrain of strategic-tactical reading. To think about the possibilities of theory poaching, I want to move on to consider a specific case study. For, as John Hartley has rightly noted:

> [C]ultural studies was focused obsessively on the supply side. Questions about the uses to which literacy in reading – including cultural studies – might be put

had not been asked . . . Even writers like [David] Morley, famous for
championing the cause of empirical audiences in research, showed no interest in
a move across from the supply to the demand side of cultural studies' own
enterprise. None of the Readers [chunky volumes of key readings – M H]
investigated the readers of cultural studies as such . . . No curiosity was
expressed about readers as empirical persons engaged in the activity of doing
cultural studies (Hartley 2003:171–2).

This is a vital observation: Hartley is pointing out that for all its focus on readers, cultural studies/theory has paid scant attention to its very own readers: 'While much passion was expended on insisting that media audiences needed to be known, usually by means of empirical . . . investigation, little energy seemed to go into making similar inquiries into cultural studies' own audience of readers' (Hartley 2003:172).

Michel de Certeau's work on textual poaching, as outlined above and in Chapter Three, gives us one way into the empirical study of reading cultural theory. De Certeau famously emphasizes the manner in which reading, viewed as poaching, is not a passivity in the face of the text, but is rather a set of ruses and ways of using that text (1988:169). It is de Certeau's invocation of the active ordinary reader that has so appealed to cultural studies/theory (Chartier 1995:90–1). But de Certeau also notes that on rare occasions, readers can mark texts as they read: 'the child still scrawls and daubs on his schoolbooks; even if he is punished for this crime, he has made a space for himself and signs his existence as an author on it' (1988:31). By contrast, de Certeau suggests that the TV viewer has no place of his own as 'he cannot write anything on the screen of his set' (1988:31). For de Certeau, the romanticized reader is always somehow absent and protean, always elsewhere and incapable of being brought to light as an object of study. Readers' assumed 'quasi-invisibility' (de Certeau 1988:31) occurs through not having created their own products, instead using those imposed upon them by media industries.

This stark contrast between the scrawling child and the media consumer would seem to have broken down via forms of new media interactivity, where readers can text or email their responses to media content. In any case, the notion that readers have no place of their own had already been challenged via work on media fandom and fan-produced 'fanzines' (Jenkins 1992:3). Readers are increasingly more likely to 'make spaces for themselves,' in de Certeau's terms, though these spaces may be restricted in certain ways (Andrejevic 2004). And where cultural theory is concerned, one such space, and one such practice, occurs via the annotating of theory books by students. Martin Barker and Thomas Austin observe a few such annotations in one book of film theory: 'I'm a first year (male) student and this essay just seems to me a load of jargon; Well, I'm a second year (female) student and I agree – this entire book is just pants'. Barker and Austin inform us that ' "pants" . . . is a 1990s young person's term for something that is . . . rubbish' (2000:vii). These students' annotations are used by Barker with Austin to support their argument that film theory needs re-inventing minus its jargon (see Chapter Two).

Student annotations and additions to a published text can be described as 'marginalia'. H. J. Jackson has undertaken a study of this 'familiar but unexamined phenomenon'

(2001:4), pointing out that 'marginalia represent the actual responses of actual readers' (2001:253). Yet these are still textualized traces of reading activity rather than 'the thing itself' (Hartley 1999:495). Jackson suggests that marginalia, even using 'highlighter to mark significant passages' (2001:1), are material traces of reading that convert the text-reader relationship from a private one-to-one affair into a rather more promiscuous dialogue:

> Annotation introduces [at least] a second voice where writers and publishers intended only one; the reader talks to the book. . . . For readers who cherish the intimacy of reading, who hear only one voice at a time and cannot selectively shut out another, annotations in a book are not merely a distraction, they are a disaster (2001:242).

Marginalia partly reconfigure the reading relationship analysed by Pearce (1997), converting this into a more obviously social event, as later readers encounter not only the text itself but also its annotations. Reading cultural theory annotated by previous readers therefore becomes an experience of 'co-reading', vaguely akin to watching a DVD with an audio commentary track, but more like a textualized and less formalised version of a 'study group' (Knights 1992) where different student voices clash and resonate. Far from being a solitary, private act – though we tend to imagine readers of books as solitary (Long 1994:182) – this type of reading becomes a collective act. Reading cultural theory thus frequently becomes a type of reading-through, whether this involves reading a theory, in part, through the comments that previous students have written in a library-held or second-hand book, or through the responses of one's peers in a seminar, or through textbook commentaries. In the next section, I will discuss examples of marginalia, all of them added to the published text of my own first book, *Fan Cultures* (Hills 2002). I teach a module annually at Cardiff University, Cult Media and Fandom, and as a result there are six copies of *Fan Cultures* in the short-loan section of the university library. But how have real readers used this theory book?

Highlighting and annotating

To provide some context to this exercise, Chapter 3 of *Fan Cultures* concerns autoethnography, which means (in this case) analysing one's own media fandoms. It provides examples which students can use to aid them in their coursework assignments. Material from the book's Introduction through to Chapter 4 is directly relevant to this coursework assignment, since students have to relate theories covered here to their own experience. Chapters 5–8 and the book's Conclusion then provide material that, along with lecture presentations and set readings, form the basis for exam questions. Arbitrarily numbering these library copies of *Fan Cultures* 1 to 6, we encounter the following marginalia as evidence of readers' activities:

Book 1:

- The text is fairly heavily underlined in large, wavy blue pen lines from the Preface through to the first few pages of Chapter 4. Quotes are asterisked, as on page 15, and a comment is added on p. 75. At this point the text is discussing Scott Bukatman's analysis of his comic book fandom:

'I don't read superhero comics anymore. I'm probably not as worried about my dick as I used to be. Well, that isn't exactly true – but I know longer deal with it by reading about mutant muscle men and the big-titted women who love them' (Bukatman 1994:93) Superhero comics are . . . proposed as something vaguely dysfunctional that can be used to assuage a sense of not matching up to a masculine ideal.

    To this, a reader has added: 'like listening to "tuff guy"' , relating this notion of a masculine ideal to a rap/hip-hop track by Half-A-Mill. After the markings at the beginning of Chapter 4, this copy is clean.

- A further reader has added a few pencil lines to Chapter 1, some of which repeat underlining already made in ink (p. 29), some of which are new (p. 27).

Book 2:

- Pencil underlining and comments are added to Chapter 3. On page 65, the beginning of Chapter 3, this same reader has added 'fans interpretations are not questioned' (sic) and on page 89 in white space at the very end of Chapter 3, the same reader has added:

Dawsons Creek and Beverley Hills 90210, School programmes, hoping my childhood was like these, small geeky kid, tried mirroring a prom with our ball, Shanon Doherty, Katie Holmes similar individuals, Sexuality? Ethnicity? Narratives?

Coming at the end of my own autoethnography, these appear to be notes for the student's coursework autoethnography. They indicate TV programmes that the student is or was a fan of, and emphasize aspects of their cultural identity – 'Sexuality? Ethnicity?' – which they are required to analyse.

- Another reader has underlined in blue ink one paragraph in Chapter 3 and a lengthy, indented quote (from Harrington and Bielby (1995:136) on p. 107), as well as other sections in Chapter 4 (p. 104) and Chapter 3 (p. 88).

Book 3:

- Heavy use of orange highlighter pen runs from the Preface and Introduction through to the Introduction's closing summary on p. 21. This highlighting then stops abruptly at the beginning of the section 'The rest of this book . . .'. It does not recur after this point.
- Single and markedly wavy pencil lines, for example, on p. 74–5 and straight, double-underlining (of the phrase 'endless self-interrogation' on p. 73) occur in Chapter 3. These appear to hail from two different readers.

Book 4:

- Almost entirely clean, although there is some underlining at the beginning of the book's Conclusion (p. 172).

Book 5:

- Again, an almost entirely clean copy, although some very faint underlining appears in the Conclusion (p. 177).

Book 6:

- The Preface (as with 'Adorno' and 'Winnicott' on p. xiii), Introduction and Chapters 1–4 are frequently underlined in light pencil. Darker, heavier shading is used for greater emphasis (as with 'Marxist perspective', 'use-value' and 'exchange-value' on p. 33). This is seemingly done by the same reader. This reader has underlined material in the notes (p. xiv) and also material contained in end-of-chapter summaries (e.g. p. 44).

- Some material is also double-underlined in pencil, such as the word self-absent on p. 7, which may indicate a further reader's activity.

- Another reader has used pink highlighter pen to pick out a few blocks of text in Chapters 3 (p. 88), 4 (p. 106–7) and 8 (p. 170).

What can we deduce from analysing these material marks as traces or representations of readers' activities? Well, these textual poachings indicate that readers are doing a number of useful things. Some, such as the user of pink highlighter pen (Book 6) and the blue inker (in Book 2) appear to be selecting quotes and material that can be used to represent wider arguments put forward in the book. They are unhinging chunks of text from the whole book in order to use these metonymically, as parts that stand in for the whole. The tendency to highlight or underline material towards the beginning or end of various chapters often works in the same way, since this is where major lines of argument are being introduced or recapped.

Other readers, such as the pencil underliner in Book 6, lightly underscore detailed explanations of specific concepts such as 'use-value', and then mark the name of the concept itself in darker underlining. This suggests that the reader concerned was working towards an understanding of specific jargon rather than selecting material to quote *per se*. Much of the pencil underlining in various copies is similarly of single terms judged to be significant, for example, 'self-absent' in Book 6 and 'endless self-interrogation' in Book 3. Or, pencil underlining is of key authors cited in the book – Adorno and Winnicott in Book 6, indicating readings that aim to engage with cultural theory as an intertextual matrix (see Chapter Two here).

Where readers have added comments to the text, these suggest that they are relating cultural theory to their own experiences – either choosing an example ('tuff guy') that is closer to their experience than Scott Bukatman's comic book fandom, or beginning to generate a skeletal outline of their own autoethnography ('hoping my childhood was like these') rather than passively consuming words on the page. However, given that there are surprisingly few readers' comments, and no sign of direct dialogue between readers, we can infer that these consumers of cultural theory (a) tended to respect the text as a library-held artefact, and (b) tended to treat reading as a privatized, one-to-one text-reader interaction, following what Elizabeth Long calls 'the powerful . . . picture of the solitary reader' (1994:182) in our culture. The relative cleanness of Books 4 and 5 suggests that readers may have refrained from marking texts previously clear of marginalia, for as H. J. Jackson has noted, marginalia can be considered 'book abuse' as much as book use (2001:234).

There is much evidence of instrumental reading, which is only to be expected given that the notion of tactical reading (see Chapter Three) suggests that readers will take away meanings relevant to their pre-established interests. Examples of this are the orange highlighting in Book 3, where the reader has worked on the Preface and Introduction before concluding their reading at precisely the point where the rest of the book is set out. Also, Book 1 is marked only in those chapters that relate to student coursework, otherwise being clean, while four of the six copies are predominantly marked in Chapter 3, which most directly sets up the coursework assignment. There is little evidence that these library copies are being approached as whole books. Of course, this could be due to the fact that these are short-loan library copies, meaning that students are materially compelled by time and monetary pressures to focus only on certain sections.

If this brief study has given some insight into how actual readers actually read, then it may be worth concluding this chapter by indicating how readers of cultural theory can best move towards carrying out strategic-tactical theory poaching rather than more clearly instrumental and tactical reading. Strategic-tactical reading does not just apply theory, but rather challenges and criticizes cultural theory's frameworks in order to refine and develop new insights. Rather than assuming that such elite work is the property of expert academics (see Hills 2002), how might students best work towards producing their own skilful readings? What do students need to do to succeed in the realm of theory culture?

Succeeding: Using cultural theory as a strategic-tactical reader

Doing well academically means, to a great extent, internalizing the values of theory culture. It therefore means 'doing as scholars do' rather than treating Theory as just words on a page, and sometimes alien-seeming words at that. Reading correctly, and getting reasonable marks for reading as one's tutor expects, falls closest to the domain of strategic reading. By contrast, reading instrumentally and selectively resembles tactical reading, that is, reading in line with a set of pre-established aims. But this opposition between strategic and tactical reading neglects creative rereading – reading that works on cultural theory rather than simply recognising and repeating it. Such transformative readings introduce new ideas or new lines of thought by working through preceding concepts.

At this point, an uncharitable reader may complain that I am somehow implying that students are able *en masse* to adopt the role of a Freud or a Marx or a Derrida, creating strikingly new theories out of old. I am not suggesting such a thing. Neither am I ruling out the possibility. Instead, I am opposing the lowest common denominator notion that undergraduate students should only iterate and repeat theory, while postgraduates may, in time, become able to work with theory, only reaching full academic accreditation as they produce original insights. This hierarchy, frequently naturalized in theory culture, works to defend an academic status quo and a deeply strategic fixing of readerly expertise and elitism. Against such a view, I am suggesting that we consider students at all levels of higher education as being capable of meaningfully critiquing and developing cultural theory in relation to their own interests and investments. Student readings can achieve strategic-tactical aims, even if these readings may not always be as revolutionary as those instigated by the most transdiscursive of authors. Rather than implying that students are lesser readers who should repeat others' readings and passively rehearse correct readings, I am arguing for a more respectful view of the creativity and activity of apprentice theorists. Such an argument has been made for media audiences, but not for cultural theory's audiences. It seems curious that although cultural theory/studies scholars frequently argue against a 'derogation of the lay actor', they often proceed to play out just such derogation in relation to incorrect readers and their readings.

In a sense, strategic-tactical readings cannot be entirely prescribed, prefigured and standardized as correct or incorrect, since they do not only follow texts. Such readings appropriate or take something from cultural theory, twist its existent materials into new shapes. These are appropriating and critical readings. Through such practices, readers of cultural theory gradually become 'more active or interventionist . . . less passive or receptive' (Johnson *et al* 2004:172). Such responses also cannot be instrumental, since to read creatively and transformatively calls for an engagement with the intertextual matrix of theory rather than with a text assumed to be symbolically bounded and singular. Hence, these readings are both partly strategic – occupying the proper place of cultural theory – but also partly tactical, treating cultural theory as something to be taken from, and simultaneously refined, reworked and re-energized. The guiding image of this type of reading is thus that it, somewhat combatively, does things with cultural theory. Strategic-tactical readings can operate in any number of ways, and I will now, non-exhaustively and in no special order, outline a few of these.

Strategic-tactical readings can focus on indications of the theorist's affiliations and group memberships. Does the writer align him- or herself with cultural studies or cultural theory? If the text is a book complete with acknowledgements, then who is acknowledged? Where is the writer based? By googling some of the names contained in acknowledgements, or checking them in library catalogues, readers can start to get a sense of the social networks that accompany the theorist's work. This can be important, as we may be able to map the type of work with which this theorist wishes to associate him- or herself. Another way of doing this is to consider which theorists are cited approvingly and which are criticized. Again, by researching some of these names, we can start to contextualise the current theory within cultural theory's intertextual matrix, which will enable us to consider what, if anything, is novel and distinctive about the current theory in relation to rivals and alternatives. Note that this approach requires reading outside and beyond the bounds of the specific text in order to gain a sense of context. Often lecturers work to provide contexts for their students' reading, but textbooks and secondary commentaries can also be useful supports within this process. By building up an idea of how any given theory relates to the broader field – and theory's intertextual matrix – strategic-tactical readings can then play tricks and ruses with this sense of context by forging new links between writers, playfully positioning a theory in a different context to the one in which it usually supposed to operate or be fixed, or elaborating on the established context in such a way as to challenge how a theory has itself poached from its predecessors.

Taking Stuart Hall's 'Encoding/decoding' essay (1980) as a sample text to be read, in terms of affiliation, we could note that it is printed in the book *Culture, Media, Language* which actually bears the logo of the Centre for Contemporary Cultural Studies, University of Birmingham. An opening essay by Hall introduces the work of the Centre; Hall is one of the editors of the collection, and the book's cover blurb tells us that the CCCS 'has played a pioneering role in the development of cultural studies'. By studying 'para-texts' (Genette 1997) – all the materials that precede and follow the book itself, ranging from book cover to blurb to acknowledgements, dedications, prefaces and so on – we can begin to establish a sense of academic context and the social networks that Hall's work emerges through and alongside. Fairbairn and Fairbairn (2001:91) stress the importance of this type of 'active reading', noting that good readers make use of the 'structural features of [academic] books' such as their blurbs and publishing histories.

We can also consider the range of Hall's references in this essay: he cites Karl Marx approvingly in opposition to how 'Traditionally, mass communications research has conceptualized the process of communication' (1980:128), and returns positively to Marx later in the essay (1980:129–30). Writers in media studies such as Philip Elliott (author of *Making of a Television Series: A Case Study in the Sociology of Culture*, 1973) are cited (1980:129), as is US mass-communications scholar George Gerbner (1980:131), placing Hall's work in relation to then-current media studies. Hall then goes on to approvingly cite Italian literary theorist Umberto Eco on 'codes' of meaning (1980:132), following this with a positive reference to the work of structuralist Roland Barthes (1980:133). Then, on page 135, Hall introduces the only lengthy indented quote in his essay. This is therefore clearly important for the development of Hall's own argument. It comes from a speaker at an event held at the University of Leicester (the essay's notes tell us this: see 1980:295n12). And Hall disputes the ideas put forward. This is very much not an approving quote, instead Hall writes immediately: 'Our quarrel here is with the notion of "subjective capacity", as if . . . the interpretative level were an individualized and private matter' (1980:135). He then sets out the different categories of decoding (see Chapter Three). Consulting the notes for 'Encoding/decoding' gives us a fuller sense of other theorists used by Hall although not always directly referred to in the main body of the text. By reading the text and its para-texts closely, we can suggest that Hall is writing as some type of Marxist, or at least that he is poaching from Marx, that he is also adopting structuralist ideas, and that he is strongly opposed to subjective explanations of decoding, which are linked to work at the University of Leicester and to traditional mass-communications research. Having reconstructed a sense of how Hall's work connects into cultural theory's intertextual matrix, we can ascertain what is distinctive about his essay: it attacks a subjective version of audience meaning-making head on, and uses structuralist work on linguistic codes to support this. We can also note that Hall is attacking the linearity of a previous sender/message/receiver model of communication.

How, then, can we use this as the basis for a strategic-tactical reading? Well, we could playfully shift the context of Hall's work – what if his break with the traditional model was not as clear as he argues (1980:131)? What if we viewed his own work, counter to his expressed intentions, within the context of mass-communications models? We could then argue that actually Hall's model does not entirely do away with the sender-message-receiver model, especially as his diagram (on p. 130) has arrows moving from a sender via a message to a receiver, even if these three moments are retermed 'encoding – programme as meaningful discourse – decoding'. Indeed, this critical, strategic-tactical reading of Hall's has been put forward by one of the leading cultural theorists to have applied and revised encoding/decoding, David Morley. He notes that one problem with the model is that it implies 'the notion of television as conveyor belt for a pre-given message or "meaning"' (1992:120). My point here is not that student readings should reinvent this particular wheel. Rather, by following techniques of strategic-tactical reading, I am suggesting that it is entirely possible for apprentice theorists to arrive at conclusions akin to those produced by experts. As Steven Miles has usefully observed:

> You will gain considerable confidence if somebody has the same interpretation as yourself. . . . theory is not written in stone. It is there to be interpreted and discussed in a critical fashion. . . . you should not underestimate the benefit of secondary sources . . . [Although] never a substitute for original ones, . . . they might provide you with that extra bit of confidence in your own ability to read . . . theory (Miles 2001:13).

Engaging with Hall's original work, and perhaps some secondary commentaries, the student reader does not after all need to be familiar with every arcane aspect of cultural theory's intertextual matrix, nor do they need to know a lot about television production *per se*. Instead, they need to be open to reconstituting the context of a theoretical work and open to exploring how this work is positioned in relation to theory's intertextual matrix.

As well as challenging encoding/decoding for its partial replication of an idea that it seeks to distinctively break away from, we can also assess Hall's borrowings from structuralism. By tracking his references, it is clear that Hall is working across disciplines, relating structuralist literary theory to media theory. But he does this while also citing Karl Marx on the 'passage of forms'. This introduces a necessary tension into Hall's position. He uses structuralism as his source of ideas about en- and de-'coding', but links these ideas to a Marxist-derived model of cultural power. It is partly the collision of these very different theoretical lineages which results in Hall's model fixing power on the side of encodings (just as Marx fixed power in the ruling class), despite the fact that the decoding part of Hall's argument should grant social and cultural power to audiences as decoders by virtue of their socially situated decodings (see Chapter Three). Further strategic-tactical readings of encoding/decoding could therefore creatively challenge Hall's specific linkage of structuralism and Marxism, viewing this as a problematic blend of incompatible schools of thought, rather than accepting the model as a 'holy whole' (Ekegren 1999:116).

Strategic-tactical readings can focus on the rhetorical systems of the given theory – how does it rhetorically seek to persuade the reader of its legitimacy and validity? Does it repeatedly use certain classes of metaphors, or specific images, to achieve these aims?

Staying with 'Encoding/decoding' as our example (primarily because it is a short and influential piece of cultural theory which has already been introduced in Chapter Three), we can note how Hall systematically refers to encoding as happening in a place apart from other social processes. 'Production structures of television . . . draw topics from other sources', and these production structures are a 'differentiated part' of the wider social whole (1980:129). Encoded and meaningful TV discourse then achieves 're-entry into the practices of audience reception' (1980:130). Hall therefore uses a spatialised language: encoding has its own proper place here (resembling de Certeauian theorizing), while decoding does not, despite the fact that 'before this message can have an "effect" (however defined) it must first be . . . meaningfully decoded' (1980:130). Hall's rhetorical structuring of TV's 'meaningful discourse' as emerging through professional, production practices that are spatialized helps to lend weight to his notion that encoding is powerful. But it would be entirely possible to emphasize not the space-bound nature of TV production but, in place of this, the need for TV messages to be comprehensible to large numbers of viewers. In this case the matter or myth of space-bound power held by a kind of TV centre would start to appear far less self-evident.

The reader can also consider how Hall uses scare quotes – ' ' – around certain terms. He is rhetorically consistent in this practice. His systematic placing-in-quotes works to destabilise certain ideas, or to indicate that he does not passively accept particular concepts. Strategic-tactical readers should, then, not only be on the look-out for who is referenced and quoted, but also for which established concepts are used while simultaneously being challenged. Hall refers to TV's ' "effects" (however defined)', as well as to the 'use' that TV messages are put to, and the 'gratifications' of TV audiences (1980:130–1). Similarly, he puts quote marks around 'source' and 'receiver' (1980:131). These tiny marks frequently speak academic volumes. They indicate that Hall is refuting source and receiver models as well as subjective theories of audiences, who are said to use texts for the gratifications they provide. Indeed, the traditional models Hall (1980) was criticising were 'uses and gratifications' theory and 'media effects' research (see Morley 1992:51, who also puts 'effects' in scare quotes). One mark of strategic-tactical reading – working to creatively transform ways of thinking – is that it systematically borrows terms and encloses them in scare quotes to demonstrate a new-found distance from the assumptions written into those very terms. French (post-)structuralist Jacques Derrida does something rhetorically similar when he suggests crossing out specific theoretical terms on a page so that the objected-to words will remain visible underneath marks of their erasure or critique. This practice is called placing a concept 'under erasure' or *sous rature* (see Norris 1982:69). Placing words under erasure and systematically placing them in scare quotes both work to indicate that a strategic-tactical reading is underway, and that key concepts and terms are being revised. These terms constitute the very ground across which the theory poacher travels.

Theoretical affiliations and ruptures can thus be marked typographically and rhetorically as well as through the grander sweep of references and direct quotes. Reading for scare quotes is helpful because it allows us to note that sometimes cultural theorists are quoting even when they are not directly providing referenced quotations. Of course, some of these indirect quotes (in scare quotes) may also be approving ones – just as direct references can be approving or disapproving – and so it remains important to relate the use of scare quotes to the overall context of a theorist's argument.

Strategic-tactical readings can focus on the stories that are told by a theory – how does this theory use specific narrative structures? What resolutions, if any, does this theory or story have? Does this theory narrate its superiority to alternative theories?

Essentially, Hall's essay tells the story of a 'new and exciting phase in . . . audience research' (1980:131). It, or Hall, is therefore a protagonist in the very events recounted.

'Encoding/decoding' is thus a highly performative piece of cultural theory, we might say, it acts to do something with and to theory (and thus our view of the world) rather than simply describing or reflecting a state of affairs. The proposed resolution of this narrative is the emergence of Hall's encoding/decoding model itself, and thus the essay ends rather abruptly as soon as Hall has detailed his three reading positions: 'dominant', 'negotiated' and 'oppositional'. The sequencing of these reading positions is also narratively interesting, as there is no necessary reason for Hall to present them as dominant, negotiated and oppositional. By contrast, I introduced them as dominant, oppositional and negotiated earlier, in order to emphasize their 'thesis-antithesis-synthesis' structure. By concluding on the oppositional code and then adding only the flourish of a one-line paragraph, Hall shifts performative register from theorist to activist, exhorting his readers to action: 'Here the "politics of signification" – the struggle in discourse – is joined', he conclusively proclaims (1980:138). It is worth noting how odd this actually is, standing as the conclusion to a major essay in the field of cultural studies/theory. It is almost as if Hall has broken off mid-thought. There are none of the niceties and civilities of a closing summary or a rounding-up. Instead, 'Encoding/decoding' announces that we have decisively shifted into the era of a politics of signification, suggesting that its readers must now take sides in this struggle.

The fact that Hall narrates a tale that culminates in his own emergent theory is an aesthetic structuring that may go some way towards accounting for the continued appeal of this essay, as well as for the force it has had on other academics. There are few comparably self-conscious, self-narrated pronouncements of novelty in cultural theory, although Derrida's 'Structure, Sign and Play in the Discourse of the Human Sciences' (1978[1966]) may be one, given that Derrida also concludes by referring to 'a birth . . . in the offing' (1978:293) by way of concluding his strategic-tactical reading of structuralism which prefigures and announces an emerging post-structuralism.

Hall also sounds notes of wariness, suggesting that his depiction of TV will 'crudely characterize' the processes involved, as well as observing that 'Beginnings and endings have been announced in communications research before, so we should be cautious' (1980:131). This tone of humility, and again, Hall's self-awareness that he is using a narrative structure, both contribute to a sense that he is not merely asserting a 'new and exciting phase in so-called audience research' (1980:131), but is instead carefully and authoritatively weighing up its possibilities.

Strategic-tactical readings can focus on the basic assumptions of any theory – what has to be true for this theory to work as it does? What are the essential aspects of the given theory and what do they assume?

By considering cultural theory through the image or metaphor of a series of sedimented layers, strategic-tactical readings can seek to excavate theory, pursuing its most deeply buried levels. Even where cultural theory appears to be challenging common-sense ways of thinking as well as previous disciplinary schools of thought – as encoding/decoding does – it still tends to replay and carry specific assumptions. For example, Hall makes a number of assumptions. He assumes, for instance, that we can entirely bracket out the 'subjective' matter of reading, and that this is, in other words, of no consequence or theoretical importance: 'Of course, there will always be private, individual, variant readings. But "selective perception" is almost never as selective, random or privatized as the concept suggests. The patterns exhibit, across individual variants, significant clusterings' (Hall 1980:135).

Reading this attentively, it seems contradictory. Lacking confidence in our reading, we might even feel a sense of confusion – the poor, disempowered reader confronting a powerfully encoded text. Have we missed something? But we can take solace in Miles's argument that 'the student of . . . theory should not assume that he or she is somehow ignorant or stupid. More often than not . . . confusion is caused by the fact that the theorist him- or herself is confused' (2001:12–3). Readerly confusion can therefore be a useful guide to problems in theory, rather than a sign of the reader's lack of cultural competencies and training as an academic reader (though it can be this too). So, apprentice theorists might want to listen to their confusion more, if you like, seeking to determine whether their confusion is productive and can be used as the starting point for a critical reading.

And here, Hall's argument seems to be confused. He suggests that there are 'always . . . private, individual readings', something he has opposed up to this point since such readings could be infinitely variable rather than being patterned in relation to preferred readings. But then he takes away the notion of privatized readings by asserting that even here, clusters of meaning exist. So-called privatized readings, which two sentences previously were said to always exist, now actually don't exist at all according to the encoding/decoding model. In short, the essential aspects of encoding/decoding theory – that readings are socially patterned into fixed categories – require a foundational assumption. At the most sedimented level of this instance of cultural theory, there lies a presupposition that is never fully backed up: it is assumed that there can be no meaningfully or significantly individual readings. Although 'no doubt some total misunderstandings . . . do exist' (1980:135–6), where readers are not within 'the limits and parameters' which encoding has set up, these misunderstandings are not of analytical significance for Hall (though Lewis 1991:123–57 addresses the misunderstandings and confusions of news viewers). One possible strategic-tactical reading and reworking of encoding/decoding would therefore involve reintroducing the notion of strongly individualized readings. However, this would threaten to bring the whole theoretical edifice toppling down. The fact that such a critique has not been forwarded to date suggests that cultural theory/studies has tended, as an interpretive community, to share Hall's Marxist-sociological assumption that individual readings are only ideologically or falsely individualized.

Strategic-tactical readings can focus on the conceptual distinctions and divisions that sustain the given theory; what opposed conceptual units is the world broken into? Which of these primary concepts are valued or celebrated by the theorist and which are devalued or denigrated?

This type of reading can be characterised as 'deconstructive' (after the philosophy of deconstruction established by Jacques Derrida; see Norris 1982). Paula Saukko has outlined key tenets of deconstructive reading:

> it challenges taken-for-granted . . . concepts . . . it is interested in uncovering the binaries that underpin the language . . . we use to make sense of reality. . . . [d]econstruction aims to destabilize binaries by unravelling the way in which binaries render the other side of the equation invisible and natural (2003:135–6).

The binaries (any set of opposed terms) that deconstructive readings attack can be things such as 'mind' versus 'body', 'masculine' versus 'feminine', 'nature' versus 'culture', or even 'writing' versus 'reading'. This type of approach is useful for illuminating how theoretical frameworks persistently tend to establish binaries and then prioritize one of these opposed terms over the other. Continuing to pursue the example of the encoding/decoding model, we know that Hall sets up and opposes the two concepts that give the model its name. But which of the two does his writing tend to prioritize or value, and which does it tend to devalue? These processes of (de)valuing are not always immediately evident. It appears, though, that Hall's model prioritizes encoding, since it is this that comes first in the model, and there can be no decoding without a prior encoding. A deconstructive reading of Hall's model would attempt to destabilize the encoding/decoding binary by arguing that these conceptual units cannot be kept apart from one another. Deconstruction works to blur binaries by demonstrating that terms set up against one another actually interpenetrate. The devalued term occurs within the valued term: 'Deconstruction is not simply a . . . reversal of categories which otherwise remain distinct and unaffected. It seeks to undo both a given set of priorities and the very system of conceptual opposition that makes that order possible' (Norris 1982:31).

Deconstructing the conceptual units of the encoding/decoding model would involve suggesting that encoding's prioritization is false, since all encoding requires an auto-decoding. I can only know that I've encoded this book by reading back the sentences I've written – the supposedly primary act of encoding is invaded by its supposedly secondary Other, decoding. And media professionals encoding a news report must, similarly, initially decode their own report in order to establish that it makes sense and follows certain conventions. The devalued term (decoding, which Hall views as being limited by encoding) invades the conceptual space of the valued term, encoding. We can therefore read Hall's work deconstructively by arguing that decoding is more significant and central than Hall permits it to be.

A deconstructive approach to de Certeau's theory of reading-as-poaching is also possible. Such a reading would take de Certeau's conceptual building blocks or units – strategy and tactics – and assess which is prioritised in his work. Addressing exactly how de Certeau uses the terms 'strategy' and 'tactics' calls for careful consideration. Yes, de Certeau fixes strategy as the more powerful force, but the entire thrust of *The Practice of Everyday Life* (1988) lies in uncovering the multiple and diffused workings of tactics, those 'art[s] of the weak'. Whether or not we can conclude that strategy and tactics constitute a clear binary opposition (see Highmore 2002:154–6; Buchanan 2000a:86–7), it is evident that de Certeau celebrates tactics as opposed to strategy, just as John Fiske (1989, 1992) and Henry Jenkins (1992) have tended to when using de Certeau's theory. De Certeau's prioritisation of tactics is even implied in the phrase 'art of the weak' (1988:37). Strategies are not represented as possessing an art: they are impositions, working to militaristically fortify space. It is the artful that de Certeau values, championing tactics against the disciplining work of strategy. But as I noted in Chapter Three, de Certeau's model assumes that power is fixed in place: he devalues strategy for its exercising of power, and values tactics for the way they convert a lack of power into successful ruses. A deconstructive reading would suggest that tactics are at work within strategies, and that again there can be no clear separation of these terms into a binary opposition. If we consider the deconstructive possibility that tactics may infiltrate strategic attempts to control and manage institutions, then we can begin to reconceptualize a scenario in which power is not definitively held by one group or institution, but is self-fragmented, and subject to internal struggles and re-creations. Indeed, blurring together strategy and tactics is exactly what I have done in this chapter. I have put forward the notion that rather than accepting a binary opposition of strategy (academics' correct readings) versus tactics (students' instrumental readings), we can consider strategic-tactical readings in which cultural theories are not just responded to correctly but are also critiqued and poached from.

As Gary Hall points out, 'Deconstruction is an enactment of a certain problematizing reading' (2002:3). It makes problems for prior conceptual units and oppositions rather than reading a theory in its own terms and so repeating it. Deconstruction therefore necessarily 'remains closely tied to the texts it interrogates' (Norris 1982:31). In Derrida's work, we can find what amounts to a provisional definition of strategic-tactical reading:

> Within the experience of following [a theory] there is something other, something new, or something different which occurs and which I sign. . . . That's what I call a counter-signature . . . which both confirms the first signature [the theory that has been read], and nevertheless is opposed to it. . . . A counter-signature is this strange alliance between following and not following [a theory], confirming and displacing (Derrida 2003:10).

Deconstructive readings are very close; they do not simply oppose a theory but nor do they mechanically replicate it. Instead, they inhabit its binary oppositions and conceptual units, and twist these into new configurations. Such readings are hence both strategic, a deconstructive reading remains a correct reading of sorts, and tactical, since they introduce 'something other, something new' through an engagement with cultural theory's binary oppositions.

Strategic-tactical readings can focus on the limits to a theoretical explanation. What does a theory not say? What does it rule as being outside its remit? All forms of cultural theory are abstractions and models of the world. This means that they cannot explain 'everything' and will always possess limitations.

Deconstructive reading does not have a monopoly on strategic-tactical reading. A range of theorists more closely linked to structuralism have also read in ways that supplement and extend prior texts of theory, both following and not following prior cultural theory. One such type of structuralist reading has been termed 'symptomatic reading'. Philosopher Louis Althusser, along with Etienne Balibar, puts forward this notion in *Reading Capital*, where it is argued that Marx's work can be read to uncover another text 'present as a necessary absence in the first' (1970:28). Colin Davis has explained what is at stake in any symptomatic reading:

> What Althusser calls a *lecture symptomale* [is] a reading which 'detects the undetected in the very text that it reads', finding in the text a second text which 'is articulated in the lapses of the first' (Althusser *et al* 1996:23) . . . Although part of the aim of the symptomatic reading seems to be to pin down meaning . . . its effect is also to open up meaning to a process of supplementation which need never end. The identification of gaps or blanks in the text serves as a simple illustration of this (Davis 2001:303–4).

Akin to deconstructive reading, symptomatic reading refuses to take a text at face value and to merely replicate its sense. Instead, the text's 'symptoms' are diagnosed, if you like, just as a doctor has to interpret signs of illness in order to detect a particular malaise. Many illnesses are not immediately self-evident; instead they have to be traced through a process of detection and brought to light. For Althusser, cultural theory calls for a metaphorical process of symptom-tracking, with alternative texts being hidden below the surface of a theorist's work, and cast into the gaps and absences of the theory concerned. The metaphor of reading texts for symptoms is also indebted to Freudian psychoanalysis, and the idea that people may display symptoms of behaviour, such as phobias or obsessions, which can be read by the psychoanalyst as indicating repressed psychological material. Althusser's mode of reading suggested that 'an interpreter might understand the author better than himself' (Bordwell 1989:72). This was greatly appealing to cultural theorists and critics, of course, since it suggested that their readings could supplant or critically diagnose preceding texts. Within such a framework, the reader takes on an inflated or extreme significance. It is their reading which self-consciously adds to the text rather than working within its encoded parameters, as Hall would imply, or poaching certain elements and meanings from the text as de Certeau (1988) suggests. Symptomatic readings became quite the fashion in literary, media and film studies of the 1970s (see Bordwell 1989:71–104).

Pierre Macherey developed the notion of symptomatic reading (see Buxton 1990:12–6; Tulloch and Jenkins 1995:42–4), suggesting that 'we must go beyond the work and explain it, must say what it does not and could not say' and adding that the 'work must be elaborated, *used* . . . within its proper limits' (1978:77–8). Like Derrida, Macherey (1978:136–56) offered a strategic-tactical reading of arch-structuralist Claude Levi-Strauss in which he argued that 'Analysis is not a repetition but the production of a new knowledge' (1978:151; see Ekegren 1999:108–9). This new knowledge is realized through a process of questioning:

> We should question the work as to what it does not and cannot say, in those silences for which it has been made. The . . . order of the work is thus less significant than its real determinate disorder. The order which it professes is merely an imagined order, projected onto disorder (1978:155).

This advice is strikingly similar to the reading of Janice Radway's *Reading the Romance* enacted by Ien Ang (see Chapter Three), in which Ang (1996) reads for the absences in Radway's (1987, 1991) work, noting that the author remains silent on the matter of whether her own interventions helped to construct the community she was studying, while also writing out any notion of a feminist romance fan by presenting an opposition between academic feminists and non-academic romance fans. Rather than destabilizing binary oppositions, the symptomatic reading looks for what is not said and considers why these absences have been produced. In Radway's (1987) case, the absences marking *Reading the Romance* are concerned with defining popular readers firstly as 'real' – their community is just out there for Radway to find and study, and secondly as in need of feminist consciousness-raising, hence consoling Radway and her academic feminist readers.

Another good example of a reading which addresses symptomatic limits to a piece of cultural theory is Alan McKee's response to *Fan Cultures* (Hills 2002):

> My biggest disappointment with this book is that there is, in fact, so little of this . . . positioning [of the author] informing the writing (it is separated out in a section from pages 82 to 88). Apart from . . . [a] . . . single paragraph . . . acknowledging that Hills's relationship with theory is another form of fandom, this insight vanishes from the rest of the book (2003b:127).

McKee makes a criticism of my work that is similar to Ang's (1996) of Radway. Although, unlike Radway, I sought to analyse my own fandoms in *Fan Cultures*, I nevertheless inscribed a series of distinctions between 'the fan' and 'the academic'. Most notably, I limited discussion of my fandoms to popular media texts rather than thinking of my passion for cultural theory as another fandom. I symptomatically ruled out any concept of 'academic fandom' (Lacey 2000). There was a different book hidden in the gaps and absences of *Fan Cultures*, one which would have more centrally challenged separations of fandom and academia rather than participating, to an extent, in these distinctions and belief systems. McKee points out that it is

> only in the conclusion that [Hills] returns to the possibility that it would be useful to study 'academic subcultures' as fan cultures. I want to know – why doesn't this book do that? Why is Hills the person writing the book *before* that, the one that clears the way?' (2003b:127).

All cultural theory is limited, and cannot say everything. It cannot be perfect or unquestionable, only 'good enough' (Winnicott 1992:67) within its various contexts of production and reception. However, an awareness of theory's limits can act as a spur to further cultural production: McKee's points are, in fact, addressed here (see Part Three). Although symptomatic reading seems to open the door to endless supplements, it should not be taken as any cause to view theory as somehow futile given its always limited nature. We can ceaselessly consider further limits to pieces of cultural theory, but this does not undermine the positive, determinate achievements of such theory. Considering theory's limits also allows for dialogue between ways of thinking, just as McKee's (2003b) review of *Fan Cultures* acted as one inter-text provoking this book.

Theory's absences can, in principle, be almost infinite (Davis 2001:304), but symptomatic readings generally restrict themselves to seeking systematic silences, silences that can be taken to indicate an author's world view or set of beliefs. Hall, for example, glosses over the possibility of 'misreadings' of encoded material, and so these 'total misunderstandings' (1980:135–6) become a structuring absence in his model, being cast outside the triumvirate of dominant, negotiated and oppositional readings. Why does Hall's model not say anything more about 'total misunderstandings', given that he admits their existence? Doing so would open the door to the possibility that reader's codes might be entirely unrelated to the codes used in encoding, challenging the very logic of Hall's model, in which decodings must be related to encodings. What else is the encoding/decoding model silent about? Well, it offers a general theory – a theory said to work generally for all TV audiences – and as such it necessarily remains silent on actual, social and individual differences among audience groupings, referring abstractly only to 'a viewer' (1980:137) or 'he/she' (1980:138). General theory always takes on specific silences as it presumes to be able to explain all instances of its object of study. Hall is therefore operating within an ideology, a set of beliefs, about the range, scope and explanatory power of cultural theory – not, it should be said, an ideology that is shared by all cultural theorists, some of whom believe that theory's aims may be more modest, context-specific and situated. Nor would all cultural theorists assume that preferred readings can be objectively isolated, as Hall argues, again strongly defending the generalisability of his model (1994).

Are there also silences that structure de Certeau's theory of reading? Here, we might note that while discussing 'reading as poaching' (Chapter XII of *The Practice of Everyday Life*) de Certeau aligns this activity with a host of others such as walking in the city (Chapter VII), ordinary language (Chapter I) and popular culture (Chapter II). By constituting a host of practices within a singular object – everyday life – and applying the same theoretical recipe to these different examples, de Certeau also gives the impression of having uncovered a general theory. But this creates a systematic silence with regards to just how everyday de Certeau's different examples are. Is walking in a city really analogous to reading as a creative act? We might ponder the fact that these acts could mean very different things socially and culturally: the route one takes to a lecture theatre does not have the same significance as what one studies or learns in that lecture. As Bennett has argued:

> What de Certeau's account of everyday practices most lacks . . . is anything approaching an adequate sociological . . . description of . . . practices that would be capable of locating them within . . . specific social milieux. Instead, what is offered is a poetics of the oppressed . . . in which the prospect of understanding the specific social logics informing specific forms of resistance is traded in . . . for a generalised account of transgression (1998:174).

Like Hall, perhaps de Certeau generalises too soon. And this creates gaps in his work that, for Bennett, require a sociological filling-in, or a sociological strategic-tactical reading.

Strategic-tactical readings can focus on neologisms, on new terms that the writer coins, asking what work these terms perform in the theory. How do they push us to think differently about a situation?

De Certeau's (1988) term 'poaching' has been highly productive in cultural theory. As a metaphorical image, it does not seem obscure, and it usefully carries a sense of power relations. However difficult some of de Certeau's theorizing may be, the image of the poacher which has been popularised in media and cultural studies is immediately graspable. In a study of imagery in philosophy, Michèle Le Doeuff argues that

> the meaning conveyed by images works both for and against the system that deploys them. *For*, because they sustain something which the system itself cannot justify, but which is nevertheless needed for its proper working. *Against*, for the same reason – or almost: their meaning is incompatible with the system's possibilities (1989:3).

Neologisms usually carry certain imagery either directly, or in their wake. By introducing new metaphors into cultural theory they attempt to provoke new ways of thinking. Following Le Doeuff's argument, we can observe how neologisms convey specific imagery but also pose difficulties. For instance, the poacher is a recognisable figure, but our common-sense understanding of the phenomenon of poaching may then limit how we think of the finer details of de Certeau's theory. The term 'poaching' may partly work to reinforce a reading which views strategy and tactics – gamekeeper and poacher – as pitted against each other. By the same token, the notion of poaching works for de Certeauian theory by naturalizing the fixed power relations that are assumed in the general-theoretical model. Since de Certeau offers no definitive evidence for strategy always being powerful while tactics are always weak, his image or neologism of reading as 'poaching' props up that very assumption, making it appear persuasive.

Similarly, Stuart Hall's use of encoding and decoding as neologisms works to push us towards breaking with a linear view of a message travelling from sender to receiver. The imagery of 'coding', drawn from structuralism, directs us to think of media texts as being subject to different codings, just as one can code a message differently. Communication is de-naturalized through such a neologism, and converted into a matter of the construction of meaning. However, the difficulty with relying on an image of the code to do this work is that it also tends to defeat Hall's theoretical system: the general use of a code is, after all, to encrypt a message which our chosen recipient can then decrypt and plainly understand. Coding, in a 'common-sense' version of the term, is what actually guarantees that a message gets through to just the right person. This hardly helps to emphasise Hall's argument that 'there is no necessary correspondence between encoding and decoding' (1980:135).

Focusing on neologisms and their imagery allows a strategic-tactical reading to indicate how cultural theory attempts to legitimate its new ways of thinking through stock images, while also considering how neologisms may partly work against a theorist's expressed aims. Such readings do not merely repeat and follow theory – whether it is of poaching or decoding – but critically explore the conditions of theory's innovation and circulation.

Strategic-tactical readings can focus on any examples that the theory puts forward to explain or sustain itself. Do these examples work in the way that the theorist tells us they do, or can they be challenged? What if we selected other examples? Could we start to demonstrate ways in which the theory may not work as clearly as it is supposed to? These need only be thought experiments – we can imagine and hypothesize counter-examples in order to complicate or challenge a theory.

For instance, Michel de Certeau's (1988) examples of the practices of everyday life concern activities that we might think of as relatively ordinary: consuming, reading, walking. But we could multiply his examples: is sleeping a practice of everyday life? Or what about dreaming? These are surely quotidian activities that we all do much of the time. What of peoples' daily routines and habits? By considering these as examples, we can begin to see that de Certeau's cases are restricted to how 'we' use imposed cultural artefacts or systems, and do not concern what might be thought of as involuntary acts such as sleeping, dreaming or habitual routines, despite the fact that these are significant within cultural meanings of everydayness. De Certeau's notion of 'everyday life' is thus not rooted in the feelings and experiences of everyday life, in its rhythms, repetitions and routines (see Giddens 1984; Silverstone 1994:18). Instead, everyday life becomes a series of impositions on the self that are creatively and calculatedly twisted to the self's agenda. The perhaps less-than-creative or less-than-heroic phenomena of habituation and 'down time' are not adequately theorized. Hence examples that may play up these aspects of everydayness are minimized by de Certeau.

Alternatively, we can consider the examples I gave in *Fan Cultures* (2002:3–8) regarding what it means to be an academic. I discussed academics' commitment to rationality as restricting the type of work they produce (2002:4), and I also stressed the community-based norms of academic writing (2002:8). My discussion remained at a fairly abstract level, and in response to these generalizations, Mark Duffett proposes new examples:

> [Hills's] model of the researcher also tends to be based upon academic norms. Much less is said about institutional pressures that come, for example, from academic publishing and how they shape acceptable work via commercial market research and peer review. I would have liked a more realistic portrait of the sociology of research publication as performance. This might have helped Hills to recognize the further restraints and guidance mechanisms that shape academic research in cultural studies (Duffett 2004:256).

This is a perfectly fair criticism. By introducing new examples – how do the commercial pressures of academic publishers limit academic work? – Duffett therefore highlights that it is not only academic norms and ways of thinking that restrict what can be said in cultural theory. It may also be commercial pressures, that is, market forces (and for a more adequate theorization of this, see Chapter Five). What this shows us is that theorists' selections of examples can often be extended and expanded upon. New examples may not fit so readily into the theoretical framework espoused, thereby helping the strategic-tactical reader to extend and critique it.

Strategic-tactical readings can focus on moments where the theorist defends their theory from possible attacks by other schools of thought. This very specific rhetorical device or defence is called 'prolepsis', meaning to anticipate and answer objections in advance. Such moments are a rich source for strategic-tactical readings as they hint at ways in which the cultural theorist feels his or her work may require bolstering against critique.

I have frequently used key theories of reading as examples thus far, linking this chapter back to the previous one. However, in this case I would like to take an example even closer to home than *Fan Cultures*: can we see prolepsis at work in this chapter? Looking back to page 77, I have written:

> an uncharitable reader may complain that I am somehow implying that students are able . . . to adopt the role of a Freud or a Marx or a Derrida, creating strikingly new theories out of old. I am not suggesting such a thing. Neither am I ruling out the possibility. Instead, I am opposing the lowest common denominator notion that undergraduate students should only iterate and repeat theory, while postgraduates may, in time, become able to work with theory, only reaching full academic accreditation as they produce original insights. This

hierarchy, frequently naturalised in theory culture, works to defend . . . a deeply strategic fixing of readerly expertise and elitism.

We can recognize this as an instance of prolepsis via the manner in which it anticipates criticism. The difficulty with proleptic defences is that no author can ever have enough of them: strategic-tactical readers will always be able to supplement a text by reading it for its inevitable limits and absences. Prolepsis is especially useful for the reader, however, as it indicates tensions in any theoretical argument. Considering this particular example of prolepsis, we can ponder what further questions it raises. Clearly, I am concerned not to be seen as wildly exaggerating the possibility of new theory being created by apprentice theorists, although this concern occurs against a backdrop where students are all too frequently represented as 'lacking' in contrast to professionalized academics (Hartley 2003:150). My rhetorical example is rather extreme: very few academics will ever achieve what Freud, Marx and Derrida achieved. But this proleptic moment draws our attention to a specific anxiety: by opposing what I've termed 'the derogation of the student', am I falling into an overly optimistic or celebratory mode? Just as audience 'activity' has been romanticized and exaggerated (see Fiske 1989), am I romanticizing the reading activities of cultural theory's students? My proleptic defence indicates that a binary opposition of active reading versus passive reading could be mobilized to devalue my own argument: in this case *How To Do Things* . . . would be dismissed for moving too far away from passive models of reading (reading as the reproduction of correct interpretation). Of course, strategic-tactical readings are not just tactical: they are not purely active, nor do they occur wholly in opposition to 'correct' readings. Being strategic-tactical, they are more correct than correct, working to overhaul prior theory by inhabiting its absences, weak spots, imagery and assumptions. As strategic-tactical responses, they testify to the fact that we cannot divide strategy and tactics into a securely 'dichotomous logic' of 'a' versus 'b', but must also consider intra-group power struggles within the ruled (Karner 2004: 267) and the academic or institutionally 'ruling'.

My hope is that this chapter might act as an incitement to strategic-tactical readings, having sought to demystify such practices by breaking them down into some component techniques. I have also emphasized the materiality of theory – its written-ness and its argumentative shape – rather than assuming that it possesses some magical authority, alien-ness or grandeur. In any case, if students are treated and positioned as if they are incapable of carrying out creative, critical re-readings (as in Larsen 1997), then lecturers will only have themselves to blame when their prophecies become self-fulfilling. The most important precursor to successfully critiquing cultural theory is, quite simply, having the confidence to try. As long as cultural theory is thought of as difficult, remote and alien words frozen on the page, and as something produced by strange, daunting beings called 'cultural theorists', then it will seem an impossible task.

By way of moving towards this chapter's conclusion, here is one further defence against anticipated critique: some may feel that this series of strategic-tactical readings presupposes an overly combative image of reading. After all, isn't it most important to understand cultural theory? We could deploy a range of much more peaceable, pleasant metaphors and images for reading, where reader and theorist find themselves harmonising, reaching agreement, exchanging views, or becoming immersed in dialogue. Since I have been using and revising Michel de Certeau's work, however, and since I have also been emphasising modes of critical reading which evaluate, challenge and contest cultural theory, I have (re)produced a somewhat militaristic image of the encounter between cultural theory and its readers. (Note that, as authorial prolepsis, this works to shift the blame for militaristic imagery on to others). It would be wise to recall Fairbairn and Winch's cautioning note that '[s]cholarship is not, or at least should not be, a form of blood sport' (1996:208). And Ian Craib has similarly warned that 'one of the . . . [possibilities] . . . of theory . . . seems to be that destructiveness can be acted out under the guise of rational argument' (1998:152) in 'logical hatchet work'. Poaching from theory does not, after all, mean savaging or demolishing the work of others. It is not, or should not be, academically institutionalised aggression. (Proleptic defences can be more or less successful, of course, and may actually draw attention to the very argumentative weaknesses they were designed to fix. Although this paragraph has hopefully worked to remind us that strategic-tactical readings should always be tempered by a sense of fair play and dialogue, rather than simply attacking others' arguments, it could still be countered that any de Certeauian model of theory poaching remains irredeemably laden with metaphors of power, conflict and struggle).

All of the forms of strategic-tactical reading I have outlined here represent ways of succeeding as an apprentice theorist. All of them are applicable to any piece of theory reading one is obliged to do. To an extent, of course, these modes of reading presuppose that a level of understanding has been achieved: strategic-tactical readings may not always emerge straight away, or even on a first or second reading. They take time and effort to work towards:

> your first reading . . . might involve identifying the three or four key themes identified by the theorist. Your second reading might involve fleshing out those themes. You may identify particular quotations that really get at the crux of what is being said . . . A critical interpretation [that is, a strategic-tactical reading – MH] may not come until a third or even fourth reading, or at least when you have considered some of the secondary texts (Miles 2001:13).

Through this process, cultural theory can come not just to be understood, but it can also be raided, creatively poached from, appropriated, and even (bearing in mind my provisos above) critically assaulted:

Affiliations and referencing – can we reconstruct scholarly contexts of debate?
Systems of rhetoric – how are we persuaded?
Stories that are told – especially, how are these resolved?
Assumptions made – what has to be taken for granted for the theory to work?
Units of conceptual definition and opposition – can these be deconstructed?
Limits to the theory – can these be read symptomatically?
Terms used to provoke different ways of thinking – do these hinder as well as help?
Examples used – can we add to these and so complicate the theory?
Defences indicating weak(er) points in the argument – can we locate and use these?

In Chapter Five I will address how we might best produce cultural theory. What processes are involved in writing theory, and how can this activity itself be theorised? If reading is one of the main things we tend to do with cultural theory, then writing is no less important. Of course, following Hall's encoding/decoding model we might assume that writing cultural theory, or encoding it, is primary while reading and decoding are secondary and less valuable activities. Despite the common-sense idea that we can only read what has already been written, which obviously renders writing primary, perhaps writing cultural theory can only be done after we have read widely. Writing emerges out of reading, in this case, and in the structure of this book. Cultural theory's consumption supports its production. Theorists set out new ideas, pen critical responses, and perform their own strategic-tactical readings, as theory's 'reception . . . ultimately leads towards self-production' (Marshall 2004:44).

chapter five

Writing Cultural Theory

Although there have been significant theories of reading in cultural theory (see Chapter Three), there has generally been less of a focus on writing, and this despite cultural theory's '*written* mode' (Branston 2000:27). It can fairly be said that 'the starting point for cultural studies is generally consumption' (Marshall 2004:10) and hence that 'the problem of media producers has been neglected in recent media and cultural studies' (Garnham 2000:84; although see Murdock 2003). Cultural theory has tended to reproduce a deep-rooted binary opposition, that of reading versus writing, where the activity of reading has seemingly been valued over the symbolic production of writing. This has also been viewed as a social division of labour – while the 'mass' reads or consumes, a specialized minority or 'knowledge class' (Frow 1995:96; Garnham 2000:84–5) writes or produces.

It would be mistaken to conclude that writing has been altogether effaced from the agendas of cultural theory. In certain areas, such as ethnography, the anthropological study of cultures, based on the analyst being there for a length of time via fieldwork, much attention has been paid to how the ethnographer's encounter with a culture is written up. In books such as *The Ethnographic Imagination: Textual Constructions of Reality* (Atkinson 1990), *Writing Culture* (Clifford and Marcus (eds) 1986), *Reading Ethnographic Research* (Hammersley 1998) and *Tales of the Field: On Writing Ethnography* (Van Maanen 1988), a range of authors have explored issues raised by the written-ness of ethnography. This strand of work, in marked contrast to much other cultural theory, has been described as 'obsessed with the question of writing' (Augé 1999:37). Recalling my conclusion to Chapter Three, it may come as no surprise that 'writing research' has been taken to task for its 'self-referential' quality (Back 1998:292), as if reflecting on how, and under what conditions, knowledge is produced is unimportant. Such critiques assume that academics should simply get on with finding things out, failing to address how these findings have to be mediated through narrative shapes and rhetorical structures.

Writing has, then, found a specific niche as a topic in cultural theory. In this chapter, I want to consider ways of connecting reading to writing rather than viewing these as contrasted terms, either logically, or through divisions of labour. I will also consider ways in which the professionalized writing of cultural theory is itself a commodified activity akin to other forms of media production, examining cultural theory's 'critical industry'. Finally, in a section mirroring the guidance on strategic-tactical readings given in Chapter Four, I will conclude by examining how apprentice theorists might best create cultural theory. To begin with, how has writing been contrasted against various Others in cultural theory?

Contrasting and careering

As I've already noted, it's not always easy to separate out reading and writing. Theorists' writings are typically composed, at least in part, of readings of other theories. The activity of reading can also involve writing, whether this is note-taking or highlighting passages of text. Despite the difficulties involved in separating reading from writing, cultural theorists have tended to proceed as if these can be separated out. For instance, the much commented-upon 'death of the author' and simultaneous 'birth of the reader' (Barthes 1977:148) proclaimed in literary and cultural theory may seem to strike at ways of thinking about authorship as a privileged source of meaning, but it also pits author and reader against one another in a zero-sum power struggle, implying that cultural theorists should choose between championing readers or writers. After Roland Barthes's (1977) announcement of 'the death of the author', cultural theory has recurrently found itself refereeing between writers and readers, seeking to de- and re-value writing.

The work of (post-)structuralist Jacques Derrida (1976 and 1978) forms another tributary here. Derrida has taken the devaluation of writing as one of his themes, arguing that Western philosophy from Plato to Saussure was marked by logocentrism, or 'the craving for self-presence' (Norris 1982:29) assumed to be guaranteed by speech. Although Derrida (re)values writing against speech, while Barthes devalues authorial writing in favour of reading, both theorists nevertheless open new ways of thinking about writing by reworking its place when set against specific Others (reading and speech).

Derrida (1976 and 1978) argues that writing cannot be securely contrasted to speech as Saussure and many other thinkers have assumed:

> *Voice* . . . [provides] . . . a metaphor of truth and authenticity, a source of self-present 'living' speech as opposed to the secondary lifeless emanations of writing. In speaking one is able to experience (supposedly) an intimate link between sound and sense, an inward and immediate realisation of meaning . . . Writing, on the contrary, destroys this ideal of pure self-presence. It obtrudes an alien, depersonalized medium, a deceiving shadow which falls between intent and meaning . . . Against this tradition, Derrida argues . . . that writing . . . must be conceived as prior to speech (Norris 1982:28).

Derrida's deconstructive reading of the speech and writing binary argues that speech cannot fulfil its promise to guarantee self-presence and immediate meaning: instead, speech is infected by writing's 'secondariness' and non-immediacy. When we believe that we are expressing ourselves, we are already structurally divided between the 'I' that thinks it is being spoken and the 'I' that is enunciated as a pronoun in language. The speaking self and its spoken-ness therefore cannot purely co-incide, being subject to the same mechanisms of supplementation, detachment and self-difference as writing (see Bhabha 1994:36). To assume that speech is full and live while writing is somehow empty, dead words on the page is to subscribe to a flawed world view or ideology of logocentrism, in Derrida's (1976) terms. Derrida terms his new science of writing 'Grammatology', thereby enacting the beginnings of deconstruction, depicted as railing against a vast, transhistorical 'conspiracy' or logocentric 'metaphysics of presence' (see Norris 1982:29) that is coded into preceding texts of philosophy. Other critics have suggested that Derrida's own deconstructive approach to writing versus speech is, however, caught within the logocentric terms which Derrida himself opposes. In *Orality and Literacy* (1982), Walter J. Ong complicates Derrida's account by arguing that logocentric philosophy was bolstered rather than challenged by print culture, reflecting full self-presence as much through typography as through speech. Ong notes that Derrida does not provide any 'description of the detailed historical origins of what . . . [is called] . . . logocentrism', and his critique argues that logocentrism was never as univocal as Derrida assumes: Western philosophy's 'metaphysics of presence' was partly the metaphysics of speech but it was also the metaphysics of print and writing (see Hall 2002:3).

Lending credence to Ong's (1982) argument, an (allegedly) inherent linkage between writing and rational, detached thought – and hence good theorizing – appears in influential commentaries in media and cultural theory such as Marshall McLuhan's *Understanding Media* (1967) and Neil Postman's *Amusing Ourselves to Death* (1985). McLuhan contrasts spoken and written words, viewing speech as reactive while

> writing tends to be a kind of separate or specialist action in which there is little opportunity or call for reaction. The literate man or society develops the tremendous power of acting in any matter with considerable detachment from the feelings or emotional involvement that a nonliterate man or society would experience (1967:89; see also McLuhan 1962 on 'typographic man').

McLuhan suggests that visual culture sustains more emotionality and symbolic attachment than typographic culture, and thus that 'nearly all the emotional and corporate family feeling is eliminated from . . . [literate man's] . . . relationship with his social group'. The typographic self is 'emotionally free to separate from the tribe and become a civilized individual' (1967:92). This cutting-apart of typography and everyday life results, we are told, in a situation where literate man is freed 'from the tribal trance of resonating word magic' (1967:94). There is little sense of Derrida's monolithic and totalising 'metaphysics of presence' here: although speech is viewed as more reactive or present than the written word, this presence is not simply valued over writing viewed as secondary. Instead, the written word acts as an insulating, rationalizing space that frees its users from the tribal trance of magic speech which threatens to over-take the rationally civilized self.

In his attack on television as a technology leading to cultural degradation, Neil Postman also equates writing with rational, detached discourse. Citing Ong (see 1985:19), and professing a personal debt and loyalty to McLuhan's work (1985:8), Postman analyses 'typographic America': 'from its beginning until well into the nineteenth century, America was as dominated by the printed word and an oratory based on the printed word as any society we know of' (1985:42). This 'printed orality' (1985:43) takes printed text as its model, and engages in closely argued, detailed exposition: lectures dealing with cultural theory, or scholarly conference papers to be read out, would be contemporary examples.

Postman (1985:62–3) argues that in typographic America the printed word dominated all forms of public discourse rather than only occurring in academic settings. The now-historical version of America analysed by Postman is said to have been 'word-centred' rather than 'image-centred' (1985:62). Its typographical mind-set promoted values of detachment, objective analysis and rationality (1985:52–3). Postman diagnoses such values as having come under attack through the rise of television and the image. His account of the typographic mind again subordinates speech to writing: valued public speech is 'printed orality', that is, speech that attempts to emulate the printed word. There is no sense here of the 'logocentric metaphysics' which Derrida perceives, and challenges, as an 'uncritical tradition' in Western philosophy from Plato onwards (Derrida 1976:46). On the contrary, Postman persistently devalues speech as secondary, positing it as less rational, less detached, and less analytically composed in comparison with the written word.

Could we not conceptualize writing outside of these persistent contrasts? It seems that either the reader or the writer is viewed as 'powerful' (Barthes 1977), or writing is (de)valued as primary or secondary (Derrida 1976 and 1978). Alternatively, writing is a fall from tribal emotional connectedness (McLuhan 1967) and an escape into typographic rational culture, aligning it with the valued side of a rational versus emotional binary (as in Postman 1985). Ong himself values writing, as does McLuhan (1962 and 1967), for the 'distance . . . [it] provides for consciousness as nothing else does' (Ong 1982:82). Rather than conceptualizing the writing of cultural theory as essentially distancing cultural theorists from social life, or relating the writing of cultural theory to the non-self-'presence' of theorists' voices, we could instead take a rather less lofty, generalizing view. The writing of cultural theory can be placed, much more specifically, within a 'career framework' (Stebbins 1992:69), avoiding grand-theoretical contrasts against reading or speech as Others.

I will now outline some key work on 'career paths' in consumption and production activities – not focused on the writing of cultural theory *per se* – before relating this work to cultural theory's consumption and production. The body of theory I will consider is useful because it does not oppose consumption and production – for this, we can substitute reading and writing – but rather views consumption (reading) as potentially leading to production (writing). I will argue that career frameworks therefore provide one way to think about consumers who are also producers, avoiding 'a radical separation between readers and writers' (Jenkins 1992:45).

Robert A. Stebbins has analysed *Amateurs, Professionals and Serious Leisure* (1992). Serious leisure, unlike more casual leisure, is distinguished by the fact that its pursuits:

- require perseverance
- tend to lead to 'careers' even for amateurs
- involve 'significant personal *effort* based on specially acquired *knowledge, training,* or *skill*' (Stebbins 1992:6)
- tend to allow for the 'recreation or renewal of self' (1992:7)
- involve a surrounding 'unique ethos' (1992:7) akin to sub-cultural or 'idiocultural' activities (see the next chapter)

- lead to participants' self-identifying with their enthusiasms, that is, viewing them as important aspects of their cultural- and self-identities.

Stebbins suggests that serious leisure unites professionals (those paid to pursue their enthusiasm) and amateurs in any given field, and furthermore that one can map individuals' amateur-professional career paths through broad phases:

- **Beginning**: An interest in the activity takes root, abruptly or gradually, and at this stage one is pre-amateur, having yet to develop 'a substantial awareness of the pursuit itself' (1992:71).

- **Development**: Here 'interest in an activity . . . becomes systematic and routine' (1992:74), but is subjected to contingencies beyond the control of the neophyte, such as 'parental, moral and financial support' (1992:75). This career stage includes the 'pre-professional amateur – the person who is consciously preparing for professional work in his or her pursuit' (1992:81). Among this amateur group, Stebbins includes 'students in university undergraduate . . . programs' but excludes 'graduate students who are more accurately described as junior professionals' (1992:47). Despite this exclusion, he appears to include graduate students as 'conditional pre-professionals', who are those 'considering becoming professionals in their field, if certain conditions were met . . . e.g. "if I earn a doctoral degree"' (1992:46).

- **Establishment**: 'practitioners . . . move . . . beyond the status of learner of the basics' and establish themselves as 'known' and reputable in their field (1992:82–3).

- **Maintenance**: The practitioner has attained status within their field and has to work to conserve this in the face of competition and contingencies (1992:88–9).

- **Decline**: Marks the twilight of an amateur-professional career through a fading of the practitioner's abilities. Although this can be highly marked in sports, it can be greatly deferred outside sporting pursuits.

Stebbins's model is similar to that put forward by H. F. Moorhouse in his study of hot-rod enthusiasts. Moorhouse also views amateurs and professionals as interlinked in an 'enthusiasm', seeing them as being surrounded by 'the interested public' and then 'the general public' (1991:22–3). Moorhouse notes that 'to this we must add a notion of process since individuals move in and out of various categories' (1991:22–3). Nicholas Abercrombie and Brian Longhurst draw on Moorhouse and Stebbins to suggest that a generalisable media 'audience continuum' can be identified, ranging from the 'consumer' at one extreme end to the 'petty producer' at the other (1998:140–1). Petty producers are 'those who have perhaps . . . become . . . professional' and who are 'returned . . . to general capitalist social relations [rather than being within the ethos of a subculture – MH]; as producers they are as much at the mercy of structural forces as the consumers at the other end of the continuum' (1998:140). Abercrombie and Longhurst suggest that their consumer-producer 'continuum may represent a possible career path under certain conditions', a suggestion that is developed by Garry Crawford (2003 and 2004) in work on sports fans.

Substantially building on Abercrombie and Longhurst's approach to consumption and production activities, Crawford sets out a 'career progression' of sports fandom which moves from the 'general public' through to 'interested', 'engaged', 'enthusiastic', 'devoted', and 'professional' participants before concluding with those who are involved in administering and running professional sport. Crawford stresses that this is not a continuum of typologies, but is rather made up of 'points along a career trajectory', points along which individuals may progress as well as 'regress [or] leapfrog . . . or move in and out of this [entire] career structure' (2003:227–8). Thinking of cultural consumption and production within a career framework has a number of benefits, not the least of which is that:

> . . . the use of the term career moves away from restrictive typologies and dichotomies that . . . force individuals into often ill-defined and rigid 'types' . . . and allows for a more fluid and dynamic understanding of the structure of a community and the nature of an individual's progression (Crawford 2004:41).

This framework can be related to the writing of cultural theory: theory is produced both by amateurs (usually students) and professionals (usually university-based academics). Although the production of theory occurs as a type of work for both parties, it remains akin to Stebbins's 'serious leisure' insofar as it unites professionals and amateurs – recall also that Stebbins suggests that undergraduates can be thought of as pre-professional amateurs, having freely chosen to pursue specific studies requiring perseverance and the acquisition of specialist knowledge. Thinking of the writing of cultural theory through the lens of careerism, which is not to morally impugn such work, gives us a way out of conceptualizing writing as logically opposed to reading or philosophically opposed to speech.

In place of these fixed dichotomies, we can explore writing as part of a career progression. Approached in this way, writing does not simply emerge out of reading as I suggested at the end of the last chapter. More precisely, neither reading nor writing are primary or secondary, since although writing depends on reading (Agger 1990:92), reading also depends on encountering writing, itself produced out of previous reading(s). This indicates a 'dialectical [interwoven] relationship between reading and writing' (Agger 1990:87): we cannot identify which is primary or secondary. Any such separation of writing (production) and reading (consumption) – and accompanying (de)valuations of each term – becomes pointless from a dialectical, 'career frame' perspective.

Having said this, it is insufficient merely to point to the blurring of reading and writing. Rather like Jenkins (1992), Abercrombie and Longhurst (1998) and Crawford (2004), P. David Marshall's recent work on 'the cultural production thesis' (2004:11) moves in the direction of exploring consumers who are also producers. Marshall, too, argues that the 'dichotomy of production and consumption' (2004:103) needs to be challenged. But despite calling for a move from the 'readerly' to the 'writerly', and from the 'art of making do' to the art of 'making' (2004:10–11), Marshall offers little sense of the career progressions and social logics that may actually facilitate and sustain, or impede, these moves. His call for a move from reader to writer hence appears to be overly abstract, rather than allowing for consideration of how one might move, in different ways, between being a reader and a writer. While Marshall's work on cultural production lacks a career frame, the previously considered audience continuum (Abercrombie and Longhurst 1998) and enthusiasm model (Moorhouse 1991) lack an adequate focus on cultural production. Abercrombie and Longhurst argue that skills (and types) of production increase as you move from 'consumer' to 'petty producer' (1998:148), implying that consumption remains passive while production is more skilfully active, and failing to address the dialectical relationship between consumption and production (or reading and writing). Similarly, although Moorhouse allows for dynamic processes whereby people can move between his different categories, production still appears to be separated off from consumption. Crawford's more flexible 'career points' model (2003:226–33 and 2004:38–49) therefore offers the most promising possibilities for considering cultural theory's writing. It can be applied and appropriated as follows:

- **General public**: Those who may have an interest in cultural theory: possibly students considering taking the subject, but also cultural consumers more generally. They are an amorphous, relatively unknowable 'pre-audience'. They are not yet readers and writers of cultural theory.

- **Interested**: Those who begin to take a more specific interest in cultural theory/studies, but who may not yet be enrolled on a dedicated degree programme. They may have begun to read some cultural theory, probably only secondary texts or commentaries, but may not yet be writing cultural theory.

- **Engaged**: Those who freely choose to participate, as amateurs, in the production of cultural theory: neophyte or apprentice readers and writers. They may tend to predominantly read secondary commentaries as well as some work in the original. They have begun to write theory, usually applications of prior theoretical models demonstrating comprehension of these works.

- **Enthusiastic**: Those beginning to feel a sense of commitment to the subject, who could be undergraduates considering postgraduate study. They have repeatedly and successfully written cultural theory and have begun to immerse themselves in relevant reading. They are nascent strategic-tactical readers, articulating challenges to prior theory in their own writing.

- **Devoted**: Non-professionals who are nevertheless generally affiliated and self-identified with cultural theory/studies: they could be Stebbins's 'conditional pre-professionals' (1992: 46). They may have considerable time to read (especially as postgraduate students), but are likely to be insecurely authorised to commercially produce cultural theory. They are effective strategic-tactical readers, adept at challenging a range of cultural theory, using these critiques to construct new approaches.

- **Professional**: Accredited academics who are authorised to commercially write cultural theory, but paradoxically may lack the time to read new work and keep up to date with their field (Agger 1990:92). They oscillate between applying and critiquing cultural theory, aiming to articulate their own sense of good theory which is connected to a precise sense of social and theoretical affiliation ('where they stand' within ongoing disciplinary debates).

- **Apparatus**: Those involved in running and administering the industry of cultural theory, such as commissioning editors and other cultural workers in publishing. Although professionals can move across into this career point, 'members of this group most frequently enter into this position directly due to their expertise or experience' (Crawford 2003:233). This career point is thus linked with others, but is also relatively disarticulated from them. Participants in theory's apparatus are likely to read a lot of cultural theory while not generally writing it. Reader-writers can emerge in the form of 'professionals' who have moved into this career point.

Whereas Crawford's model stresses to-and-fro movements (that is, one can move from engaged to enthusiastic or vice versa) with regards to the production of cultural theory, movement tends to be more unidirectional. It is evidently possible to cease being a professional academic but maintain levels of devotion, enthusiasm, engagement or interest. Similarly, those who are devoted at one point may fall back into levels of interest, even moving back into the general public if they decide not to pursue an academic career or maintain any links to cultural theory. Students can drop out of their studies, for instance. These backward steps are, however, made less likely by the fact that unlike sports supporters' 'careers', career progression in cultural theory is articulated with forms of accreditation and educational qualification. This is not always via any one-to-one correspondence, so an individual does not automatically move up the career ladder by gaining new qualifications. One could move through engaged-enthusiastic-devoted levels while an undergraduate: no new level of qualification would necessarily be required for these commitments and skills to develop. And although one cannot generally progress to the status of a professional academic without some kind of postgraduate qualification, even here there are exceptions to this rule.

As career progression and self-identification with cultural theory develop, the social pressures of serious leisure become increasingly significant. Cultural theory's reader-writers may, for example, begin to display 'continuance commitment', which Stebbins defined as 'the awareness of the impossibility of choosing a different social identity . . . because of the imminence of penalties involved in making the switch'. Stebbins goes on to argue that amateurs can opt out more freely than professionals, whose continuance commitment is necessarily much higher (1992:51–2). Yet, despite the fact that Stebbins includes some prospective graduate students in his case studies, he fails to note that there may be high opt out costs for undergraduate and postgraduate students just as for professional academics. Cultural theory, we might say, has unusually high continuance commitment in relation to non-academic serious leisure: it carries the moral weight of official and legitimate education, and surrendering it as a commitment therefore involves challenging cultural scripts of the good (educated) self. Crawford terms his career model of sports fans a 'moral' one in that 'the development of a sport fan often involves changes in the individual's own identity . . . and significantly how they categorise and judge their own and others' behaviour' (2004:42). Yet the notion of a 'moral career' appears to be more directly true for readers and writers of cultural theory, for whom both the production of theory, and possible renunciations of this, can be intensely moral acts (see Chapter Six).

This career framework usefully stresses the constant interconnections between reading and writing cultural theory at each career point (with the possible exceptions of interested individuals and those within the industry apparatus). It also stresses the different, characteristic relations between reading and writing at different career points, such as the professional who writes a fair amount of cultural theory but does not read as much, or the devoted reader-writer who, relatively speaking, writes less and reads far more. There is no clear, definitive or binary separation of reader and writer to be had on this account. Instead, there are different social logics, and career phases, through which reading and writing are articulated. In the next section, I will consider how certain of these logics – the professional theorist dealing with cultural theory's apparatus – concern cultural theory's commercialization.

Publishing, commercializing and mediating

Lorna Sage focuses on the work of the professional writer, testifying to the dialectic of writing and reading by arguing that commercial book reviewing involves 'writing reading':

> To write reading you must spot and exaggerate and semaphore all the signs, insert yourself between author and real reader, make over long texts into short, alliterative sentences, perform reading as surrogate and advocate, and at all costs help to keep the trade in words alive (1998:262–3).

This writing reading does something with words, being a performance intended for publication. As such it is akin to Lynne Pearce's notion of 'making a reading' (1997:220), where the personal self-reflection or memorializing reverie of the 'reading process' (1997:220) is disciplined into a proper professionalized writing reading. Sage suggests that reviewing commercially is 'very different from . . . academic' work, although 'it's a difference of relatively recent origin . . . what I'm calling "writing reading" used to look like a continuum' (1998:263) ranging from commercial reviewer to scholar. This continuum of writing reading is said to belong to a different era, now that 'academic criticism and literary journalism have grown further apart' (Sage 1998:263). However, Sage then challenges this contrast. Academic writing, too, can be conceptualized as 'performing' reading – as having a kind of literary quality. It is not just reviewers and fiction writers who have to make it new through literary performance, but also cultural theorists:

> [T]he more interesting implication lurking here is that it is the academic critic not the novelist or poet who is the heir to the avant-garde literary project of making it new, art which took the form of utopian anti-art and demystification. Post-structuralist critical writing – elusive, shadowy, self-renewing, prolific – becomes a new, rival genre [to literature] (Sage 1998:269).

Or as Angela McRobbie has put it, 'not everybody can be an artist, poet or writer', although in her view cultural studies' writing often does approximate to literary or poetic art (see McRobbie 1999:103–4). Jeffrey Wallen argues, *contra* McRobbie's optimistic view of cultural theory-as-artwork, that:

> We now continually have a shift from a cognitive to a performative strategy – from the attainment and transmission of knowledge to an insistent playing out of the ways that words 'actually do things'. A focus on the performative aspect

of language draws attention to the ways in which language engages others and accomplishes an action. Under this dual imperative of performance and performativity, the critic's own person often becomes the vehicle for insight, impact and success (1998:105).

Wallen sees this shift toward performative cultural theory – having an impact on its audiences rather than just telling them something – as highly problematic. For, if it is 'performers that matter' as much as the substance of what is being written (1998:105), then cultural theory is seemingly fatally contaminated by logics of celebrity (see Chapter Seven) and industry. Ted Striphas (2002) further addresses these questions, placing commercial book publishing at the core of cultural studies. Striphas focuses on what Crawford's (2004) career model terms the industrial 'apparatus' of any amateur-professional enthusiasm. Examining the contemporary writing of cultural theory must, inevitably, mean thinking about how such writing is produced not just by lone, 'heroic' writers (Brodkey 1987:54–5) but also how it is mediated by commercial publishers. Since it is the career fate of the professional academic to write commercially, how can we structurally separate the writing of cultural theory from the writing of, say, a genre novel, given that both are commodities to be sold in the marketplace?

Abercrombie and Longhurst's (1998:140) caution with regards to the 'petty producer' may apply just as well to the professional cultural theorist: he or she too is, like the consumer, prey to social relations of capitalism. The commodified writing of cultural theory means that theory is necessarily a part of 'the culture industry' (Adorno 1991). Indeed, critical theorist Ben Agger has suggested that 'it is important to catalog academic work alongside employment in the entertainment industries . . .' (1990:77).

The operation of commercial academic publishers has frequently been a cause of concern to left-wing cultural theorists. In her essay 'Banality in Cultural Studies' (1990), Meaghan Morris infamously criticized the standardization of cultural studies writing, implying that there was a submission to commodification taking place here (see also Robbins 1996:186). Morris's accusation toys with the fact that cultural studies has tended to oppose the culture industry thesis of Frankfurt School writers such as Max Horkheimer and Theodor Adorno. Horkheimer and Adorno (1973) subjected popular culture to Marxist critique, viewing it as a standardised 'mass culture' incessantly repeating formulaic clichés. Adorno described this as a 'levelling down process' of mass culture where 'any and every product refers back to what has already been preformed', resulting in a 'pre-digested quality of the product' (Adorno 1991:58). Meaghan Morris appropriates these terms of critique, when she challenges cultural theory/studies to confront its own commodified standardisations:

I get the feeling that somewhere in some English publisher's vault there is a master disk from which thousands of versions of the same article about pleasure, resistance, and the politics of consumption are being run off under different names with minor variations. Americans and Australians are recycling this basic pop-theory article, too . . . cut free from . . . context, as commodities always are, and recycled . . . the vestigial *critical* force . . . tends to disappear (1990:21).

Morris's nightmarish vision is of a wholly mechanized cultural theory, a 'vast banality machine' (1990:21) resembling the mass culture of Theodor Adorno's criticism: 'Morris' jab at the unnamed English publisher and its master disk signals her frustration with book publishing as a key industry . . . involved in the banalization of cultural studies' (Striphas 2002:441). Morris develops this theme in later work, again pondering how commercial publishers have limited cultural studies:

> I recently asked a senior editor where innovation might come from in a world of textbooks and doorstoppers. . . . Of course, publishers rarely order you to confine yourself to these forms. They will say that your excellent book on an unusual theme sadly 'doesn't have a market'. This usually means that they can find no-one who teaches a course with a similar title to your book . . . It is already quite hard to publish anything original or heterodox in cultural studies (1998b:504).

The commodification of cultural theory is seen as an evil that scholars are subjected to. Market forces work to homogenize theory in chunky readers/doorstoppers and introductory textbooks assumed to have nothing new to say. Andrew Wernick observes how the 'key to success for academic books is getting them included on course lists . . . the course-credit system [in contemporary universities] . . . shapes the end market, determining the kind of product which must be produced to match' (1991:174). And just as student numbers on courses matters, so too does the size of the market, making America a more lucrative market for 'the chic category of cultural studies' (Grossberg 1996:135). In the world of commercial publishing, cultural studies seemingly slots into a market niche. Commercial pressures do not only restrict what can make it into print, and in what form, they also dictate how long books will stay in print:

> saleable topics may have a short academic life once saturation point is reached in the market . . . [and publishers] may pump out vast numbers of books while giving any one title only a few months to succeed before pulling it . . . It means you can publish a book that few people . . . may ever see before it disappears. Your book may be unobtainable by the time the slow machinery of academic reviewing has passed word out through the journals, two or three years later, that your work is important (Morris 1998b:502).

There is a powerful clash of temporalities here, as a market rationalization of 'what's hot now' intersects with theory culture's more glacial processes of evaluation and assimilation:

> Academics . . . those working in 'culture', are about the *longue durée*. . . .
> A book, an academic book can last ten to fifteen years [as something new, notable, and 'informative' – MH]. It can take four years to write. Research grants are for two to three years. What a different time scale journalists operate on. As does the entertainment industry. What an extraordinary set of – time and budget – constraints they operate under. In a sense they are an 'industry', a 'culture industry' (Lash 2002:73).

Lash partly agrees with Ben Agger's thesis in *Fast Capitalism* (1989), arguing that media theory no longer purchases any distance from the world it analyses: 'theory will be increasingly in the same genre as information, as media' (Lash 2002:65). Although theory today cannot supposedly offer any transcendent critique – that is, a critique from outside commodified culture – for Lash it continues to operate on a slower time-frame, the *longue durée*, rather than being caught up in speedy production. But it is exactly the newly compressed time of writing reading that Agger highlights in his work, where 'few pause before the written word' (1990:92) any longer, and where scholarly writers are compelled to produce the 'academic commodity form' of journal articles or textbooks (1990:136). Agger (1989, 1990) and Morris (1998b) are far less convinced of theory's inherent slow time than Lash, it should be said, whose argument appears to bracket theory off from its own cultural and commercial contexts. In the UK context, pressures hailing not only from publishing's commercial operations, but also from governmental Research Assessment Exercises, add a further compulsion to publish in a timely manner (see Strathern 2000; Brew 2001; Schlesinger 2001; Evans 2004; Furedi 2004). And Jeffrey Williams, writing of the US situation, has also observed theory's acceleration:

> Contemporary . . . scholarship hardly exists for the ages but is extraordinarily transient . . ., with an average life expectancy . . . of only a few years. This in turn influences the cycling of critical approaches and theoretical models, which move through the scene within a few years . . . In a certain determinative sense, these changes are linked to the increasing capitalization [commerciality and profit-making – MH] of academic publishing (Williams 2000:29).

The publisher Routledge comes in for a fair amount of bashing in these accounts: Meaghan Morris even terms her model of hyper-commercial publishing 'the "Routledge" model' (1998b:502; see also Striphas 2002:442). Making a similar move, Jeffrey Williams argues that US university presses, traditionally non-profit-making bastions of academic merit, have become more profit-driven, modelling themselves on commercial publishers and 'emulating the early nineties zenith of Routledge with its array of sexily jacketed, trendsetting and profitmaking books in theory and cultural studies' (2000:29; see also Hutnyk 2004:8). Routledge's vice president and publishing director William Germano has discussed the 'enigma of [cover] design' (2001:178), offering the following guidance:

> Authors . . . often confuse the cover as a selling tool with the cover as a symbol of the book. A successful cover will be eye-catching and appealing, clearly presenting title, author and any other verbal tools (words of praise; the stellar list of contributors) that your publisher needs on the outside to sell what's inside. A cover design needn't be complex to be effective. It's often harder to design a simple cover than a cluttered one. Do not expect a cover design to represent the fragmentation of hegemonic discourse in the wake of postcolonial theory (2001:179).

Covers aren't about capturing what's in a book, they are about selling it. Designs are simple and direct, while theory is difficult and cerebral. This marked contrast between images and words appears to partly replay a McLuhanesque (1967) dichotomy between visual and typographic cultures. And as selling tools, book jackets may draw visually on the very cultural short-hands, stereotypes and forms of common sense that cultural theorists are aiming to challenge in their written work (for a rare example of tensions between cover designers and authors being discussed in a commercially published academic book itself, see the commentary 'About the cover' in Tulloch and Jenkins 1995:vii).

However objectionable a book cover may be to its authors, it will nevertheless carry their names. The academic proper name is put into circulation by publishing, working as a signifier detached from the flesh-and-blood person so designated, and hence operating as an 'author-function' (Foucault 1979). The proper name accompanying all academic publication reinforces the individualism of theory culture, and its focus on scholarly reputation:

> [I]t isn't enough that your book should be excellent . . . there has to be some reason for your book to stand out in the shops and catalogues from the dozens . . . of similar titles . . . pouring out of Routledge, Duke, Minnesota, Cambridge, Oxford . . . A good title, subtitle and book design helps. Mostly, I'm afraid, potential readers will be looking at your name (Morris 1998b:503).

Giving this advice to graduate students, Morris observes that 'I live on my "name"' (1998b: 503). The proper name is a sign of the quality of a professional scholar's work. It is, in a sense, a brand: 'the proper names of fashionable theorists have a function equivalent to that of successful brand names' (Goodchild 1996:7; see also Bourdieu 1988:263–7). This scenario resembles 'other sectors of commodified cultural production. Familiar and prestigious names help move the merchandise with which they are creatively associated' (Wernick 1991:175). Andrew Wernick also notes that the 'authorial moniker, like any brand-name' can have an auto-promotional effect: favourable reception for one book title can translate into an increased print run and greater marketing efforts for an author's following work, enhancing 'the selling power of the authorial name' (1991:175). Given this commercialization and promotional culture, some writers have advocated a refusal of

> the personalisation of knowledges and affects . . . If refusing to think of music in terms of names and faces is effective (and it is), then why not talk about ideas in the same way. Shut up about Derrida – let's talk about deconstruction . . . Stop dreaming of being a . . . brand, a commodity sold to the highest bidder. Write collectively under assumed names (Gilbert 2003a:107).

Or, for that matter, professional academics might choose to write anonymously. But the lure of the brand(ed) name, even for scholars who profess their left-wing credentials, appears to be strong. How many of the self-professed (neo-)Marxists writing in cultural theory/studies today have challenged the commodification of their academic proper name, either surrendering royalties, or writing under assumed names? Most, if not all, seem content to inhabit the capitalist system, thereby being placed within the critical industry of cultural theory, working to produce relatively standardized and commodified critiques of capital.

By publishing commercially, and circulating their brand name, professional academics can take on a kind of virtual identity:

> When writers talk about their work, the self is always prominent. Their written names offer them a substitute for the self, a representation of the self . . . and

an extension of the self. Basically, their written names appear to offer them another form of identity . . . writers [can] 'know' each other on the basis of nothing more than their written names (Macdonald 2001:195).

Where 'the name is the fame of the game' (2001:193), academic names can circulate as ghosted versions of their corresponding 'doxic' or flesh-and-blood individuals (Bourdieu 1988:22–3), being reduced and inflated by virtue of their virtuality, and becoming blank spaces for readers' projections: 'I constructed Carolyn Steedman and Valerie Walkerdine [authors of *Landscape for a Good Woman* and *Schoolgirl Fictions* respectively – MH] as powerful mentors. Although I only "knew" them through their writing, I built up images of the "real" woman behind the text' (Lacey 2000:37). The brand name takes on a virtualized life of its own, almost magically causing readers to feel connections and identifications with cultural theorists whom they do not know in any conventional sense beyond the mediated encounter of reader and writer. Academic brand names thus circulate through networks of 'para-social' interaction; though the reader feels as if they have a relationship with a writer, this is in the first instance only one-way or illusory, like a TV viewer who talks 'back' to an on-screen newsreader (Giles 2000:128). J. B. Thompson discusses this type of 'mediated quasi-interaction' as offering 'non-reciprocal intimacy at a distance' (Thompson 1995:219). However, the terms *quasi*-interaction and *para*-social imply that there is something dysfunctional about these relations. David Giles (2000:128) usefully reminds us that para-social interaction with an actual, living writer means that we can potentially meet them, just as Joanne Lacey eventually worked with Valerie Walkerdine (see Lacey 2000:44–5; Giles 2000:140–1; Moran 2000:154).

The circulation of academic proper names along with professional cultural theorists' writings means that as well as building reputations, theorists become linked to specific topics. Published writings tend to fix an image of the academic-as-brand, so that scholarly 'epistemic individuals' (Bourdieu 1988:22–3) – constructed, mediated personae, if you like – tend to connote areas of expertise. Charlotte Brunsdon observes this phenomenon at work when she interviews fellow feminist Ellen Seiter. Seiter recounts how her early work on soap opera has trailed her, so that although she has worked on other topics, 'it's like gum on your shoe or something you can't get rid of' (Brunsdon 2000:208). Brunsdon interprets her interview transcript as follows:

Ellen's perception of her research on soap opera being like 'gum on [her] shoe' provides a tactile metaphor for the *identities that are constructed for academics through bibliographies, reviews, and references*. Long after she has moved on to other work, the invitations and citations she receives nominate her as a soap scholar . . . [O]nce academic research enters the public domain it acquires a certain autonomy (2000:208, my italics).

The commodification of scholarship does not only affect the forms that published writing can take in the marketplace via the 'burgeoning industry' of textbooks (Bennett 1998:20). It also extends the writer's self into a virtual, mediated terrain, with the result that 'doxic' individuals (real people) can feel a sense of alienation or misrecognition in relation to their 'epistemic' selves (their brand). The commercial circulation of names-as-brands helps to construct restricted identities for scholars, as Brunsdon points out. The authorial name is 'an identification tag, which circulates independently of the . . . individual, and which functions . . . as a vehicle for whatever significance . . . that name has come to acquire' (Wernick cited in Moran 2000:67).

Publishing as a professional theorist may bring some financial and reputational rewards, and form part of a career progression, but it can also create tensions between actual and virtual selves, or 'disembodied images' (Moran 2000:58). The commodified writing self confronts the actual writer, displaying the 'mystical character' of commodity-fetishism (Marx in McLellan 1977:435). Through this process, 'the object that labour produces, its product, stands opposed to it as something alien, as a power independent of the producer' (Marx cited in Lury 1996:41). Joe Moran has argued that 'the literary [or cultural theory – MH] celebrity conforms to Marx's definition of the fetishized commodity' (2000:9). That is, the individualized figure of the theorist-as-brand-name comes to stand in for the social, communal nature of cultural production, where cultural theory is generated in relation to, and through, an intertextual matrix of inspiring 'textual others' (Pearce 1997).

Where accounts of commercialized cultural theory bemoan the negative impacts of commerce (as I have done thus far), they mobilize a binary opposition between 'authentic' non-commodified academic writing and 'inauthentic' writing viewed as being commercially circumscribed. This contrast occurs in Agger (1989 and 1990), Hutnyk (2004), Lash (2002), Morris (1998b) and Williams (2000). However, we can challenge this view that cultural theory's critical industry unilaterally represents a fall from non-commodified grace. Simone Murray has argued that

> a . . . mainstream/separatism divide . . . suffuses extant commentary about feminist publishing. In its relentless binarism, it is a model that has too often served to straightjacket commentary into arid debates over political 'credibility' versus market 'responsiveness' . . . it is striking how inadequate this static binary model has proven to the task of describing the multiple paradoxes within which academic feminist publishing now operates (2004a:124).

Murray suggests that any mainstream/separatism way of thinking simply cannot deal with the diversity of the publishing sector, which includes:

> independent feminist presses . . . feminist/women's studies lists within independent [publishing] houses and university presses . . . feminist lists within mainstream houses. . . . 'gender studies' publishing across the academic sector . . . and mainstream trade publishing of 'women's books' which may, to a greater or lesser extent, incorporate feminist approaches (2004a:124–5).

And in his analysis of academic publishing and cultural studies, Ted Striphas makes a similar point, again cautioning against viewing commercial pressures as singular forces or processes working to de-authenticate cultural theory/studies. Like Murray, Striphas considers how cultural studies is published not just by commercial academic presses, such as Routledge, but also by 'not-for-profit' university presses and 'strongly profit-driven' trade presses (2002:443).

Further, Striphas argues that within this tripartite system, practices 'vary widely from press to press'; even 'some commercial academic presses emphasize publishing more "original", scholarly titles over textbooks and course readers' (2002:444). Stressing the 'differences that exist across the publishers that together comprise the university presses, the trades and the commercial academic presses' (2002:444), Striphas suggests that although Meaghan Morris's (1998b) ' "Routledge" model' of hyper-commercial academic publishing may have some truth to it, publishing does not only impact detrimentally upon the form and content of marketable academic output. In fact, Morris is not purely critical of commercial academic publishers, even the metonymic Routledge: 'The "Routledge" model has had a huge impact in diversifying the range of topics and approaches that academics can respectably take up, and in democratizing, to some extent, the market for academic books' (1998b:502).

This democratization of cultural theory by commercial publishers has been viewed as fundamental to the rise of cultural studies by John Hartley. Rather than assuming in advance that commerce and cultural theory must represent opposed terms, Hartley re-examines the role played in popularising cultural studies by publisher Allen Lane, founder of Penguin books. In fact it is Lane's second imprint, Pelican Books, launched in 1937, which can be shown to have aided the rise of cultural studies in the UK (Hartley 2003:22). Pelicans were cheap, mass-market non-fiction books, aimed at 'a vast reading public for intelligent books' (Lane quoted in Hartley 2003:23). They included titles on science, astronomy, history, politics and economics. Hartley points out that:

> The connection between Pelicans and cultural studies is direct. Many of the works that are now recognised as founding texts of cultural studies itself, or of one of its contributing disciplines, were published, increasingly as originals, by Pelican Books [including] *The Uses of Literacy* – Richard Hoggart: Pelican A431, *Culture and Society* – Raymond Williams: Pelican A520, [and] *The Making of the English Working Class* – E. P. Thompson: Pelican A1000 (2003:23–4).

It is striking that the detailed account provided by Hartley is not a common feature of cultural studies textbooks. Instead, these foundational links between commerce and cultural theory have tended to be ignored or glossed over, with the origins of cultural studies appearing instead as authentic matters of pure thought and anti-commercialist political idealism. Cultural theorists may well have typically erred in favour of prematurely opposing cultural theory and commerce, as Striphas (2002), Hartley (2003) and Murray (2004a) argue.

If cultural theory and commercial forces of mediation cannot be viewed as antithetical, indeed if they have been productively intertwined from the very formation of something called cultural studies, it still seems as though academic publishing, like academia, demarcates itself as relatively autonomous from mainstream interests and tastes. Recognizing the persistent boundedness of academia and its publishing houses alongside the interpenetration of cultural theory and commerce, I would suggest that Sarah Thornton's (1995) taxonomy of mediation is relevant here. Thornton distinguishes between 'mass media', 'niche media' and 'micro-media' (1995:122, 137, and 151), relating each of these to the formation and development of specialist subcultures (see Chapter Six). Broadly speaking, subcultures can, for now, be considered as specific taste cultures that set themselves apart from what they construct and view as 'the mainstream' (Thornton 1995:114–5). Thornton points out that the role of the media in relation to subcultural formation has rarely been explored academically, other than via the assumption that the media act negatively on subcultures (Thornton 1995:151–2). This should sound rather familiar, of course, as it closely replays the assumptions through which scholars have typically thought about commerce and cultural theory. Both subcultures and theory culture have sought to position themselves as authentic, as opposed to a suspect and commercialized mainstream.

Against these assumptions, Thornton indicates that the media do not simply co-opt and commodify subcultures; they are also instrumental in sustaining them. Through 'micro-media' (1995:137–8) such as flyers or fanzines, subcultural participants can communicate with one another. And through niche media such as the music and style press, subcultures are baptized and symbolically organized:

> [niche] consumer magazines . . . categorize social groups . . . [and] generate the self-consciousness required to maintain cultural distinctions. They give definition to vague cultural formations, pull together and reify ['fix in place'] the disparate materials which become subcultural . . . The music and style press . . . do not just cover subcultures, they help construct them (1995:151).

Thornton concludes that far from tainting the authenticity of subcultures, commercial and consumerist media 'and other culture industries are integral to the processes' (1995:160) through which subcultures develop. Again, this should sound familiar. It replays the logic of more recent scholarly debates over cultural theory and commerce, being akin to John Hartley's (2003) recovery of the importance of Pelican books for cultural studies. Commerce, on these accounts, is not an external force imposed on theory culture (or subculture). Commercial motivations and practices are already inside theory culture, being a part of its infrastructure (Hodkinson 2002:114–28). Viewing commerce and media as internal as well as external to subcultural formations, rather than always being extraneous and hostile to them, takes us back to Abercrombie and Longhurst's (1998:140) 'petty producer', and Garry Crawford's caution that we should address the industrial 'apparatus' (2004:49) that exists for, and partly alongside, any enthusiasm. Adopting such a view offers one way to avoid the assumption that cultural theory properly occurs only outside or against commodification:

> Rather than requiring an escape from 'the media' or 'the market' . . . relative autonomy suggests that the forms of consumption and communication which facilitate and construct the grouping in question [here, cultural theorists and theory culture – MH] are, to a certain degree, distinct or separate from those connected with outside cultural amalgamations (Hodkinson 2002:109).

This captures the role of commercial academic publishing remarkably well. Cultural theory is itself material and existent, a part of the world, not a pure set of transcendent ideas that we magically absorb. It does not (and cannot) escape from the market and mediation into some mystical other realm. Arguably, theory culture could not sustain the self-consciousness of itself as a shared (local, national and transnational) enterprise without the 'niche' mediation of commercial publishers, and the 'micro' mediation of academic conferences, presentations and lectures. And despite sometimes crossing over, cultural theory sets itself apart from a mainstream Other, thus being served and partly constructed by its niche mediators. However, these 'niche media' are not 'subcultural consumer magazines' (Thornton 1995:155); they are typically 'theory-cultural consumer books'. In this case, the 'cultural politics of the book' (Murray 2004a:125) and the scholarly journal are such that academics appear to primarily communicate within their own group. This is not necessarily cause for condemnation (Wallen 1998), as Jeremy Gilbert has indicated:

> The . . . complaint that academics spend too much time talking to each other misses the point that the teaching which those academics deliver to students is in large part a result of the talking they do with each other: either literally or via publications. The fact that an article in a refereed journal may only be read by . . . a few hundred specialists, does not mean that those people will be its only effective audience. Presumably it will have some impact on their teaching and their research and the teaching of people who read that research. So its direct audience may be small, but its 'mediated audience', if you like, may be much larger (2003b:156).

Gilbert's view of mediation here encompasses both 'niche' and 'micro'-media in Thornton's terms, reflecting on the publication of academic writing and how that writing is drawn upon in lectures and teaching. This indicates that any perspective on cultural theory/studies which ignores its own processes of mediation fails to take into account the very life blood and 'transmission' (Debray 2000:7) of theory. To lament cultural theory's commodification is to fail to perceive how commercial, niche-mediation contains and constructs scholarly 'talk'. Of course, to celebrate cultural theory's commercial nature is also to ignore the possibilities for alternative forms and contents offered by non-commodified writing. The path between pro/anti alternatives to theory's commerciality may lie in recognizing that theory and commerce are necessarily and inevitably interconnected, with both positive and negative consequences. Commercial forces do not guarantee cultural theory's fall from grace, but nor do they automatically secure its redemptive democratization.

In this section I have focused on the professional cultural theorist, neglecting other kinds of 'writing reading' (Sage 1998). It is all well and good to consider the virtual self that confronts the commercially published writer, but what of writers who are earlier in their careers, such as those who are engaged, enthusiastic or devoted, in Crawford's (2004) terms? What of writing not for publication, but for grading and assessment? These writers are less likely to be concerned with forces of commodification and more likely to be concerned with what it means to write successfully. Just as I addressed effective reading in the preceding chapter, I will now consider how apprentice theorists can best produce their own micro-mediated cultural theory for an initial readership of one or two (usually tutors and external examiners).

Creating: Writing cultural theory for purposes of assessment

As Laurel Richardson bluntly states, 'writing matters' (1997:86). It is how we present our ideas and our readings of others' work. However, it is not particularly helpful to simply counsel writers that the use of jargon should be avoided. For, as I have already noted (in Chapter Two), one scholar's jargon is another's precise and conceptually helpful terminology. Nor is it especially helpful to vaguely refer to a need for clear writing:

> It is not enough to say that theory must write simply and lucidly. As Marcuse (1964) has shown, this is extremely difficult where the universe of discourse is nearly closed and words robbed of their critical meanings . . . Plain talk is muddied where cultural meanings are largely determined by [forms of cultural power] . . . Neither lucidity nor opacity is a sufficient political posture (Agger 1992:161).

Rather than focusing on whether one writes clearly or not, or uses jargon or not, it is more productive to consider how writing reading re-presents the words of other preceding theorists. Writing cultural theory is always concerned with how to use theory's intertextual matrix. It is for this reason that referencing and bibliographies are so important. These are not merely the pedantic fussing of academics. Instead, as I demonstrated in the previous chapter, referencing is a part of how cultural theory displays its affiliations, connections and ruptures with established schools of thought. Accurate referencing in the body of written theory, coupled with an accurate and full bibliography, are thus the essentials of writing theory. It is impossible to indicate how one has creatively poached from, or expertly applied, a given theorist unless this process is followed. Referencing and bibliographic work are not presentational devices added to an argument when one writes theory; they are not matters of style rather than substance (*contra* Stokes 2003:166–7). They are nothing less than the *sine qua non* of writing cultural theory. It is common for apprentice theorists to feel somewhat intimidated by the mass of theory available to them: where should one start? What is most important to include in a piece of writing? Starting with one or two overview articles or textbooks can help to narrow down one's focus, identifying core theorists and their approaches:

> Students learn that they must say something about all the people who have discussed 'their' problem [essay topic, theme or concept – MH] before them. Nobody wants to discover that their carefully nurtured idea was in print before they thought of it . . . and in a place they should have looked (Becker 1986:136).

Identifying major authorities and approaches in a field is only half the battle. Writing cultural theory also calls for authors' arguments to be evaluated. This requires a basic attitudinal stance: do not assume that just because something is stated by an authority, or included in a key approach, that it is incontrovertible. Much cultural theory is likely to be persuasive, plausible and productive, but it nonetheless remains just a model of the world with essential limits and absences. As Howard S. Becker (1986:141) has cautioned, the ideal of scholarly writing is not merely to recap previous thinking, it is to contribute to this thought, to make readers say 'That's interesting!' as they see how new data and new examples do not entirely fit into preceding frameworks. The point is to 'use the literature', not to 'let it use you' (Becker 1986:149).

The process of writing underlying an original piece of cultural theory may begin with a writer's hunch, and their sense when reading a theory that it cannot be right in some respect, however minor. This intuition can come from personal experience as much as from other reading: we can assess existing theories to see if they relate in any way to our own (seemingly unrepresented or contradictory) experiences. For example, when I wrote *Fan Cultures* (2002), I did so as somebody who had been a fan of specific TV shows all my life, and as someone who had read the major scholarly work on fandom. My own experience of fandom – as highly argumentative, factional and hierarchical – did not neatly line up with what I had read, academically, about media fans. But rather than using this as a reason to castigate cultural theory – after all, what if my experience was not representative? – I related my intuition that something was lacking in fan theory to a range of alternative theoretical work. This engagement provided ways of conceptualizing, and refining, my initial hunch.

Another route into the writing of critical and original theory occurs when, reading about one aspect of cultural life, the reader-writer thinks that it reminds them of something entirely different. This initial spark can again become the seed of a creative piece of poaching, as cultural theory is transferred from one area to another, providing a new way of thinking about a specific phenomenon (see, for example, the following chapter on theory culture as a subculture). Personal experience, and its hunches and intuitions, should absolutely not be viewed as alien to cultural theory: such theory often provides a vehicle for mediating cultural experience, elevating it to the status of shared, intersubjective material, and seeking ways to structurally or systematically explain our lived experiences. C. Wright Mills argues that this shuttling back-and-forth between the minutiae of biographical data and larger issues of social structures/systems is an essential component of the 'sociological imagination' (1970:12–3). No details are too small to be overlooked or written out of cultural theory: the fictional detective's 'radiant empiricism' (Atkinson 1998:109), scrutinizing all the details of everyday life, informs the writing of cultural theory. Pertti Alasuutari goes so far as to argue that 'the sociological imagination' (which we can suggest is centrally akin to that of cultural theory) arose out of the very same nineteenth-century social-cultural conditions which produced the detective story:

> [T]he development of the modern, individually centred society contributed to the growth of both detective stories and sociological imagination. The link, however . . . is an indirect one: the object of deduction, whether in urban everyday life or in detective stories, is not to identify individuals but to *classify* and in this way to gain valuable clues for further inferences (1998:22).

The writing of cultural theory calls for a similarly imaginative engagement, where the individual case is transmuted into a classifiable instance (re-considered as part of a class/category/system):

> I have to be able to move in and out of my . . . [experiences] . . ., I have to be able to bring different, distancing [theoretical] discourses to bear upon my experience, to make that experience both private and public, to account for it both as a specific cultural practice and a systemic instance (Fiske 1990:89).

Fred Inglis makes a related point when he notes that 'the best way to make theory out of practice is to practise. We turn to the experience and the facts which interest us, and look for the patterns which give experience its meaning' (1990:193). Cultural theory is necessarily written by insiders – we all exist 'in' culture – who are also always partly outsiders, even when analysing their own cultures. Theory production requires breaking with common sense, as best we can. Writing cultural theory therefore means adopting a critical but engaged stance, writing from within and without a specific 'situatedness' (Simpson 2002). This 'insider-outsider' status of the writer is true even when an academic analyses academia; this too involves the theorist partly evading the common sense of theory culture 'proportionate to the power of his theoretical and technical powers of objectification . . . to objectify his own position' (Bourdieu 1988:15; Bourdieu *et al* 1994; Becker 1986:128).

Of course, not all cultural theory will immediately seem to relate to our experiences, nor will all such theory provoke intuitively critical responses, but it is always helpful not to screen out or *a priori* devalue what Lynne Pearce (1997) would term the personalized 'reading event' – how we feel when we read something, and how we relate affectively and subjectively to words and concepts. Wherever possible, neophyte writers of cultural theory should seek to produce theory that means something to them, making theory production relevant to their own sense of self rather than assuming that producing cultural theory is merely about making something that looks like theory. To think in this latter way is to approach cultural theory as an alien genre, trying to ascertain what attributes it has, in order to clone these qualities. This approach makes a certain amount of sense. If we wanted to write a science fiction novel, we would probably read lots of such novels in order to find out whether we need to include starships and robots in our own effort. But approaching any genre as alien, we are likely to mistakenly model our efforts on non-representative texts, or we might assume that a genre is far more fixed and repetitive than it actually is, perhaps even mistaking one subgenre for the whole thing. Writing-as-mimicry is therefore always a hostage to fortune, being open to a number of problems: what is the 'ur'-text to be mimicked, and what are the essential qualities of the genre of writing that we are seeking to copy?

It is generally more profitable not to try mimicking cultural theory. Such imitation flattens cultural theory into dead words on a page rather than considering it as a force in, and of, the world, and as something to be done – a process to be entered into, a series of ideas to be related to the self. Imitative theory writing treats cultural theory as a product rather than a process: it doesn't matter how I get to the end-product, as long as my product looks and reads like theory – it has a number of references, the semblance of an argument, and uses theoretical languages. One way of carrying out process-centred writing is, quite simply, to write readings: all the techniques of reading advocated in the last chapter can be used as the basis for disciplined writings. Good writing requires careful reading: the two cannot be divorced as separable activities. It is only by assessing the uses and limits of previous theories that we can begin to write our own cultural theory, applying but also refining established concepts. And we can seek help in this process: we can look for what others have said about the theories we are interested in – or that an assignment requires us to focus on – considering how these theorists' work has been evaluated, and considering whether and to what extent we agree with commentaries. Even if an assignment is based on a theme or a question, and does not seem to call for an engagement with specific theorists' work, it is always helpful to move back from the essay question to an established body of work, and hence to discover who the relevant key writers are in this field. Usually lecturers will have done part of this work for their students, indicating who the key theorists are in a field, and linking types of enquiry to theoretical 'maps' (see Inglis 1990:194–207).

Another part of the process of producing cultural theory is to collect (note down or copy out) any quotes that strike you as being particularly interesting, or opposed to how you would usually think, or even that you feel especially sympathetic towards. Rather than pursuing quotes that enable you to back up or challenge a specific argument – which is also, of course, a useful way of working – this more general process of collecting resonant, provocative quotes may better allow you to articulate your own theoretical vision, and express your own arguments. This is because by mining books or articles for quotes that strike you as especially memorable or useful, you are building up general resources from which to build a potentially wide range of arguments. Indeed, Howard S. Becker notes that 'I am always collecting such prefabricated parts for use in future arguments' (1986:144), and this is something which also tends to characterize my own scholarly reading. Sometimes a very good memory is enough to take one back to an apposite, relevant quotation, but it usually helps to record these nuggets or 'modules' (Becker 1986:144). Such quote-taking may seem unfocused, but if one selects quotes that seem personally intriguing or striking then there is a good chance that they will become a useful, imaginative part of one's theoretical resources at a later date. Selecting quotes that seem to be linked by theme or imagery also means that when one comes to write, this process can be informed by new links made across subject areas or topics, rather than quotations coming only from sources that explicitly or directly deal with a set topic. For example, one may not assume in advance that a study of Arthur Conan Doyle's Sherlock Holmes stories (Atkinson 1998) would be relevant to writing about writing cultural theory, but I have made such a link here. Collecting assorted quotes in advance of any given essay writing, rather than simply for a specific task, allows one's written arguments and evaluations to exhibit a greater range, flexibility and creativity. Of course, one also has to more instrumentally collect quotes relating to the exact matter in hand!

C. Wright Mills testifies to the importance of making new connections between previous theoretical quotes and ideas when writing theory. Describing his own academic practices, and how he wrote a study of the 'power elite' in society, Mills notes the importance of keeping a 'file – which so far must seem . . . more like a curious sort of "literary' journal" ' (1970:220). Keeping and maintaining such a file '*is* intellectual production. It is a continually growing store of facts and ideas' (1970:220). Mills then remarks on the importance of not just looking for quotes, ideas and material in obvious places:

> I examined my entire file, not only those parts of it that obviously bore on my topic, but also those which seemed to have no relevance whatsoever. Imagination is often successfully invited by putting together hitherto isolated items, by finding unsuspected connexions . . . As you rearrange a filing system, you often find that you are . . . loosening your imagination. Apparently this occurs by

> means of your attempt to combine various ideas and notes on different topics. It is a sort of logic of combination, and 'chance' sometimes plays a curiously large part in it. In a relaxed way, you try to engage your intellectual resources, as exemplified in the file, with . . . new themes (1970:221).

Mills writes that this imaginative 'logic of combination' can also be stimulated by literally throwing together seemingly unconnected quotes gathered for different pieces of work, 'mixing up their contents, [and trying] to be receptive to unforeseen and unplanned linkages [between ideas]' (1970:233). Of course, when ideas are connected in new ways, these linkages still need to be related to disciplinary norms and narratives: for example, linking individualistic and psychological 'uses and gratifications' approaches with encoding/decoding work in audience research would cause considerable problems since the basic assumptions underpinning each are so completely different, if not hostile to one another. Care needs to be taken when seeking new links between ideas, but Mills's 'relaxed' sifting of theories for points of overlap, or points of maximum contrast, can be extremely helpful.

It may sound extremely odd to advocate 'throwing one's notes in the air' (Craib 1992:118) and seeing where they land and whether new connections between thoughts and quotes are randomly provoked (see Morrison 1998:110 on Theodor Adorno's unusual approach to empirical research). But this seemingly 'irrational' production of rational theory according to Craib is a way of avoiding being over-protective of one favoured theory, such as a model which may blind us to other ways of thinking:

> If I commit myself to a theory, then I have to protect it; my attention is directed away from the world I am trying to understand and towards problems of logic and coherence and towards attacks on my position from other positions [see the previous Chapter on 'prolepsis' – M H]. . . . [T]he theory might become the most important part of my life. Everything has to be made to fit, everything else translated into it, at the expense of paying attention to the world that the theory is supposed to help me understand (Craib 1992:118; see also Craib 1998:140).

Although Craib draws on a problematic separation of 'theory' and 'world' here – magically excluding theory from the world as if it were not a material, real form and force – his point is nonetheless useful. A kind of 'commutation test' (McKee 2003a:107–110) where elements of theories are imaginatively shuffled around, or where aspects of different theories are recombined, can help to revitalise ways of seeing. As Craib and Mills hint, a positive approach to intellectual production on the part of students (and lecturers) is not to over-commit to theories that are assumed to securely and magically explain everything. Being too secure with one theory can be a difficulty rather than a bonus, blinding oneself to alternative ways of thinking that could explore different aspects of a situation. Equally, displaying an anxious, insecure attachment to cultural theory, where all theories are felt to be untrustworthy, too difficult or too demanding, will make writing cultural theory very difficult. Like Mills's 'sociological imagination', the creative imagination of cultural theory requires a combination of security and insecurity, a 'relaxed' stance to theory which allows different approaches to be freely juxtaposed and used.

Consequently, writers of cultural theory – whether novices or professionals – should take care not to over-structure the process of writing so that all creative jumps and leaps are excluded in advance. Whilst it is important to plan one's written work, and its argumentative structure, such a plan should not be made prematurely nor too forcefully. Otherwise, the writer can make it difficult, if not impossible, to add anything creatively or personally felt to the exercise, instead feeling as if they are just compliantly repeating the already said. Where writing cultural theory is only felt as compliance, and as a fitting in with the already written, then the process of writing has become subordinated to the product of writing, fetishized as a lifeless thing. This sometimes occurs when students, anxious about the process of writing theory, over-structure their preparation so as to minimize the risk of getting it wrong. They also thereby minimize moments of challenge, critique and creativity in their work, failing to throw it all up in the air within the writing process. For example, students studying fandom at Cardiff University have occasionally assumed that they might receive better marks for repeating my own ideas from *Fan Cultures* (2002). This entirely erroneous assumption emerges through product-centred thinking. Good marks are not awarded for imitating what is said by one's lecturer; they are typically awarded for adding to the already said, whether by virtue of criticizing it, challenging it, or applying it in new contexts, creatively making it anew. It is focusing on the process of writing reading that results in the best marks. It is finding out what matters to the writer personally through this process of production and reflection:

> I write because I want to find something out. I write in order to learn something that I didn't know before I write . . . I was taught, though, as perhaps you were . . . not to write . . . until my points were organized and outlined. No surprise, this static writing model coheres with mechanistic scientism . . . [it is a mechanical exercise, assuming that the world can be scientifically and objectively mapped – MH]. But, that model of writing . . . has serious problems: *It ignores the role of writing as a dynamic, creative process*; it undermines the confidence of beginning . . . researchers because their experience of research is inconsistent with the writing model; and it contributes to the flotilla of . . . [academic] . . . writing that is simply not interesting to read because *adherence to the model requires writers to silence their own voices* (Richardson 1997:87–8, my italics).

Here, Laurel Richardson is advocating a more 'spontaneous' approach to writing, one that is personalized and does not emerge through an overly structured process. However, the resultant written product is still likely to be expressed in a structured, argumentative form, for example, moving from an introduction through to a number of major points, including prolepsis and counter-argument, before then rounding up with a conclusion, the transition from each stage to the next being made smoothly via signposting such as 'in the next section I will argue that' or 'I will now go on to consider . . .' (see Fairbairn and Winch 1996:77).

In short, good academic writing tends to follow a specific form, as Katie Simon observes in 'Inside the Idea Factory' (2004). However, this form is not inevitably antithetical to 'the imagination in academia' (Simon 2004:117). Instead it offers a set of expository devices that one's creative writing readings need to be worked through. Simon refers to the following techniques for effective academic writing:

Begin with an anecdote that will hook your reader.
A Thesis is your one ruling idea about your topic thus it is always an assertion.
Control your tone.
Make clear and helpful transitions.
Return to your initial anecdote.
Give concrete examples.
Look beyond your thesis in a concluding paragraph (2004:113–7).

For other versions of good structure, see Green (2000:319–20) and Stokes (2003:154–70).

These are helpful points, although there may not be one entirely monolithic set of norms underpinning scholarly writing, as Simon suggests (2004:114). Some academics may not favour beginning with an anecdote, or returning to this later on: if the word count is particularly tight, it may be beneficial to begin immediately with one's main argument without a hook or anecdotal flourish. Other theorists, such as Richardson (1997), evidently favour the inclusion of a more personal voice in their writing, following feminist work indicating that 'the personal is political' (see Wolff 1995; Wise 1990 and Hills 2002:77–81). Other cultural theorists, following the social-scientific 'writing model' attacked by Richardson, will tend to expunge 'I' as a personal contaminant, but this is a fairly extreme stance. It is preferable to consider that the use of 'I' does not essentially invalidate academic argument. If one is expressing an opinion, such as, 'I think that de Certeau's work is unhelpful', then this is clearly not good academic writing. But if one is articulating an argument, that is, 'I think that de Certeau's work is unhelpful because, as I'll argue, it is based on a rigid binary opposition between . . . [etc etc]' then the use of 'I' is in no way a difficulty. Instead, the writer here is indicating how they have constructed their own writing reading of de Certeau, making this part of an argument backed up by textual evidence and interpretation. If it not clear whether you are expressing an opinion or an argument in your writing then consider first whether you are generalizing without evidence, and/or assuming something to be self-evidently true, and second whether you are drawing on evidence to support some kind of limited generalization, and/or corroborating or challenging your starting assumptions by using other cultural theory. The first instance is an opinion, offered up without evidence, while the second constitutes an argument. Both, or neither, may involve the grammatical use of 'I'; it is the structuring and corroborating of an argument, as opposed to the free-standing status of an opinion, that is the crucial distinction. Strictly speaking, opinions cannot be undermined via any challenge, since they are a matter of belief, as in 'in my opinion the moon is made of cream cheese'. Now, even if you prove to me that this isn't so, I can still reserve the right to hold my opinion, refusing to listen to your nonsense about moon rock. Our opinions are not generally so firmly held, and are sometimes open to revision on the basis of new evidence. But it is a necessary openness to revision that distinguishes an argument about the moon's composition, or about any matter of cultural theory. An argument, unlike a pure opinion, has to be based on 'a respect for available evidence' (Craib 1998: 140). And an argument, unlike pure opinion, constructs knowledge through 'scrupulous avoidance of unsupported generalisations (the student's most frequent failing, it has to be said)' (Green 2000:322). Note that cultural theory can degenerate into opinion rather than argument, even where the formal trappings of argument seem to be in place. This is the danger of becoming overly, if not dogmatically, committed to one theory: theorists then defend this as a belief which cannot be invalidated, rather than as an argument open to testing, revision and creative challenge.

In the previous section, I addressed commercial academic publishing as the 'niche' mediation (Thornton 1995) of cultural theory. The writing of cultural theory for student assessment can be viewed more as a 'micro' mediation, since such writing is generally intended for a readership of only one or two. This is not to devalue micro mediation in relation to niche mediation: though neither reaches a mass readership, there is no moral hierarchy or evaluation implied in these terms. However, since we are dealing here with micro media, this should bring home to any non-professional writer of cultural theory the importance of considering their audience. Although not writing for a market, the student is still, in a sense, writing for his/her lecturer or tutor. This doesn't mean repeating the specific lecturer's work is going to bring especial credit, as I've already noted, but it does mean that it would be wise for the apprentice cultural theorist to pay attention to the substance and form of their lecturer's own writings. Are they are a (post-)structuralist committed to clever word-play and to tracking variations in readings? Are they a feminist for whom it is important that cultural theory illuminates the personal? Are they a Marxist for whom it is important to unveil powerful forces operating in culture as part of a critique of capitalism? Or even a bit of each? What do they value and what do they devalue?

I have known lecturers who purposefully withhold their own writings from students for fear of otherwise affecting and colouring their students' work. And other lecturers may be deliberately vague about their own predilections with regard to the production of cultural theory, for much the same reason. However, there seems to be a strange double standard at work here: these lecturers are happy to adopt specific, argumentative positions in relation to the broader academic community, but are seemingly not happy for their students to perceive, and make use of, the positioned or situated nature of their work. This implies a further derogation of the student, who is not extended the same courtesies as the professional theorist. On the whole, mind you, it will often be perfectly clear where a lecturer or assessor stands on certain debates, and how they are affiliated to certain strands of cultural theory (see the previous chapter on strategic-tactical readings). What values are embodied and performatively enacted by these lecturers, both in the seminar room and on the page? What do they say, and what do they do through that writing? (criticising capitalism/reading deconstructively/challenging gender norms/encouraging, or not, the intersection of the personal and the theoretical/ critiquing representations of race or class/championing popular culture/conserving the prestige of high culture). Thinking carefully about these issues of performativity – what lecturers do with cultural theory – can provide vital clues for the student aiming to become a successful cultural theorist. Again, this is not to argue for the compliant reproduction of any lecturer's performance of cultural theory. It is simply to point out that where micro-mediation is concerned, the student writer should cultivate an awareness of their readership.

Finally, there is the vexed matter of when a piece of theory writing is finished. The production of cultural theory can include many drafts. Published theory rarely gives any indication of the amount of reworking that has taken place: the product typically masks the processes that have generated it as argumentative exposition literally over-writes activities of discovery, reflection, quote collection, throwing it all in the air and planning. This is also partly why students go astray when they fetishize finished products over processes of writing: processes cannot be adequately 'read off' from products. H. F. Moorhouse puts it rather well on the final page of *Driving Ambitions*: 'any book is just the draft that gets printed' (1991:227). Similarly, any essay that gets graded is just the draft handed in. These facts are partly a result of cultural theory's expansive intertextual matrix. Furthermore, theory often tackles questions and issues which tend not to have definite answers – 'What is culture?' – but which can still illuminate, complicate and renarrate our common sense ways of thinking about the world. Cultural theory's openness and provisionality mean that there is always more that can be said or written.

This has significant consequences. Firstly, what gets left out of any piece of cultural theory can be as important as what goes into it. Writers of theory are required to pay attention to what they cannot cover in the space of 2500 words, say, or even in the 85,000 words of a PhD thesis. Necessary limits need to be flagged up, and absences attended to. Such absences should not be wholly pragmatic or accidental ('I couldn't get that book from the library' isn't a useful admission of a limitation), but should instead be given a logical rationale, as in 'I will focus here on active audience theory as exemplified in the work of John Fiske (1989)', or 'I will discuss theories of subculture beginning with the CCCS tradition, since this has been the major influence in cultural studies work' (see the next chapter), or 'recent work in this area includes the following . . .'. Logical rationales for focusing down, and thus clearly demarcating what gets included and what excluded, can involve taking an exemplar, arguing for the relative importance of a certain approach or tradition, possibly even using a time-frame as a cut-off point. Whatever inclusion or exclusion rationale is used should also relate logically to the assigned task. It is important to ask yourself what you need to leave in and what you can dispense with given your chosen (or imposed) topic

Secondly, deadlines clearly count for something in terminating the otherwise potentially interminable writing of cultural theory. The fact that theory production is subjected to time constraints at all levels of production (commercial and otherwise) indicates that it is important to manage one's time effectively when writing, and to fit as much work as possible into the writing window. Doing things with cultural theory should ideally involve doing as much as you can. Counter-intuitively, though, this is not the same thing as assuming that if you have worked on an essay for ten days then it will necessarily be better than one written overnight:

Equating time spent and quality may . . . be empirically false. . . . Writers can worry a piece to death, fussing over adjectives and word order until readers respond to the effort that went into the polishing more than to the thought the prose was supposed to convey. More work may not produce a better product. . . . [T]he more we think about it, the more we may introduce irrelevant considerations and inappropriate qualifications . . . until we bury the thought in . . . ornamentation. (Becker 1986:131).

Essentially, then, it is most important to establish a writing routine that works best for you in terms of:

- reducing anxiety and risk while . . .
- allowing for creative engagement, and also . . .
- reducing the possibility of floating off into over-fussiness at the same time as . . .
- allowing time for different drafts to be read back, evaluated, and carefully structured in line with relevant norms of academic writing.

Taking these points in sequence:

- Reducing anxiety often amounts to discussing ideas with others and planning your writing, but not over-planning or working too compliantly, so that all creativity and personal engagement are stifled.

- Allowing for creative engagement means making use of strategic-tactical readings, and approaching writing as writing reading where critical responses to previous theories are integrated into the theme or topic of the essay. It also means making use of the 'reading event' (Pearce 1997) or process, where readers respond personally, affectively and intuitively to cultural theory ('this doesn't seem right to me – what about . . .?'). Such responses can be stimulated by the kind of tricks advocated by Mills (1970), being worked over to generate a new series of connections between theoretical concepts or to rework established concepts.

- Reducing the possibility of over-ornamentation can mean preventing oneself from continually adding to sentences, perhaps using clear headers and subheaders to structure work in progress. These subheaders – key points or stages in an argument – can then be removed from the final draft, having served their purpose of breaking an argument into manageable chunks, and acting as a kind of logical scaffolding.

- Reading drafts back and allowing time to revise them means that it is foolhardy in the extreme to finish linearly writing a first draft (that is, arriving at your conclusion very close to a deadline). Always build in time to reread and revise. Better yet, have a fellow theorist read back your work for typographical errors, grammatical errors and points of murkiness, as well as for structural and argumentative weaknesses. And consider your audience – the reader who will be assessing your work.

Although writing cultural theory may involve never arriving at an absolutely final conclusion, only stopping at temporary points imposed by time and logical rationales, this 'endlessly-deferred narrative' (Hills 2002:134) of theory can be appealing and pleasurable rather than a source of intimidation or hand-wringing. That there can always be more to find out, more to explore, and more to say or write may after all inspire a sense of working together within an enthusiastic community on a set of shared concerns. And it can also reinforce a sense of cultural theory as a type of artwork, always displaying a duality of reference both to other theory and to the non-theoretical world, and capable of being done with more or less virtuosity (in the eyes of different communal factions).

Across this chapter, I have argued that writing cultural theory cannot be disconnected from reading theory. It therefore becomes important not to oppose reading and writing. One way round contrasts between reading and writing (and related grand-theoretical binaries) is to set these terms and practices within a 'career framework' (Stebbins 1992). Writing cultural theory professionally for publication or, as an amateur, for purposes of student assessment, tends to involve types of fetishism. This can be commodity-fetishism in commercial academic publishing, or a common-sense version of product-fetishism in theory's micro-mediation between student and lecturer. Analysing writing means striving to 'admit the presence of language itself, to allow it to occupy a palpable place in our [theoretical] work' (Simon 2004:117) rather than assuming that theory is a set of pure, transcendent ideas captured on the page. It means approaching writing as a social process, partly sustained by an industrial apparatus inside and outside the contemporary university. This niche or micro mediation, this critical industry outside the terrain of so-called 'mass culture', can have positive and negative outcomes. It can allow theory to reach and affect new readerships as well as restricting theory to commercially profitable forms. Sarah Thornton's (1995) work on niche and micro mediation, which I have appropriated here, originally emerged in a study of a specific subculture. Bearing this in mind, in this chapter I have observed how a range of cultural theorists assume that authentic cultural theory is non-commodified, whereas inauthentic theory is commodified. This opposition does something performatively with cultural theory, using it to imagine and mark out cultural boundaries around theory culture which is then set apart, as sacred, from the profane (ordinary) world of capital and commerce. But why have theorists so often imagined that authentic cultural theory is anti-commercial and outside the mainstream and its ways of thinking? This sounds remarkably like the way that subcultural participants think about themselves, and it is this link that I will address in the next chapter, as well as thinking about links between cultural theory and popular culture. Is cultural theory really so far away from what it studies and objectifies, or does it also enact and perform subcultural and pop-cultural styles and narratives? I will also constatively introduce theories of subculture and popular culture in Chapter Six, although the analytical emphasis of Part Three is more on the performative (what cultural studies/theory does in the world) rather than the constative (what cultural theory says about the world). In the next part, I will therefore consider how a range of cultures, including celebrity and fan culture, are described in theory, as well as how these practices are performed by theory culture itself.

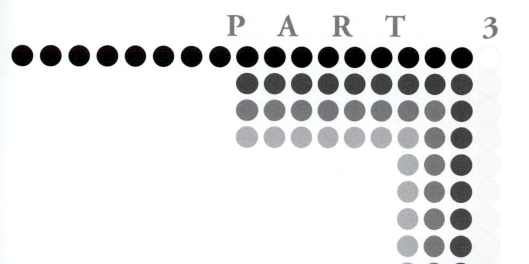

PART 3

Exploring Theory Culture

chapter six

Being Set Apart: Subculture and Pop Culture

Here, I want to consider how cultural theory has been performatively positioned in specific ways, setting it apart from a range of subcultural and popular-cultural Others (see McKee 2002a:311). In *The Philosophical Imaginary*, Michèle Le Doeuff notes the break with *doxa* (ordinary, common-sense thinking) which constitutes philosophy as such:

> [Wherever] one looks for a characterisation of philosophical discourse . . . one always meets with a reference to the rational, the concept, the argued, the logical, the abstract. Even when a certain coyness leads some authorities to pretend that they do not know what philosophy is, no agnosticism remains about what philosophy is not. Philosophy is not a story, not a pictorial description, not a work of pure literature (1989:1).

And as I have already argued in Chapter Two, cultural theory tends to be thought about, and justified, in similar terms. Although not being the same disciplinary entity as philosophy, cultural theory nevertheless partakes of a modernist philosophical discourse – its critical rationality is imagined and set apart from contaminating Others, being constructed as a pure authenticity. This setting apart of cultural theory is, however, not a natural fact – rather, it is a construction of the theorist's cultural identity. One could just as well re-imagine cultural theory as something popular, something telling us stories about the moral life, seeking to affect and move us, always energized and crackling with life's transformative vitality. While there is now a veritable mini-industry for books which find philosophy in hip popular culture (see Hanley 1997; South 2003; Irwin 2002; Greene and Vernezze 2004; Rowlands 2005), there are no comparable vehicles for cultural theory. Why should philosophy be amenable to crossing over into a cultural mainstream while cultural theory deploys difficult language (Culler and Lamb 2003) and marks out its authentic distance from pop culture? One explanation may be that while cultural theory/studies takes popular culture as its object of study, philosophy generally does not. Philosophy can deign to be found within the spaces and texts of 'the popular' by virtue of its relatively secure cultural legitimacy. By contrast, cultural theory is less culturally secure, if you like; it does not possess the serious history boasted by philosophy, and is constantly in danger of being confused and abjectly muddled with its objects of study. Conservative derogations of popular culture all too easily become derogations of media and cultural theory as frivolous, insubstantial and 'not proper subjects' (see Barker with Petley 2001). In such a context, 'Theory' defends its seriousness by defending its boundaries, cutting itself authentically apart from the popular.

In this chapter and the next, I will contest cultural theory's self-presentations as 'set apart' and 'set above' a range of Others, including fans as well as popular culture. I will suggest that theory should be reconceptualised as part of the contemporary cultural world. Setting theory apart from and above the culture it analyses means fixing artificial limits to what can be done with cultural theory/studies. It means marginalizing theory's actual links to storytelling, and its consumers' experiences of affective, emotional fandom (see Chapter Seven), falsely emphasizing the 'allegedly complete rationality of theoretical work' (Le Doeuff 1989:2).

Focusing on how cultural theory has been produced as apart from the mainstream of popular culture, I will firstly consider the concept of subculture. This has been of great significance to cultural studies, allowing theorists to champion sectors of cultural production outside the academy which have also sought to set themselves apart from mainstreamed Others. Cultural studies' well-documented focus on subcultural resistance can be re-examined as a mirroring of its own cultural position. Subcultural theory, in my account, does not just say something constatively about the world. It also performatively validates cultural theory as analogously set apart and resistive. Cultural theory projects, emphasizes and legitimates its own political concerns through pre-existent subcultures, testifying to its own subcultural status and authenticities. Stressing this ethic of connection, where Theory does things to and with its 'objects of study', does not mean criticizing such theory as lacking. Rather, it means positively recovering the insistent performativity of cultural theory as a project – a projection and a task.

Having considered how Theory sets itself apart from cultural Others, hence becoming subcultural, I will then address Theory's further links to the popular in terms of its storytelling capacities. What stories does cultural theory tell, even while it adopts the guise of authentically rational critique? While cultural theory/studies claims to be detached and set apart from both subcultures and popular culture, it nevertheless does things with these dimensions of Othered culture, articulating and narrating its own cultural identity and value system. Theory culture, in short, has been produced out of and through its objectified Others, rather than confronting them as a pure observer.

Distancing and mirroring

The concept of subculture has a long history, one which has recently been explored by Chris Jenks (2005). Jenks points out that although the 1970s work of the Birmingham School (the Centre for Contemporary Cultural Studies, CCCS) is often taken as a modern starting point for subcultural theory (as in Cohen 1972; Hall and Jefferson 1976; Mungham and Pearson 1976; Willis 1978; Hebdige 1979), the notion of subculture was actually used, in its contemporary conceptual form, as far back as 1945 in American Sociology (Jenks 2005:7; see also Tolson 1997). Despite this prefiguring, the term 'subculture' (as used in cultural theory/studies) carries a range of attributes: 'the prefix "sub", which ascribes a lower or secondary rank to the entity it modifies, gives us a clue to one of the main assumptions of this tradition of scholarship – . . . "subcultures" are subordinate, subaltern or subterranean' (Thornton 1997:4). Subcultures are of interest to cultural theorists for the way that they interact with cultural power. Such cultures can be youth cultures subordinated to the generational power of adult or 'parent cultures' (Clarke et al 1976:14), and they can be social groups subordinated along dimensions of class and gender (Powell and Clarke 1976:227). Being variously subordinated in relation to 'dominant' cultures (Clarke et al 1976:16), subcultures can also be loosely or tightly organized:

> Some sub-cultures are merely loosely-defined strands or 'milieux' within the parent culture: they possess no distinctive 'world' of their own. Others develop a clear, coherent identity and structure. Generally, we deal in this volume only with . . . 'sub-cultures' . . . which have reasonably tight boundaries, distinctive shapes, which have cohered around particular activities, focal concerns and territorial space (Clarke *et al* 1976:14).

A specific version of subculture is thus enshrined at the beginning of CCCS work, and this subcultural type has most frequently been analysed in cultural theory/studies: the subculture as set apart from a mainstream or parental cultural world, as bounded, coherent and distinctive. Such a definition practises a gesture of conceptual exclusion, appearing to marginalize and subordinate the study of loosely defined subcultures (although these are still said to merit the term), as well as those which may not be resistant. When Patrick Fuery and Nick Mansfield (2000) offer a Venn diagram of subculture meant to indicate the degree to which different types of culture overlap with 'the ideological mainstream . . . [of] . . . white late-capitalist patriarchy', it is the bounded circle of subculture which intersects least with that representing ideology (2000:24–5). We are matter-of-factly informed that 'subcultures tend to operate outside of . . . dominant ideologies, often offering sites of resistance to such ideological contexts' (2000:27).

The structured and bounded version of subculture prioritized here is clearly identifiable, meaning that it can 'provide an effective point of departure for . . . research' (Bennett and Kahn-Harris 2004:15). And such subcultures' construction against dominant culture makes them an effective site to explore for political resistance to mainstream-ideological belief systems and norms: a 'dichotomy between subcultures and an undifferentiated "general public" lies at the heart of subcultural theory' (Clarke 1990:84). The general public or the mainstream (Thornton 1995:93; Hollows 2003:36–7) are assumed to be monolithic, degraded and inauthentic exemplars of commercial conformity or 'straightness'. By contrast, subcultures are represented as 'resistant', artful and 'authentic' to the very extent that they are set apart from their imagined Others. More than this, Gary Clarke argues that Dick Hebdige's work (1976 and 1979) focuses 'on subcultures at their innovatory moments . . . his concern is typically for the "art" of the innovators' (1990:83 and 86). Subcultures are viewed as most authentic upon their emergence, subsequently selling out or being incorporated into dominant culture as more people become involved and the subculture's initial resistance and energy are diluted: 'the distinction between originals and hangers-on is always a significant one in subculture' (Hebdige 1979:122). Subcultures are repositories of authenticity: they are identified as authentic when set against their out-group (the mainstream), while some subcultural participants are even more authentic, having been there from day one.

We can add one further dimension of subcultural authenticity: that of 'distinctive individuality' (Muggleton 2000:63). Here, subcultural participants demonstrate an awareness of a coherent, bounded, self-identified subculture but proceed to differentiate themselves, however minimally, from any singular group identity or uniformity. Like originals versus hangers-on, this is another in-group

> distinction where subculturalists are quite aware of the socially shared dimension to their individuality – the individual look *within* the group. . . . [The] diversity of this group . . . enables it to accommodate a range of looks and tastes, allowing each member to maintain a sense of simultaneous similarity and difference . . . This allows one both to fit in and yet stand out within a group (Muggleton 2000:67).

Subculturalists also stress their individuality by narrating their entry into a subculture as one of authentic personal choice rather than the mere imitation of a given subcultural look (see Widdicombe and Wooffitt 1995:143 and 149). This form of self-authenticity indicates that subcultures are permeated by the concept and ideal of individualism (see Chapter Seven on 'theory stars'), and so may not be as resolutely resistant to dominant values as cultural theory has implied. As Paul Hodkinson has pointed out, the cultural-theoretical

> assumption of subcultural authenticity reflects not just Marxist theoretical preoccupations, . . . but also an uncritical acceptance of the more exaggerated claims to authenticity of the subcultural participants themselves . . . The tendency to locate both ['dominant'] media and commerce in an oppositional relationship to subcultures is a particularly problematic element of most subcultural theory (2002:12).

Cultural theorists have recently sought to complicate accounts of subculture, reacting against Dick Hebdige's 'canonical' work or 'orthodoxy' (Jenks 2005:4; Muggleton 2000; Hodkinson 2002). Writing in the wake of other major CCCS studies of subculture (see Muggleton 2000:3), Hebdige self-reflexively related the conceptualization of subcultures to the cultural theorist's self-identity. Unlike the more soberly constative models of subcultural 'genesis of style' offered in, say, Clarke (1976:183), or Powell and Clarke (1976:223 and 227), Hebdige linked subcultures to the very role and identity of cultural theory. Subcultures were used to speak to and about cultural theory/studies:

> Barthes . . . understands . . . the 'mythologist' . . . can no longer be one with the 'myth-consumers'. For, like Barthes, we must live an uneasy cerebral relation to the bric-à-brac of life . . . The cord has been cut: we are cast in a marginal role. We are in society but not inside it, producing analyses of popular culture which are themselves anything but popular (Hebdige 1979:139).

This has been viewed as a 'gloomy' conclusion, but while appearing to indicate the 'inevitable gulf that separates the intellectual' from the subculturalist (Beezer 1992:115) it also enacts its own gesture of scholarly autonomy. The cultural theorist had initially hoped to identify with his subcultural objects of study, thereby no longer being 'alone in reading significance into the loaded surfaces of life' (Hebdige 1979:18; see Chaney 1994:39). Instead, he is 'condemned to a "theoretical sociality" (Barthes 1972) . . . confirming the distance between . . . everyday life and the "mythologist" ' (1979:140). But if this destroys any direct unification of theorist and subculturalist, it also works to make the cultural studies scholar more subcultural than their studied subculture. It is the theorist who is 'in society but not inside it'; it is the theorist who is unable even to identify with the already marginalised subculture. Such theoretical 'set-apartness', Hebdige seems to be implying, must remain present – even in relation to those Others who have already cut themselves apart from dominant society and ideology – in order for the cultural theorist or mythologist to retain their distinctive cultural identity. Although Hebdige's language may seem despondent (condemned, alone, uneasy), there is an implicit heroism to his sub-subcultural hiding in the gloom. Recognizing Hebdige's affiliation with the ideals of resistant subculture, other cultural studies scholars have applauded the subculturalist style of his work:

> Hebdige's . . . seminal *Subculture: The Meaning of Style* displays all the signs of the 'cut up' method which, he argues, punk borrowed from Dada, surrealism and from William Burroughs to give it the distinctive, jarring, torn, broken, angry and splintered aesthetic (McRobbie 1999:103).

Seemingly a punk theory as well as a theory of punk (see also Miklitsch 1997), Hebdige's proclaimed distance from his subculturalists thus mirrors and out-does any supposed subcultural distancing from the mainstream. The self-identity of the theorist is styled as being more remote from the ideological mainstream than that of any ordinary subculturalist. This gesture of oppositionally and authentically breaking with dominant cultural forces – that which defines subcultures for cultural theory – is incessantly re-enacted in cultural theory itself. Subcultures offer the hope that cultural theory's project of being set apart, politically and resistively, can work to represent culturally subordinated others. Yet at the same time, cultural theory threatens not only to represent subcultures as points of identification, but rather to become another subculture in its own right.

Each of the forms of authenticity that subcultures are said to construct (anti-mainstream, anti-newcomers, anti-group-identity) recur within theory culture. By 'asserting itself as a transgressive force' (Belghazi 1995:171), theory culture enacts the same anti-mainstream authenticity as subcultural activity. It is (institutionally) bounded, as subcultures have been said to be, and even allegedly carries its own subcultural style:

> One can always spot the theory crowd . . . Their dress, manner and tastes set them apart . . . just enough to support the illusion, the simulation, of their difference . . . [T]his involves adorning oneself in black clothes and carrying a well-thumbed copy of Lacan's *Écrits* or, if one is less impecunious, wearing a leather jacket . . . while networking at conferences (Agger 1992:188).

And in terms of intracultural distinctions, theory culture also sets pioneers against followers, originals against hangers-on, and 'stars' against their acolytes (Eagleton 2003:1–2, and see Chapter Seven). Theory culture's authentic oppositionality can, just like that of subcultures, be co-opted or degraded through the possibility of 'selling out' (Kendall and Wickham 2001:164) or being incorporated into capitalism:

> If, at an earlier moment, the resistance of theory could be analogized to the energy that fuses the traditional Christian promise of otherworldly salvation, such resistance can probably be . . . recharted, at the turn of the new millennium, as part of the unstoppable momentum of a prosperous multinational capitalism (Chow 2003:104).

Furthermore, theory culture's participants do not merge into one uniform group identity, since they, too, pursue distinctive individuality via the production of cultural theory. This generates the irony of subcultural theorists attacking Hebdige's work in order to differentiate their theory-cultural selves from 'traditional subcultural theory' (Hodkinson 2002:9). Theorists perform the same mechanism of distinctive individuality which characterizes subcultural affiliation: one enters theory culture by challenging other participants' theories (see Chapter Four), and these challenges, however minimally, should express some distinctively individualizing difference. Paul Hodkinson notes how new scholars' 'desire to *put some distance between themselves and traditional subcultural theory* has been partially responsible for the coining of a . . . plethora of new terms to replace subculture' (2002:19, my italics), while David Muggleton (2000:4) reproduces a subcultural anti-mainstream logic within theory culture by positioning Hebdige's work as a cultural-theoretical 'mainstream' to be resisted (see also Miller and McHoul 1998:x).

Hebdige's heroic, scholarly distancing is cited and recontextualized in these new theoretical 'distancings' and 'anti-mainstreamings'. What is done with cultural theory is a performative setting apart from a range of Others, whether this is the work of a previous generation of theorists having attained the power of a 'orthodoxy', or the cultural production of subculturalists outside the academy. By distancing their work from the by-now theoretically mainstream likes of Hebdige, scholars have begun to shape what's been termed 'post-subcultural theory' (Muggleton 2000; Hodkinson 2002; Muggleton and Weinzierl 2003; Stahl 2003; Bennett and Kahn-Harris 2004; Martin 2004). But before I address post-subcultural theory, in the following section I want to briefly focus in more detail on cultural studies' interest in subcultures.

Politicizing

For the CCCS, subcultures represented a significant Other which could sustain and reflect their politicizing of contemporary culture. By approaching subcultures as 'resistant' (Hall and Jefferson 1976), Marxist-derived cultural theory could be read into and across the cultural world. Its theorists proceeded by

> identifying with cultural minorities . . . Rather than seeing youth culture as a problem that has to be reconciled to the social order, . . . subcultural research was oriented to its subjects . . . as inarticulate deconstructionists [inarticulate political activists and challengers to the dominant ideology] (Chaney 1994:39).

However, this 'identifying with' also meant that CCCS cultural theorists were rarely actual participants in the subcultures they studied. For these theorists, what was important was not reflecting the experience of subcultural participation so much as politicizing subcultures via a big theory like Marxism: 'The brand of cultural studies they purvey remains confined within . . . abstracted political narratives, rather than engaging the stories by which social actors navigate their reality' (Sherwood et al cited in Muggleton 2000:4). Another of the CCCS investigators of subculture, Paul Willis, makes this clear when he argues that:

> the [participant-observation] principle . . . has directed followers towards a profoundly important . . . possibility – that of *being 'surprised'*, of reaching knowledge not prefigured in one's starting [theoretical] paradigm. The urgent task is to chart the feasibility, scope and proper meaning of such a capacity. . . . It is vital that we admit the most basic foundations of our research approach and accept that no 'discovery' will overthrow this most basic orientation (1980:90).

This insight is generally reproduced as an argument for the power of 'participant-observation' (temporarily taking part in the cultural activities that one is studying) to produce surprising new knowledge for the cultural theorist (Ang 1991:110; Moores 1993:48; Morley 1998:493; see Hills 1999). But Willis's point does not simplistically celebrate surprise. Quite the reverse, his 'theoretical "confession"' (1980:90) limits any shock to the theory system, prioritizing whatever theory is used 'at the outset' – Marxism in the case of Willis's (1977) *Learning to Labour* and his (1978) *Profane Culture*.

The CCCS turn to subcultures therefore makes sense within a specific, politicizing framework, one which positions cultural theorists not as wholly autonomous from society, as if they can transcend and escape from their social, material contexts into a realm of pure ideas, but rather as representatives and champions of the interests of specific material, social groups, and thus as representatives of a definable, left-wing politics. Stuart Hall (1992:280–1) appropriates the term 'organic intellectual' from Marxist Antonio Gramsci to mark out this distinction. Gramsci contrasted 'traditional' intellectuals to 'organic' intellectuals (1971:5–14), describing the traditional type as putting 'themselves forward as autonomous and independent of the dominant social group' (1971:7; see Femia 1987:130–1). By contrast, the 'organic intellectual' belongs to a social group and gives 'it homogeneity and an awareness of its own function not only in the economic but also in the social and political fields' (1971:5). This type of intellectual represents, for Gramsci, a material, class interest (for example, the working class, though they can also represent the dominant, ruling class; see Bellamy 1997:35). Such intellectuals are thus 'grounded in society without losing [their] "adversarial" potential to further . . . [critical] social movement[s]' (Robbins 1993:12). They do not imagine themselves to be entirely set apart from social, class interests, as would the idealist and traditional intellectual valuing pure ideas over material contexts and struggles.

Viewed in this light, CCCS theorists were never interested in just constatively describing the cultural world. To criticize their work for failing to match up to some subculturally experienced 'actuality' as if it were the 'whole truth' (Muggleton 2000:4), and as if the politicizing work of Theory could be bracketed out, misses this fact entirely. The Theory of cultural studies always performatively politicized culture and tried to act upon it:

> We were trying to find an institutional practice that might produce an organic intellectual . . . we weren't sure we would recognize him or her if we managed to produce it. The problem about the concept of an organic intellectual is that it appears to align intellectuals with an emerging historic movement, and we couldn't tell then, and can hardly tell now, where that emerging historical movement was to be found. We were organic intellectuals without any organic point of reference . . . we were prepared to imagine or model or simulate such a relationship in its absence (Hall 1992:281).

But as Hall concedes, the attempt 'never produced organic intellectuals . . . it was a metaphoric exercise' (Hall 1992:282; see Davis 2004:29–31). Any account of cultural studies as simply reflecting or championing the interests of Other social groups, such as subcultures, hence needs to be complicated, as does the notion of theory culture as definitively set apart from its Others. I have suggested here that there is a kind of mirroring between the concept or performance of subculture and theory culture, but this is not the broadly Marxist mirroring desired by Hall and the CCCS. Instead, it is a competitive, hierarchical and individualistic logic of subcultural resemblance. It results in a construction of the cultural theorist as more subcultural than the subculturalist, or latterly, of the cultural theorist as more subcultural than other mainstreamed cultural theories. These performances of self-identity within theory culture hinge on the same assumed anti-mainstream, anti-newcomer and anti-group-uniformity 'authenticities' as conventionally subcultural identities. My interest in 'accountable theory' across this book (Couldry 2000:126), and in a 'cultural studies of cultural studies' (Hall 2002:111), therefore means noting that theory culture is performatively implicated in 'doing subculture' as well as making theoretical pronouncements about it. However, given that post-subcultural theory challenges the accounts which I have used to characterise subcultures, and theory culture, as bounded and authentic, I will now look at these more recent re-descriptions of subculture. If we rethink subcultures as insecurely bounded (Stahl 2003; Martin 2004), as loosely organized (Bennett 1999 and 2000; Hodkinson 2002:19), or as non-anti-mainstream/anti-commerce (Muggleton 2000:131; Thornton 1995:116) then what does this do to any supposed mirroring of subculture and theory culture?

Re-defining and networking

Post-subcultural theory has struck at prior definitions of subculture. Foremost among these is the idea that *sub*culture indicates a sub-ordinate culture. This assumed subordinate-but-resistive status was what made subcultures so important for cultural studies and its politicizing project. The entire theoretical-political project(ion) of identification with a resistive Other – who nevertheless remained less authentically resistive than the cultural theorist – relies on imaging a dominant, mainstream culture. One of the moves of post-subcultural theory has been to dissolve this depiction:

> In saying that subculture has become superfluous I am . . . [arguing that] . . .
> it is not sufficient to assume that elements in a dominant culture can be
> appropriated . . . as a means of distinctive 'counter-cultural' revolt. . . . [T]he
> once-accepted distinction between 'sub' and 'dominant' culture can no longer
> be said to hold true in a world where the so-called dominant culture has
> fragmented into a plurality of lifestyle sensibilities and preferences (Chaney
> 2004:47).

And Chris Jenks, writing in a similar sociological vein, has also marked time for the concept of subculture, suggesting that it is a way of solving theoretical problems via a sleight of hand: 'our real problem resides in attempting to theorize what most of us mostly do, that is what we previously referred to as the "center"' (2005:135). Jenks argues that the notion of subculture has enabled theorists to carve society up into sealed or bounded (sub-) compartments, thus avoiding the question of what subcultures share with the centre or with the dominant ideas in a society, and evading 'growing difficulties in identifying the centre, the mainstream' (2005:135; see Couldry 2003). Jenks ultimately concludes of subculture, 'my sense is that the idea has run its course' (2005:145). This is true for him because he rather problematically suggests that cultural theory should be purely constative rather than performative, that is, it should only describe the world rather than seeking to politically and morally act upon it. Jenks asks

> analytical questions about the reasons why . . . theorist[s] elected to realize the
> world in subcultural terms. . . . [W]hy does the . . . youth cultural theorist wish
> to constitute their object of attention as something discontinuous with the
> centre, the society, the common culture? At what point does the theorist decide
> that the interests within their designated subculture can no longer be contained
> within a more totalizing concept . . .? And of course, the reasons are never
> simply analytical, they are political and moral and thus paradoxical
> (2005:143).

Jenks thus sounds a note for theorizing which should only describe the world, as if it were a type of secondary and pure observation (Žižek 2001:9). He appears to condemn performative cultural studies for its politicizing dimensions, since it wishes for set-apart subcultures in order to champion their very resistance and mediate this in yet more set-apart, and more resistant, cultural theory. As I have argued throughout this book, no purely constative cultural theory is possible. In fact, Jenks's own condemnation of performative cultural studies as 'political and moral and . . . paradoxical' is itself moralizing and performative. It seeks to do something with cultural theory, that is, rule out certain ways of thinking, while re-affirming society's centre in the face of social fragmentation. Although Jenks charges cultural studies' work on subcultures with being 'paradoxical' (see the conclusion on performative contradiction), his work is no less paradoxical given its own desire to dissolve moral and political reasons for defining subcultures. By observing that

Jenks's work is paradoxical, I am not insulting it in the way that he seems to slight cultural studies. I would argue that cultural theory is often, and of necessity, paradoxical. In fact, this may be one of its strengths rather than a lapse, failure or weakness. Such paradoxes allow us to observe the necessary limits of pure, observational logic in the face of cultural theorists' political, communal, and moral engagements.

The dissolving dismissals of subculture furnished by the likes of Chaney and Jenks do, however, compel us to produce further rationales for subcultural theory. If the 'sub' of subcultures cannot be assumed in advance, nor even the boundedness of subcultures as a unit (see Stahl 2003:39; Martin 2004:31), then cultural theorists may wish to defend the concept as something more than mere wish-fulfilment on their part. That is, while never being purely constative, cultural theory might also attempt not to be purely performative. The project of cultural studies has undoubtedly involved identificatory projections on to subcultural Others, but to remain properly theoretical as well as political, I would argue that Theory cannot only be 'wishful theory' (Dollimore 2001:39). Oscillating between the performative 'should be' and the constative 'is', cultural theory avoids surrendering to

> 'wishful thinking' [by which] I mean the tendency to construct a theoretical world according to a usually implicit idea of what the world should be like. Since theory offers a way of ordering the world, a way out of confusion, it also offers a way of avoiding confusion where confusion, or at least complexity, actually exists (Craib 1998:145).

This tempting way out of confusion, presenting a clear account of subcultural subversion and resistance, say, also tends to make cultural theory 'self-exonerating . . . [and] hardly at all . . . self-questioning' (Dollimore 2001:39). Subcultural theory would threaten to become purely self-exonerating were it to continue to (wishfully) image subcultures as bounded and resistant while ignoring evidence that subcultural boundaries may be dissolving within contemporary society. But the arguments of Jenks and Chaney have neglected a further characteristic of subcultures. This missing factor is brought out in Nancy Macdonald's study of graffiti subculture. Like critics of the term subculture, Macdonald notes that it has 'become . . . overly vague. . . . Do subcultures, as we know them, exist . . .? Is a meaningful use of this concept still possible or even valid? Perhaps not' (2001:152). Rather than concluding with this dissolving gesture, Macdonald moves to counter it:

> But in declaring . . . subculture dead and buried, where does this leave its apparent members? As I see it, they are the ones we should be consulting on these matters as the key to this dilemma lies, potentially, in their hands. *Perhaps subcultures are only subcultures if their own members recognize themselves as such, if they themselves draw boundaries and define themselves as members of a group which is seen as standing 'apart' from others* (2001:152, my italics).

Macdonald also reclaims the 'sub' of subcultures, which need not imply being 'beneath other groups and cultures, as this would involve outsiders' own value judgements. But "sub" [could be used] as in separate from' (2001:152). On this account, the possible permeability and non-resistiveness of subcultures are attested to, but definitions of any given subculture as relatively bounded and ideally resistant remain present in the experiences and value systems of subculturalists themselves: 'A subculture may be defined as that which constructs, perceives and portrays itself as standing apart from others as an isolated, defined and boundaried group' (2001:152).

Macdonald's conclusion resonates with Paul Hodkinson's post-CCCS theorizing of Goth subculture. Hodkinson accepts that subcultures can be more fluid than CCCS accounts would predict (2002:19), and his work also indicates that forces of media and commerce play vital roles in forming and sustaining subcultures (see Hodkinson 2002:109–29; Thornton 1995). Despite these apparent indicators of a subculture that constantly seems to be dissolving into its mainstream, dominant Others, Hodkinson continues to argue for subcultural 'substance' (2004:141), and hence for the '*relatively* high level of autonomy' (2002:32) that is constructed and valued by subcultures:

> Gaining acceptance, popularity and status [in the subculture] was often dependent upon making oneself sufficiently compatible with the distinctive tastes of the subculture. It is important that such clear evidence of *relative* consistency and distinctiveness is not obscured by an over-emphasis on [subcultural] diversity and dynamism (2002:30).

We can therefore marshal two sources of evidence against the dissolving of subcultural differences and boundaries: subcultures involve their participants imagining themselves set apart from outsiders-as-Others, and subcultures, despite their fluidity, diversity and internal mediation and commercialization, continue to involve patterns of taste, value and style which have their own 'us' versus 'them' coherence. Subculture, we might say, exists in the eyes of its participants. Many aspects of the CCCS definition of subculture – boundedness/internal coherence/resistance to external norms – can thus be seen to persist, even while we recognize that subcultures are mediated and commercialized constructs as much as they are authentically set apart from these forces.

This integration of post-subcultural theory with the experiences of subcultural participants vis à vis their set apartness allows us to make further sense of theory culture when viewed as a subculture in its own right. I have already argued (in the last chapter) that theory culture is highly permeable to commercial forces, as well as being partly constructed and sustained by mediation in the form of academic publishing. Furthermore, although theory culture is also subject to many internal differentiations, such as cultural studies scholars, critical theorists, deconstructionists, Deleuzians, feminists, and a myriad of overlaps between these identities, it remains the case that participants in theory culture imagine themselves as set apart from non-academic Others. The degree of this set apartness may vary, with feminists and cultural studies scholars frequently reaching out to audiences beyond the academy, or academically representing non-academic cultural identities (e.g. fandom). In general, though, theory culture appears to display Hodkinson's relative consistency and distinctiveness (2002:30). It also satisfies Macdonald's definition of a subculture as participant-imagined and constructed (2001:152).

Some scholars have actually characterized theory culture's factions as subcultures in their own right: Lyn Thomas (1995 and 2002:11) refers to 'feminist subculture'. However, we can more accurately consider academic factions to be 'sub-subcultures' (Hodkinson 2002:191). Theory culture, thought of as a subculture, indicates the need to consider intra-group distinctions, with *sub*-subcultural identities, such as 'the deconstructionist', existing within the subcultural bounds of theory culture as a whole. One way of clarifying this internalized diversity of theory culture is to analyse what Linda Brodkey calls 'academic networks' (1987:40). Similar to the common-sense notion of networking – being in touch with significant people in one's area of work – academic networks are, quite simply, about who maintains contact with whom. Brodkey (1987:40–52) argues that feminist and deconstructionist networks can be discerned, meaning that self-identified feminists and deconstructionists tend to network with other such scholars. These networks are discernible by virtue of the fact that their members are frequently 'cultural isolates in their respective institutions and departments' (1987:44), focusing their sense of academic subculture around spatially distanced but related scholars, or focusing on 'local reading groups' that are set apart from other theory-cultural factions (1987:47). Academic networks 'serve . . . as a form of political solidarity among the members who perceive themselves as isolated from . . . their respective institutions' (1987:44). And this occurs despite the fact that deconstructionism, especially, may have achieved 'academic success' and 'academic authority' (1987:43 and 45). It is this trans-institutional and interdisciplinary networking – now often supported by online communities – which secures academic sub-subcultures as distinctively set apart. They possess their own journals, such as the *Journal of Feminist Media Studies*, or '*Diacritics, Sub-Stance, Glyph* and *The Georgia Review*' as early US supporters of Derridean work, (Lamont 1987:610), their own publications, study groups and conferences. It is this sense of being further set apart within theory culture that, I think, provokes Lyn Thomas's invocation of 'feminist subculture' and Sara Ahmed's analysis of 'feminist attachments':

> feminism involves an emotional response to 'the world', where the form of that response involves a reorientation of one's bodily relation to social norms. . . .
> It is not that anger at women's oppression 'makes us feminists': such an anger *already* involves a reading of the world in a particular way (Ahmed 2004:171).

At the same time as stressing feminism's political, cognitive and emotional set-apartness from norms of social and cultural power, Ahmed acknowledges that this can never be total. Feminism cannot think and feel itself-as-such wholly outside and against cultural power: 'an "anti-normative" politics does not and cannot suspend the power of social norms' (2004:172). This is not cause to dismiss feminism or see it as inevitably failing to meet its own standards. Rather, it means recognizing that, as an academically networking sub-subculture, feminism imagines itself as set apart, while still linking into forms of cultural power by existing within the academy. Subcultures may thus be politicized and resistant in specific ways, while simultaneously reproducing aspects of cultural norms. No (sub-) subculture is ever totally oppositional: this would indeed represent wishful theory, and a reduction of cultural complexity. For example, in the following chapter I will argue that theory culture, like many non-academic subcultures, tends to reinforce cultural norms of individualism. And feminism may also reproduce cultural norms of hierarchy and power inequality through its construction or celebration of theory stars.

Ahmed's focus on the role of emotionality in academic networking needs to be generalized beyond its seemingly natural home in feminist thought, as if the feminine and the emotional can be equated (see Ahmed 2004:170). Randall Collins has examined the more general importance of 'emotional energy' in building and sustaining academic networks. Collins argues that:

> Intellectuals are a peculiar combination of the intensely localistic and the . . . cosmopolitan . . . Intellectual sacred objects [for example, *emotionally as well as cognitively* favoured theories – MH] are created in communities which spread widely yet are turned inward, oriented toward exchange with their own members rather than outsiders . . . Intellectuals are much more self-reflexively and self-analytically aware of their group identity than are lay groups (2000:24).

Of course, the definitional exception to Collins's final point here is precisely the subculture, whose members are just as aware of their coherent, bounded distinctiveness as are academic groupings. Nevertheless, Collins argues that the 'interaction rituals' (2000:20–4) which sustain academic sub-subcultures depend on embodied, emotional encounters. Hence, despite the importance of mediated reading and writing in academia, key

> intellectuals cluster in groups . . . The personal contacts between eminent teachers and later-to-be-eminent students make up . . . kinds of chains across the generations. And this is so even though communications technology has become increasingly available. Intellectual life hinges on face-to-face situations because interaction rituals can take place only at this level. Intellectual sacred objects can only be created if there are ceremonial gatherings to worship them. This is what lectures, conferences, discussions and debates do (Collins 2000:25–6).

This clustering in specific places also means that academic sub-subcultures are typically formed through 'collaborative circles' (Farrell 2001). Anti-normative or resistant practice thus does not form in a vacuum, or entirely individually, but rather through the work of a reasonably small, tightly-knit and co-present group of participants. Such circles, not yet mediated and trans-local, are thus akin to Hebdige's subcultural 'originals' or pioneers. Their formation as circles of friends and creative collaborators

> *constructs its own subculture* . . . [as] a new theory and methodology that they introduce into their discipline . . . In the early stages of circle development, the supportive friendships within a circle enable the members to resist pressures to conform to the dominant vision of their field (Farrell 2001:270, my italics).

Michael P. Farrell's (2001) work on collaborative circles, linked to Collins's (2000) on scholarly cultural production, gives us a way to explain why it is that academic sub-subcultures – just like other subcultures – almost always have their own origin stories. In these, high-status individuals are accorded the 'authenticating' role of originators, and this authenticity is carried, through networking, across generations of mentors and disciples. Such accounts partly reflect the tendency for new academic sub-subcultures to emerge through the more intense emotions and rituals of embodied interactions. Cultural studies, then, has its originators primarily in the 'intensely localistic' form of the Birmingham School, whose mentor figure, Stuart Hall, and generational disciples – the CCCS's postgraduate students such as Dick Hebdige, Dave Morley and Charlotte Brunsdon – became the stars of this new cultural theory. And deconstructionism similarly has its originator, Jacques Derrida, along with an Anglophone origin story which ties major figures into one spatial location, a Johns Hopkins conference on structuralism in 1966:

> Paul de Man and J. Hillis Miller attended the Johns Hopkins conference and later became energetic proponents of Derrida's work, as did Harold Bloom and Geoffrey Hartman . . . As a sophisticated Parisian cultural good, Derrida's work could and did reinforce the disciplinary position of the Yale scholars, whose influence had traditionally depended partly on the display of high-status cultural goods (Lamont 1987:611; see also Brodkey 1987:40–3).

The fact that subcultures possess a structural and spatial logic of emergence does not automatically mean that their pioneers should naturally be accorded high status. It is rather a part of subcultures' characteristic set-apartness that their pioneers are accorded such status, since these honorific narratives allow subcultures to legitimate and reinforce their relative consistency and distinctiveness. Imagining oneself as being set apart from outsiders requires a narrative of subcultural identity which provides markers of when and how the (sub-)subculture distinctively became itself, when and how it was mediated, popularized or culturally extended, and perhaps even when it began to be co-opted. Non-academic subcultures and the sub-subcultures of theory culture are hence related insofar as they are ways of telling stories about cultural identity. They work to construct and imagine bounded, coherent and distinctive identities for cultural subjects who are simultaneously part of commercialized, mediated and permeable groupings.

We might therefore suggest that subcultures and sub-subcultural factions of theory culture display a form of 'false consciousness', since their material context is generally at odds with their self-presentation. But it would probably be more accurate – not to mention less derogatory in relation to both non-academic subcultures and scholarly sub-subcultures – to follow Ahmed (2004) by observing that forms of resistance are always emotionally, cognitively and habitually attached to what they resist. Subcultures are never purely outside the dominant; theory culture is never purely outside what it theorizes. If subcultures, and theory culture, really were wholly autonomous, as opposed to relatively autonomous in Hodkinson's (2002) sense, then the very cultural power they define themselves against would, in fact, no longer be powerful at all.

It may seem odd to think of cultural theory as telling tales, and as never being entirely separated from what it theorizes, but these are the threads that I will now consider in more detail, paying specific attention to how popular culture and politicizing cultural theory/ studies rely on narrative structures of good versus evil, or heroes versus villains. First, it will be necessary to examine various definitions of popular culture, considering how popular culture and cultural theory/studies may be intertwined through the matter of pleasure as well as narrative.

Othering and pleasing

Like many of the terms used in cultural theory, popular culture is not amenable to easy definition. John Storey sets out six possible ways of thinking about it, indicating that 'difficulty arises from the . . . other which always haunts any definition we might use. It is never enough to speak of popular culture, we always have to acknowledge that with which it is being contrasted' (2001:14). Storey's Others for popular culture are:

- Unpopular culture: material that is not widely liked in terms of numerical counts of its appreciators (2001:6).

- High culture: pop culture is that which does not meet criteria and standards for inclusion as high culture; it is formulaic, insufficiently artistic, ephemeral, non-exclusive and hence not culturally worthwhile (2001:6).

- Folk culture: culture that is authentically of the people, not being commercially produced. By contrast, popular culture is denigrated for its mass production and mediation, and termed 'mass culture' (2001:8).

- Mass culture: this is the inverse of the last approach since in this case pop culture is precisely defined as the culture of the people, in contrast to inauthentic, commercially imposed mass culture (2001:10).

Storey then examines his fifth and sixth definitions of pop culture, although it is unclear what the Other to popular culture is in these accounts, a difficulty reflected in the fact that he lists only four discernable Others in his summing-up (2001:14). Storey's fifth and sixth approaches are more clearly theoretical positions, whereas the four listed above also circulate in versions of cultural common sense:

- Pop culture is explained as a terrain of exchange between commercial interests and the people: this is a mixture of the opposed approaches (the third and fourth), and is presented as superseding them. Presumably the multiple Others to popular culture here would have to be 'pop-culture-as-singularly-attacked' and 'pop-culture-as-singularly-defended' (2001:10–12).

- Pop culture as a terrain which is blurred into high culture, and where such distinctions no longer hold. Again, this is a more theoretical, 'meta'-argument, since pop culture is defined against other versions of itself; here, its Other would presumably be 'pop-culture-as-securely-bounded' (2001:12–3).

This wide variation in the term 'popular culture' means that 'popular culture is defined by how it is explained and evaluated theoretically' as well as in common-sense accounts sharing aspects of these theoretical explanations (Strinati 2004:xvii). We can be for popular culture, or against it, although perhaps we may be too uncritically for it (an accusation made by McGuigan 1992), or too unthinkingly against it (an accusation usually directed at Frankfurt School thinkers such as Theodor Adorno, see Jenkins 1992). As Morag Shiach has noted, 'discussions about popular culture seem to end up reproducing one of a very limited number of . . . descriptions' (1989:200). Although these are usually broadly pro- or anti-positions, in

Storey's fifth definition we can discern a cultural studies' 'see-saw' model which tips between positive and negative views, while nevertheless tending to fall on the side of critiquing pop culture as an ideological force. On this account, although popular culture is compelled to give something to the people, it still circulates limited and limiting representations, and reinforces ways of thinking about the world ultimately aligned with the interests of big business and society's ruling elites.

Storey's examination of popular culture opens out further in his later *Inventing Popular Culture* (2003). Here, the Other of 'unpopular culture' is left to one side as unworkable: how could one ever produce a numerical audience figure above which something would be popular and below which it would be unpopular? (2001:6). New categories are added; popular culture is additionally considered as a form of art in its own right, as a globalized commodification of culture, and as the source ('root') and trajectory ('route') of our cultural identities, with contemporary consumers stitching together their self-identities out of mediated texts (see Chapter One on textualized agency). Again, these accounts do not possess obvious Others, although we might suggest that pop-culture-inflected self-identities can be contrasted to traditional self-identities based on relationships to embodied Others rather than mediated texts (Gergen 1991).

Across all these ways of thinking about popular culture, a couple of characteristics pretty much remain in place. It is rare for theorists to dispute the commodified nature of popular culture: 'popular culture usually becomes available, or is produced, because it is a commodity' (Strinati 2000:251). And this commodity status is almost always linked to notions of consumer-audience pleasure, with one of the values of pop culture being its pleasurable status:

> [A] discourse about pop idealizes fun as the summit of cultural pleasure . . .
> The pop discourse brings together the exhilarating loss of self engendered by
> entertainment and its paradoxical everydayness; a combination of the
> *wonderment* you may experience the first time you hear Elvis Costello with the
> *familiarity* of background pop [music] in the kitchen (Miller and McHoul
> 1998:3).

Or, indeed, the familiarity of hearing your favourite Elvis Costello track for the thousandth time, something which still reminds you of the wonderment you felt when you first heard it. Since accounts of popular culture usually agree on its commercial and pleasurable natures – these being the *sine qua non* of the popular – commodity-derived pleasures then tend to be subjected to all manner of hierarchical evaluation by theorists and non-academics alike. In other words, pop cultural pleasures are valued or devalued according to what they tell us about the consumer concerned. Pleasures taken in popular culture classify the person who attests to them, just as the refined appreciation of high culture classifies its devotee (Jensen 1992). In a sense, then, pop culture can be viewed less as an inherently democratizing or commercially imposed cultural force which we must choose to be for or against, and more as a system of classifications – a discursive field – through which constructions of pleasure are made meaningful.

Rather than magically producing an ineffable and untheorisable pleasure, on this account popular culture can be viewed as the cultural site *par excellence* where self-consciously cultural pleasures can be publicly ascribed to the self or to imagined Others, and where cultural performances of pleasure (and/or their evaluation) can be carried out. Pop culture allows us to make almost unceasing attributions of pleasure to imagined Others – he or she is into that band and likes that kind of music – and to evaluate actual Others on the basis of their tastes or pleasures. By virtue of its near-ubiquitous presence, popular culture provides a common ground and a set of systematic differences through which consumers can, as textualized agents, define aspects of their cultural identities. Storey draws on theories of performativity to address this:

> What Judith Butler (1999:33) argues with regard to gender identities also, I think, applies to identities in general; that is, 'an identity is performatively constituted by the very "expressions" that are said to be its results.' In this way, the performance of identity is the accumulation of what is outside (in culture) as if it were inside (in nature) . . . Popular culture is a fundamental part of this process (Storey 2003:91).

However, Barry King remarks that '[s]urprisingly given their pervasiveness as providers of identity imagery, Butler has little to say about the impact of the visual media' (2004:186) as well as having relatively little to say about the pleasures of consuming popular culture. Yet it is 'performance . . . based on popular cultural practices' (2004:193) through which elements of our cultural identities are re-produced and re-iterated, given that 'consumption [of popular culture] is perhaps the most visible way in which we stage and perform the drama of self-formation' (Storey 2003:89).

Whether this re-iteration occurs through the figure of a reviewer on amazon.com, or the crowd member at a gig, or the poster to an online forum, or the queue member for a late-night promotional event at a local store, or the impulse purchaser at a supermarket, popular culture works by producing anticipatory and reflective performances of pleasure – or, on occasions, performances of disappointment and displeasure. It is via the discourse of pleasure that external popular culture is replayed as something seemingly ineffably or magically inside our selves and identities. This cultural pleasure is commonly taken as a sign of our pure or natural interiority and selfhood, and peoples' pleasures taken in popular culture frequently feel very close to their sense of self. Pleasure itself is disciplined and ordered through pop culture, being placed into appropriate mechanisms of expression and performance. This is not the same thing as arguing that discourses of pleasure have altered in line with vast swathes of historical time such as 'eras' (Wilson 2004), nor is it quite the same as arguing that different theories, such as psychoanalysis or philosophy, carry their own constructions of pleasure (Hills 2005). Rather, it is to argue that popular culture can be viewed as apparently generating audience pleasures in people, whereas it is actually facilitating textualized agency. That is, people are busy doing things with pop culture's texts, and one of the things they do is to perform and profess their pleasures taken in certain texts, and displeasures taken in others, thereby producing a consumerist sense of their 'distinctive individuality' (Muggleton 2000:63). Consumers of pop culture generally feel themselves to be no less linked to, and simultaneously apart from, group identities and uniformities than do subcultural participants.

This popular cultural 'pleasure-performance principle' as a public marker of the natural, interiorized and privately valuing self is also evident within cultural theory. For example, Miller and McHoul perform this classificatory work in their comment above. Elvis Costello is elevated as a source of wonderment, while background pop is said to be merely 'familiar'. For these writers, it would seem that Costello deserves to be really heard rather than blending into the indistinct background of pop. Far from escaping cultural hierarchy by focusing on popular rather than high culture, cultural theory/studies has thus tended to participate in the construction of various intra-pop-cultural hierarchies via its tendency to value types of pop culture as properly resistant objects of study and pleasure whilst other arenas of pop culture remain too irredeemably mainstream to study, or to safely profess taking pleasure in. Nick Couldry has noted this tendency:

> Cultural studies began with a democratic critique of earlier elitist approaches to culture, recognizing the fundamental importance of 'popular culture': the experiences and pleasures of those outside the cultural elites . . . Now, however, our priorities must be formulated in different terms. The problem with the term 'popular culture' is symptomatic of a wider difficulty . . . [which is] the exclusions which cultural studies itself has entrenched . . . [such as] the downplaying of the 'middlebrow' or of any cultural experience which is not 'spectacular' or 'resistant' (2000:3).

Elizabeth Bird sounds a similar note when she observes that cultural studies scholars, often fan-consumers of what they study (see Hills 2002:1–21; Muggleton 2000:4), have taken for granted the goodness of their fan objects while assuming that 'other kinds of popular forms are beyond the pale' (Bird 2003:121). As Bird comments:

> There is very little cultural studies work on music that does not suit the tastes of the scholar, such as the middle-of-the-road popular and country music enjoyed by vast numbers of people: we are much more likely to read a cultural studies article about the Grateful Dead or Phish than about Garth Brooks or Celine Dion. The middlebrow consumer, the 'easy listener and light reader and Andrew Lloyd Webber fan' as Frith (1991:104) puts it, is the most ignored (2003:121).

Bird argues that the situation is similar in studies of television, where 'edgy, avant-garde, or . . . "cult"' TV such as *Buffy the Vampire Slayer* is favoured over 'successful "middle-of-the-road" offerings like *Home Improvement* or *Diagnosis Murder*' (2003:121). This scenario suggests that by treating culture more inclusively, and by aiming to take seriously the pleasures of popular culture (while still critiquing much pop culture as ultimately ideological), cultural studies/theory may have unwittingly provided a vehicle for the more or less implicit exercising of 'popular aesthetics' (Bird 2003:118) where certain popular texts are valued over others (see also Faulk 2005; During 1994:4). If this is so, then rather than existing apart from the terrain of popular culture, cultural studies/theory may have actually moved towards it, since the types of textual discriminations being made by scholars are structurally similar to those made by non-academic consumers of pop culture (the difference being that these consumers don't usually produce theory about the resistiveness, authenticity or philosophically illuminating status of their favoured popular-cultural artifacts). Virginia Wright Wexman has argued that although 'critics customarily consider themselves disinterested observers . . . [their activities lead] . . . to practical valuations of . . . texts, [and] one can view current scholarly practices in the light of these valuations. Why are certain . . . texts chosen for special attention?' (1999:77). Wright Wexman concludes that 'scholars, like others, have . . . interests at stake: we are not only critics but also consumers' (1999:89).

If there is a danger here that cultural theory/studies may, at least partly, be of a piece with other consumers' pleasure-performances, being caught up in the same networks of social identification, dis-identification, and individualization, then there is also the fact that cultural theory retains its drive to be set apart within theory culture. We might therefore suggest that many hybridised 'scholar-fans' (Hills 2002:11–2) use cultural theory as a *specific* way to articulate and value their fandoms, where this specificity means not just speaking one's fan interests, but also ideally modifying them, reflecting upon them, and critically moving 'beyond them' (Grossberg 1997b: 251). Positively assessing cultural theorists as popular-cultural consumers, we might note the following:

- Pleasure-performances of popular culture indicate degrees of cultural skill. Rather than seeing these processes as a threat to theory culture, cultural studies' scholar-fans 'hope not to be deskilled of what we know as members of a popular audience before we are thought to be adequately prepared to enter academic life' (Jenkins, McPherson and Shattuc 2002:9). Possible continuities between pop culture and cultural theory offer a way of revitalizing theory culture by challenging its previous set-apartness, allowing new research questions and topics to be posed from 'the knowledge of our guts, our hearts and our longings' (Jenkins *et al* 2002:9).

- Pleasure-performances of popular culture are, unlike much of theory culture, second nature to almost all students and apprentice theorists. Again, rather than threatening the proper carrying out of cultural theory, this provides one possible way of partly overcoming 'alienation between academic and student' (Parham 2002: 473). And more than bringing about an identification between student and professional scholar, emphasizing this commonality may also reduce 'the impression given of . . . hesitancy, among academics, about relating their intellectual and "popular pleasures"' (Parham 2002:475; see Chapter Seven).

- Pleasure-performances of popular culture also suggest a need to accept that 'lecturers and students represent different (and internally differentiated) social forces, with some common and differing interests, who may forge alliances for some purposes but not for others' (O'Shea 1998:524). Using cultural theory to read specific pop-cultural texts as obviously ideological (devalued) or evidently resistant (valued) risks leaving cultural theory to operate as an attack on, or defence of, different pre-established tastes and social forces. Instead, both lecturers and students could use cultural theory to self-reflect on how their tastes are premised on cultural exclusions and devaluations of imagined Others. This would mean forging alliances not merely in terms of potentially shared tastes and shared pleasures in pop culture, but also through analyzing the cultural hierarchies of pop-cultural pleasures.

- The pleasure-performances of popular culture have been viewed as a problem in much cultural theory, given 'the need to establish popular culture . . . as worthy of study . . . [by] . . . refusing . . . traditional modes of judgement' (Geraghty 2003:27), as well as refuting such evaluations via the 'notion . . . that to make aesthetic judgements was to impose the cultural norms of the powerful' (2003:27–8). These are well-taken points, and the latter is especially persuasive, since by favouring certain types of edgy and cult popular culture, academics are to an extent participating in a common sense devaluation of middlebrow pop culture. Geraghty argues that there is hence a case for 'academics being more explicit about the evaluative judgements that we inevitably make' (2003:40). Along with making it more difficult to sustain a sense of cultural theory as definitively set apart from popular culture, this would also mean that theory could not be used to surreptitiously reperform scholars' popular cultural pleasures, with pre-existent tastes being taken as the unannounced basis for theoretical hierarchies or conceptual distinctions.

Despite these more positive takes on cultural theory's inter-relatedness with popular culture, in some cases cultural theory will undoubtedly continue to act as a mask for its writers' pop-cultural attachments and consumer investments (see Hills 2002:81). It would be as well to concede that this situation poses very real problems, as well as opportunities, for cultural theory. It is not simply 'a good thing' (*contra* Jenkins et al 2002), but nor is it simply a disastrous loss of theory culture's 'set-apartness' from pop culture. The critiques offered up by Couldry and Bird are thus timely, because even if scholar-fans reflexively critique their fan-consumer identities, this is hardly helpful if the situation leads to a new canon of affirmed pop-cultural artifacts versus excluded, marginalized objects.

Given the connections between popular culture and theory culture that I have sought to highlight thus far, it is perhaps curious to note that writers can confidently assert the following as if it is a natural truth: 'academic writing is, by definition, not part of popular culture but analyses it from outside' (Couldry 2000:3). Couldry simply absents cultural theory altogether from the terrain of popular culture, re-iterating a sense of cultural theory as securely set apart from what it theorizes. Presumably Couldry would view the matter of scholars-as-fans of popular culture as a limited one affecting only specific cultural theorists, rather than as a more generalised or structural issue for scholars who are critics as well as consumers, existing inside popular culture as well as theorizing it.

Of course, Couldry's point could be taken only as indicating that theory does not circulate in the mass media, but since it remains the case that cultural theory is niche-mediated and commercialized – and that it appeals to reasonably large numbers of lecturers and students – it is difficult to argue that cultural studies is definitely unpopular culture in contrast to the popular, especially given the impossibility of determining any numerical threshold between the two. Despite difficulties determining what is meant by popular culture, cultural theorists seemingly proceed as if they also know, unarguably and naturally, what cultural theory is *not* (see Chapter Two). Just as the popular is frequently defined against a range of Others, so too is Theory, the popular appearing to be among them. However, in the following section I want to argue that links between cultural theory and popular culture do not emerge only through the pleasures and tastes of cultural theorists studying pop culture which they love. For, more generally than this, cultural theory also moves across the terrain of the popular by drawing on highly legible and formulaic narrative structures.

Storytelling and moralizing

In *Getting It Published*, Routledge's publishing director William Germano imparts some advice to professional academics:

> Anthologies and collections can only gesture toward a story, but the successful single-author book will have the inner line that pulls the reader through from first page to last. 'Story' is meant loosely here – it might be a genuine narrative, but it's sometimes possible even to have a theoretical argument unfold in a way that propels the reader. Whatever your subject, however scholarly, there is a sense of pleasure that should be part of the reader's experience (2001:184).

Lest it be thought that this is advice only for the professional, and not for the apprentice theorist, in the extremely useful student guide *Writing at University*, Phyllis Crème and Mary R. Lea also suggest that:

> One way of thinking about developing an argument in your writing is to think of it as your 'story': What is your story? Do you have a clear storyline or plot? Using the notion of a story may not seem very academic, but we think that it gives a good indication of the 'feel' of developing an argument (1997:91–2).

Although these pieces of craft wisdom testify to the importance of academic storytelling, both display ambivalence toward the notion that Theory might be akin to narration. Somehow, this 'may not seem . . . academic', or the idea 'is meant loosely'. While advocating the use of a storyline within cultural theory, these advisors hence still mark theory's assumed distance from the popular-cultural storyline or plot, seeking to set apart Theory even as they indicate possible links to popular cultural forms. Theories are typically thought of as being more than mere stories – to indicate that they are artful, literary, or narrativised is to slight the set-apartness of cultural theorizing as something assumed to be naturally beyond the popular and its devices. For example, Ann Game and Andrew Metcalfe note that although the sociology of culture

> is proud of its studies of artistic conventions and genre, it pays almost no heed to its own narrative conventions: *sociologists tell stories as if they weren't storytellers, and as if storytelling were a less honest pursuit than theirs*. These topics are absent from almost all introductory . . . textbooks, despite the vast bulk of these tomes (1996:65, my italics).

Similarly, Jonathan Culler (2000:287), Adam Morton (2004:31) and Michèle Le Doeuff (1989:1) have observed how the literary and storytelling aspects of philosophy, another of the currents flowing into interdisciplinary and re-disciplinary cultural theory/studies, are frequently devalued or rendered invisible by the norms and self-representations of theory culture. Culler notes the 'mode of critique and complaint' (2000:289) which characterizes much thinking on theory-as-storytelling. It is as if the narrativization of theory threatens to contaminate theory's purity and authenticity, rendering it improper or bad Theory. This common sense of theory culture is displayed, for instance, in Kevin Mulligan's (2003) attack on 'continental philosophy' and, more specifically, Derridean theory. Mulligan makes clear the either/or terms of debate at work here by explicitly alleging that such work 'stops well short of *any sort of properly theoretical activity*' by displaying 'an aesthetic dimension' (2003:276, my italics). And yet, Le Doeuff (1989) implies that storytelling in philosophy may be inescapable. Despite this, the common sense of theory culture all too often blinds theorists to the narrative functions embedded in their own work. Theory is, yet again, set apart from popular culture: it is necessarily something more rigorous and difficult (Culler 2003; Butler 2003) than the simple pleasures of storytelling, something unassimilable to popular pleasures.

For instance, if we were given the descriptive phrases 'simple story-frames' and 'appealing labels' (Morton 2004:31), and asked whether they characterized theory or popular culture, I'd suggest that we would be very likely to opt for the latter (in fact, Adam Morton recommends that philosophy should proceed by using these devices). Popular culture is frequently distinguished, in part, by its reliance on narrative pleasures (Strinati 2000:28–39). Indeed, one branch of 1970s feminist film theory was infamously initiated by Laura Mulvey via a demarcation of its own set-apartness from Hollywood's narrative pleasures: 'It is said that analyzing pleasure . . . destroys it. That is the intention of this article' (1999[1975]:60). What is at stake here is Theory's refusal of easy narrative pleasures, since these pleasures are, we are told, to be mistrusted as carriers of ideology. In this style of argument, which has quite a history in cultural theory (see Strinati 2000:28–34), popular narrative is viewed as a force acting negatively on the world, closing down possibilities for representation and reinforcing the idea that social problems can be overcome in certain ways. In short, narrative is suspect, and should not be allowed into the avant-gardist and separatist field of cultural theory. Narrative closures and resolutions are viewed as reinforcing common-sense ways of viewing the world – for example, that the hero gets the girl (heterosexual romance is made to seem natural), that individual heroism triumphs rather than collective action (collective action may threaten our individuality, whereas being an individual is the way to make a difference), and that forces of good will triumph over clearly identified forces of evil (these moral opposites are simply existent in the world).

Some theorists (for example, Robin Wood 1986 and John Fiske 1987) have even evaluated popular narratives on the basis of whether they are reactionary or progressive. This moralizing distinction largely relies on the presence or absence of narrative closure. Open-ended narratives are thought of as being good or progressive – they challenge our cultural norms and expectations by not clearly expelling monstrous forces from their narrative worlds or neatly resolving situations in favour of a conservative status quo (Wood 1986:87). Or, in Fiske's terms, they are supposedly 'producerly', meaning that these more open tales do not compel their readers to adopt a specific reading but instead 'treat . . . readers as members of a semiotic democracy' (Fiske 1987:95). In other words, audiences are free to make their own meanings. John Fiske notes that these more open, popular stories share characteristics with 'typically avant-garde, highbrow ones with minority appeal' (1987:95). This suggests that where types of popular narrative have been valued by cultural theorists in the past, they have been positioned on some kind of continuum with avant-garde culture – being linked to its assumed critiques and challenges – whilst devalued, bad pop narratives have been left to fend for themselves. Popular narratives which can be academically revalued are, thus, those which can be made to resemble cultural theory's self-representations as critical, difficult and challenging. By contrast, popular stories that are attacked, seemingly on moralizing grounds, are precisely those that cannot be made to fit the ideals and politics of cultural theory.

Moving more up to date than the 1980s tradition represented by the likes of Robin Wood on popular film narrative, and John Fiske on popular TV, it is possible to observe a partial reconfiguring of relations between narrative and cultural theory. Rather than narrative acting as an implicit mirror for the moralities of cultural theory, theory's reliance on popular narrative becomes more explicit. In this new lineage, perhaps best characterized by the work of Slavoj Žižek (Butler 2005:7), popular culture and its narratives become evidence for the correctness of cultural theory. Rather than being treated as something to be detached from, unless its avant-garde credentials can be shared with high theory, popular narrative is depicted as a kind of 'pre-theory'. It says the same kinds of things as cultural theory, apparently, but in less worked-over and less clearly articulated ways. Therefore, all that cultural theory needs to do is to mine the pre-theory embedded in popular narratives (see McKee 2002a). As well as fuelling Žižek's psychoanalytic readings of popular narrative and culture, which somehow find themselves validated and supported over and over again, this relationship is also present in Stephen Mulhall's *On Film*. Mulhall eloquently states what could be taken as the credo for this new approach:

> I see [these films, the *Alien* franchise] . . . as themselves reflecting on and evaluating . . . views and arguments, as thinking seriously and systematically about them in just the ways that philosophers do. Such films are not philosophy's raw material, nor a source for its ornamentation; they are philosophical exercises, philosophy in action – film as philosophizing (2002:2).

Catherine Belsey's *Culture and the Real* tracks through related territory, also building its arguments out of popular narratives. Belsey suggests that a range of recent fantasy, action and science fiction films represent 'a cultural symptom, indicating an increasing uncertainty about the borderline between fiction and fact' (2005:7–8), thereby inchoately grasping that there may be something outside of our cultural representations, an inaccessible kernel of the real. For Belsey, certain popular narratives thus have an 'affinity with post-structuralism' (2005:6): cultural theory is validated via popular film narrative. This certainly appears to once and for all dispense with the set-apartness of cultural theory, and its detachment from the commercial world as something high, pure or avant-garde. From popular film and its narrative pleasures being the moral enemies of avant-gardist theory (Mulvey 1999), we appear to have moved through a process of limited moral revaluation and launched into the current moment of popular narrative as pre-theory (see Hills 2003).

What this account misses, though, is that even when treated as pre-theory, narrative is still something to be worked over by cultural theory. Narrative and theory are still not seen to fully coincide, and wherever they move most closely together, this is yet again only at the cost of narrative becoming most theory-like, that is, 'seriously and systematically' dealing with topics. Pleasure and narrative may not be attacked head-on here, as in Mulvey (1999), but they nevertheless appear to become shadow-selves, shadowing Theory's moralizing valuation of its preferred forms (see Chapter Two). The more highly valued and prized versions of narrative, just as in the 1980s approaches of Fiske (1987) and Wood (1986), are still mirrors for Theory's favoured self-image.

In contrast to academic views of storytelling as something definitively Other, or as something to be rendered safe as a version of Theory, the positions of Culler (2000) and Le Doeuff (1989) are more flexible. They tolerate the co-presence of Theory and narrative without condemning or transforming storytelling. Such approaches hold out the possibility of examining cultural theory as a narrative form without immediately castigating this as bad, improper theory. They hence allow us to consider cultural theory as doing something – perhaps something valuable and necessary – with narrative, thereby getting a clearer sense of theory's workings. As writers such as Dacre (1998), Thornham (2000) and myself (Hills 2005) have suggested, cultural theory may use narrative structures primarily in order to affect and move its readers, and to clearly identify what it sees as being the evil in social or philosophical systems. It can be argued that much theory works by locating or defining monstrous forces. Particular concepts and power structures are allocated these narrative roles (see Greig 2004:224–5), and readers, along with the theorist, are positioned as heroic figures able to challenge bad powers. Readers can, for instance, challenge the powers of patriarchy (in feminism), or the powers of speech-valued-over-writing (in post-structuralism) or the powers of ideology (in Marxist-indebted theories). As Mark Edmundson puts it in relation to post-structuralism:

> Jacques Derrida's antagonist is the metaphysics of presence, the phantom-form of truth that haunts Western culture. . . . like the relentless poltergeist it is, [this] always reappears elsewhere, sometimes in the body of one's own writing. Thus the work of deconstruction . . . is never-ending (1997:40).

In a kind of 'endlessly-deferred narrative' (Hills 2002), the enemies that cultural theory pursues always threaten to out-run it, reappearing elsewhere (see Hills 2005 for more on theory horror). But this scenario indicates that theory's making-legible of evil, through a series of monstrous forces and figures, is itself reliant on the structures and pleasures of popular narrative and popular culture. This is why Belsey can read certain popular narratives as having an affinity with post-structuralism: those narrative structures are already present within the theory. Cultural theory is itself a kind of narrative.

To be absolutely clear, I am not devaluing feminism, post-structuralism and ideology-critique here. To view these cultural theories as stories which disavow their relationship to storytelling is, at most, to accuse cultural theory of characteristic blind-spots wherever and whenever it seeks to definitively set itself apart from Others such as popular culture and popular narrative. It is not, however, to argue that cultural theory is somehow inevitably weakened or contaminated by possessing narrative dimensions. 'Theory Proper' is not invaded by marauding alien forces here (see Greig 2004:225). On the contrary, I would suggest that much of cultural theory's power comes from the very stories that it tells us. For these stories are also moralizing machines. They carry a certain legibility because they draw on deep-rooted binary oppositions such as good versus evil, and construct theorist heroes versus villainous forms of cultural power or inequality. Such constructions do not mean that cultural theory is somehow fictional. Instead, I am suggesting that the performatively politicizing and moralizing aspects of theory are, ultimately, just as important as its constative and descriptive functions. Cultural theory describes the world while simultaneously identifying forces which work to restrict the powers, possibilities and capacities of cultural agents.

This means that the constative and performative dimensions of cultural theory will come into conflict on occasion (see the conclusion). Moralizing and politicizing can get in the way of more accurately describing cultural phenomena, while describing can stand in the way of productively moralizing in order to motivate readers and writers to act in and on the world, in however small a way. Yet, the energizing virtue of cultural theory is that it does both of these things: moralizing about the cultural world without accurately describing aspects of that world would be pointlessly delusional and unconvincing, after all. And describing without moralizing would be complicit with any and all identifiable ills in the world, achieving nothing other than a restatement of how the world is. By telling stories, cultural theory actively indicates and performs its values and its activisms.

Having raised and questioned cultural theory's persistent set apartness in this Chapter, in Chapter Seven I will analyze further limits to how cultural theory has been performatively positioned in theory culture. As well as seeking to set itself apart from subcultures as more-subcultural-than-subcultural, and detaching itself from popular culture and popular narratives via a distancing, avant-gardist gesture, theory culture also sets itself above a range of Others. Although it has become far more academically acceptable since the early 1990s – though perhaps still not entirely legitimate – for scholars to profess their fandom of popular culture, certain versions of fandom are still assumed to be beyond the pale. Theory is still common-sensically set above fandom, meaning that although one can be a fan of the popular, one cannot meaningfully or reasonably be a fan of theory. And while setting itself above the fan as an external Other, theory culture also installs intra-cultural hierarchies, such as a divide between theory stars and supposedly less original, innovative scholars. In Chapter Seven I will thus focus on the star and the fan in theory culture, just as I have focused on subculture and popular culture inside cultural theorizing in this discussion. If cultural theory and theory culture have been very good at identifying evil elsewhere, might we not hope to significantly identify the evils – the limits to representation, the restrictions of cultural possibilities and the generation of inequalities – in their own midst?

chapter seven

Being Set Above: Celebrity and Fan Culture

In the previous chapter I argued that theory culture can be thought of as a type of subculture, working to set itself apart from cultural objects of study. It can also be addressed as a form of storytelling, albeit again set apart from popular-cultural narratives and their pleasures. But setting apart is not the only spatial imagery that sustains cultural theory. For Theory also sets itself above a range of Others. It performs cultural hierarchies even while purporting to undermine or level them (see the conclusion for a related discussion of performative contradiction). In this chapter I want to consider two of the ways in which things are done with cultural theory so as to generate cultural hierarchies. Firstly, in the next section I will examine the phenomenon of 'academostars' (Williams 1992:1281). Why are some cultural theorists celebrated and elevated above their colleagues? And what might this subcultural hierarchy between stars and their acolytes or commentators tell us about theory culture? I will then move on to consider the relative invisibility of theory fans, since one way that theory stars differ from more ubiquitous stars is that nobody seems to want to seriously admit to being their fans. Instead, the figure of the cultural theory fan is persistently denied in theory culture, appearing to represent even more of a problem or an embarrassment than the figure of the theory star. Accepting that there is no such thing as a theory fan – that is, taking theory culture's 'common-sense' self-presentations at face value – means silencing the ways in which theory moves and affects its readers. And since affecting its consumers is one of the key things that cultural theory seeks to do, I will argue for the need to reinstate languages and experiences of fandom in relation to cultural theory itself. Writing and reading cultural theory may be about much more than simply belonging to a subculture: they may also be about relating theory to one's own personal-political experiences and ideals, thereby seeking to affect other writer-readers. Before tackling the thorny topic of theory fandom and its structural – I would say, ideological – absence in the value system of theory culture, I will address the subject of celebrity.

Individualizing and autonomizing

Theories of stardom and celebrity have abounded in media and cultural theory, with a range of scholars contributing to debates over what a star is, and how the phenomenon of celebrity should be evaluated. Richard Dyer's work (1979, 1986 and 1991) is generally considered to be a key starting point. Dyer stresses how film stars combine perceived qualities of extraordinariness with ordinariness (1979:49), while also embodying social types such as 'the tough guy' or 'the independent woman' (1979:68). Stars therefore represent society back to itself, functioning almost as cultural barometers: 'Stars matter because they act out aspects of life that matter to us; and performers get to be stars when what they act out matters to enough people' (Dyer 1986:19). By mattering so intensely, stars do emotional work as well as carrying cultural meanings (see, for example, Hermes 1999:80–1). P. David Marshall has argued that the celebrity 'represents a site for the housing of affect' both in terms of rationalizing personality into an exchangeable commodity form (1997:55–6) and in terms of representing legitimate and illegitimate versions of 'the personal':

> As in Foucault's interpretation of the author, the celebrity is a way in which meaning can be housed and categorised into something that provides a source and origin for the meaning. The 'celebrity-function' is as important as Foucault's 'author-function' in its power to organize the legitimate and illegitimate domains of the personal and the individual within the social (Marshall 1997:57).

Like an author who is posited as the source of a text's meaning, the celebrity or star appears to give rise to, and anchor, their very own authenticity and individuality. But what appears as a natural property of the charismatic celebrity is actually produced by discourses of celebrity, just as the author is so produced. Celebrity, on this account, is a culturally conferred naturalization of individuality. Graeme Turner (2004:7) calls this approach the 'most recent step towards defining celebrity' in scholarly work, identifying it in studies as diverse as Marshall (1997), Giles (2000), Turner, Bonner and Marshall (2000) and Rojek (2001). But such an approach is also implied in Richard Dyer's much earlier work, where stars are said to:

> articulate what it means to be a human being in contemporary society; that is, they express the particular notion we hold of the . . . 'individual'. . . . [T]hey are not straightforward affirmations of individualism . . . [but] . . . articulate both the promise and the difficulty that the notion of individuality presents for all of us who live by it (Dyer 1986:8).

Like subcultures, which also articulate notions of distinctive individuality (Muggleton 2000:63), stars thus necessarily invoke discourses of individualized authenticity (Dyer 1991). Audience responses to stars frequently focus on 'what the star is really like' (see Gamson 1994), treating publicity material as evidence for the reality of a star's persona behind their image, or interpreting their star image as true to their actual self. Stardom is thus dispersed across media sites and texts (Dyer 1991:136), involving deferred but sought-after personal authenticity. Live appearances can be compared with the star's mediated image, as can bits of celebrity gossip, and all manner of marketing tales. Stardom may involve a network of texts, but it constructs the notion that there is a true individual behind this proliferation of textuality. Leo Braudy calls this modern fame's 'constant tension between . . . the talked-of self and the unexpressed self' (1986:592).

But stars don't just tell the individualizing authentic, they also sell it, being among the leading commodities of the culture industry. Evaluated as a commodity, the star or celebrity has been criticized as a construction of meaning and, worse still, as a pure product of mediation where 'all efforts at persona projection obey the imperative of the box office' (King 2003:50). Rather than reflecting any authentic truth of charismatic character, the star can be viewed as a type of industrial fabrication: as someone famous merely because of their mass-mediation and not due to qualities they actually hold. This view is put forward by Daniel Boorstin in *The Image*: 'we can fabricate fame . . . we can make a man or woman well known . . . but we cannot make [them] great' (1963:58). Greatness emerges through heroic deeds, whereas modern stardom or celebrity, for Boorstin, is simply a matter of being well-known or mass-mediated. This devaluation of stardom, and its contrast to real greatness, recurs in a modified form in Chris Rojek's more recent *Celebrity* (2001). Here, Rojek distinguishes between 'renown' and 'celebrity':

> *Renown* . . . refers to the informal attribution of distinction on an individual within a given social network. Thus, in every social group certain individuals stand out by virtue of their . . . achievements . . . These individuals have a sort of localized fame . . . In contrast, the fame of the celebrity is ubiquitous. . . . Whereas renown follows from personal contact with the individual who is differentiated . . . celebrity . . . assume[s] a relationship in which the [honoured] individual . . . is distanced from the spectator by stage, screen, or some . . . medium of communication (2001:12).

In Rojek's terms, 'social distance is the precondition of . . . celebrity' (2001:12). Like Boorstin's argument, Rojek's position hinges on a separation between actually knowing and valuing someone (renown) and apparently knowing someone via their mediated image (celebrity). This reality/appearance binary makes celebrity into an essentially mediated and 'para-social' product, that is, it is not based on genuine, embodied social interactions (see Thompson 1995:219; Giles 2000:128). Celebrity is hence converted into something that is implicitly false due to its mass-mediated ubiquity, as opposed to true renown said to be based on a person's qualities.

Following the conclusions of Rojek and Boorstin suggests that there can be no theory stars: cultural theorists are, after all, not usually mass-mediated. And nor are they ubiquitous, typically being valued only within academia as 'a given social network'. Richard Burt has suggested 'just how far from real stardom the academic is. . . . The cultural critic may fantasize about being . . . recognized by everyone, but . . . he or she is actually known only by a narrow circle of people, and by almost no-one outside of it' (1998:124). This observation would seem to hold true, despite occasional scholars who prove the rule by their very exceptionality. Are the realms of celebrity and cultural theory therefore decisively distinct?

However, it is only an argument defining 'celebrity' against 'renown' which props up this conclusion. Moving beyond any common sense notion that stardom is not a properly academic attribute, we can recall the role of niche and micro mediation (Thornton 1995) within academia. It is not as easy to contrast renown to celebrity as Rojek might suppose, since this conceptual distinction relies on an opposition between 'direct'/real social interaction and 'indirect'/para-social interaction involving mass-mediation. Any such binary excludes a middle term, because between mass-mediation and direct social interaction there exists subcultural media, academic publishing being a good example of this (see Chapters Five and Six).

Theory stars can therefore be thought of as 'subcultural celebrities'. They are objects of 'subcultural, social knowledge and repeated personal contact as well as . . . emerging through common cultural currency and mediated distance' (Hills 2003:60). By not immediately ruling out the notion of theory stars, we can begin to see how stardom operates within theory culture in ways that are highly analogous to its general, cultural functioning. Theory stardom constructs individualizing authenticity through its star-function or 'celebrity-function' (Marshall 1997:57), and it also works by linking theorists' gossiped-about private (unexpressed) selves to their public (talked-of) selves. The star's academic persona is thereby constructed as a source of authenticity:

> Current theoretical assumptions and recent trends in scholarly practice have expanded the role of gossip, which has become as significant to academic stardom as it is to film stardom. Because of the widely held notion that one can only speak from one's own gendered, racial, class, sexual, or professional position, increasing numbers of literary scholars are engaged in describing their positions. Personal matters, once regarded as extraneous to disciplinary discourse, have become central to it (Shumway 1997:96).

This new-found legitimacy of the personal as a route to examining the culturally systematic has reinforced academic celebrity as the construction and maintenance, in person and through niche-mediated publications, of an individualizing star persona. For example, Susan Fraiman has analysed Andrew Ross as one 'poster boy for the new cultural studies' in the US (2003:54), suggesting that Ross's 'bad boy' persona and its 'cool . . . hipness' are partly constructed through 'ambivalence toward feminism [where] . . . a degree of antifeminism may actually be intrinsic to [such] hipness' (2003:56).

Hegelian-Lacanian synthesiser Slavoj Žižek's theory star persona, meanwhile, has been discussed as connoting a certain eccentricity, jumping wildly from idea to idea. Ian Parker writes of Žižek that the 'erratic quality of his speech in interviews, seminars and conference presentations is also present to the reader in the rapid shift from theme to theme in articles and in the pace of production of his books' (2004:4). Here, the star-theorist in real life and on the page are rolled together as expressions of a singularly authentic Žižek-ness. But this subcultural celebrity 'image' also has to differentiate the Žižekian from other star theorists' personalizing, individualizing authenticities, making an associative style of expression and a rapid turnover in published books into markers of the differentiated Žižek brand name. Furthermore, gossip about the private Žižek can also be used to support his celebrity persona:

> The stories that circulate about his stab at psychoanalysis with Jacques Alain-Miller for a year without saying anything that would give him away, and his refusal to do any administrative work connected with academic appointments are indicative . . . of what people imagine they are reading when they get drawn into Žižek's work . . . [working as] a 'symptomatic' image (Parker 2004:4; see also Jagodzinski 2004:2).

Academic readers construct an image of the cultural theorist as they consume his work, a niche-mediated celebrity image which they can then affiliate themselves with, or interpret theoretical work through. Continuing in this vein of exploring the star images of different cultural theorists, Anna Dacre has analysed the persona of Fredric Jameson as that of an adventurer in postmodernism. Dacre suggests that in *Postmodernism, or The Cultural Logic of Late Capitalism* 'we find Jameson standing outside the Bonaventure Hotel, scrutinising the building and searching for an entry point in the first of many challenges that he will face' (1998:3). Dacre cites Clint Burnham on the subject of Jameson as a kind of 'promotional' brand-name:

> Burnham, in his study *The Jamesonian Unconscious*, . . . asks if there was life before Jameson . . . 'Jameson and Butler and Spivak and Barthes', Burnham contends, 'are on the same plane as . . . *Deep Space Nine*' and *Star Trek*: . . . 'one is . . . driven . . . by the need to own or see or read the "latest" (or the "classic" or the "original")' . . . [I]f you like *Star Trek: The Next Generation* you should check out *Voyager*, or [if] you like *Gender Trouble* check out *Bodies That Matter* (Dacre 1998:1; see also Wernick 1991:175).

The star images of Burnham's quartet of theory stars have all been subjected to commentary in cultural theory. Judith Butler's status as a celebrity theorist is discussed in Jennifer Wicke's work on 'celebrity feminism' (1994:756–7). Wicke examines Butler's response to a fanzine called *Judy!* – for more on this, see the 'Fan-worshipping . . .' section below – and the publicity this fanzine received in *Lingua Franca* magazine. The fan-magazine in question contained 'spurious anecdotes of Butler's life and loves and . . . profess[ed] lustful devotion to its iconic star . . . Butler vehemently objected [to publicity for the 'zine]' (Wicke 1994:771). Butler's response alleged that *Lingua Franca* 'reengages that anti-intellectual aggression whereby scholars are reduced to occasions for salacious conjecture' and, like the original fanzine, 'signals the eclipse of serious intellectual engagement with theoretical works by a thoroughly hallucinated speculation on the theorist's sexual practice' (cited in Wicke 1994:771).

However, the irony of a theorist of performativity doing something with words – protesting so as to fix a barrier between serious theory and offensive gossip – is not lost on Wicke. Furthermore, Butler's attempted fixing of *Judy!* as 'homophobic reverie' (cited in Wicke 1997:771) may also, on the grounds of moral outrage, restrict and limit the complexity of the fandom that the fanzine performs. Wicke notes that:

> Butler may have protested too much in order to reinstate a barrier that no longer exists, if it ever did, as a rigid line between unsullied intellectual thought and the corruption of the marketplace. The theorist of performativity should not be surprised when 'serious intellectual engagement' gives way to, or even includes, more hallucinatory thoughts or desires (Wicke 1994:771).

Against such performative efforts to police and construct the boundaries of academia as alien to celebrity culture, Wicke argues that 'theory and theorists disport there [in celebrity culture] . . . [T]he academy . . . is permeable to celebrity, colonized by it and colonizers of it in return' (1994:772). This means that pure feminist theory cannot be securely contrasted to the rough-and-tumble of the marketplace and celebrity. The existence of what David Shumway (1997:98) terms 'Judith Butlerites', dedicated readers of Butlerian theory, further testifies to Butler's status as a star turn, even if these networked, communal readers have not been explicitly portrayed as fans.

Shumway also discusses Spivak's distinctive public performances as a source of star difference (1997:92), while a variety of writers have analysed Barthes's theory stardom (see, for example, Aronowitz 1994) and his niche-mediated celebrity persona as 'essentially iconoclastic' (Burke 1998:26). Jacques Leenhardt (1989:204–7) reads the last line of Barthes's last book before his death in 1980, *Camera Lucida* (1981), as a testament to Barthes's scholarly work, according it the status of a naturally occurring summing up or end-point. By doing so, Leenhardt reads the contingencies and accidents of Barthes's private life into and across his published theory, suggesting that an authentic celebrity self is captured and mediated by Barthes's publications. This is the gesture *par excellence* of the 'celebrity-function': public and private are read against or through each other as part of a total star text, the written word and the embodied performance being scrutinized for how they fit together to reveal, or defer, authentic individuality (see also Shumway (1997:96) for similar readings of the authentic individual of Jacques Derrida).

By focusing theory culture on discourses of stars-as-authentic-individualities, the 'star system' of cultural theory threatens to break disciplinary academic communities

> down into incommensurable camps. There are not many Judith Butlerites who are devoted to Stanley Fish, nor are there many Foucauldians who follow Derrida. Ironically, the individualism of the star system is at odds with the theories that many stars propound, theories promoting a knowledge grounded in communal interest [such as] . . . Marxism, feminism, queer theory . . . The star system has been and will continue to be an obstacle to such collectivity (Shumway 1997:98).

This obstacle has been recognised by other theorists. Jeremy Gilbert, for example, has noted that 'authors are the celebrities of academic culture', arguing for the need to 'refuse the commodification and personalisation of knowledge and affects' (2003a:107). Such refusal – writing anonymously and collectively rather than via the proper name – could challenge and contest what, from a broadly Marxist perspective, appears to be a cultural trap of individualism. Who cares whether Barthes's theory can be read as a reflection of his life, or whether Žižek's real life persona reflects his writing style? Who cares about Judith Butler's private life, or Jacques Derrida's dress sense? (Shumway 1997:91). Unfortunately, the answer would seem to be theory culture, given its investments in the figure of the celebrated individual.

Achieving such status, where details of gossip are read into published texts, and where a niche-mediated star image accompanies the consumption of cultural theory, theory stars are positioned hierarchically. They are set above their colleagues. We might suppose that such elevation occurs properly, that is, the work of theory stars is especially outstanding, original or productive; such is the myth of academic charisma. This is a version of the generalized argument that stars and celebrities deserve their status by virtue of their special qualities. Such a myth has been vigorously demolished in scholarly work on 'celebrity as a discourse'. This work argues that celebrity as a category is conferred on people rather than being produced by their own actions (Turner 2004:7). Yet the myth of 'naturally deserved celebrity' persists in theory culture. Stars' 'brilliance shines within the profession', we are told (Shumway 1997:90). 'Path-breaking figures' become star theorists, while lesser scholars exist in their shadow: 'Those who can, think up feminism or structuralism; those who can't, apply such insights to *Moby-Dick* or *The Cat in the Hat*' (Eagleton 2003:2). Theory culture has a curiously non-reflexive relationship to stardom, frequently celebrating the autonomy of the intellectual and thereby prescribing an individualism that 'detaches intellectuality from *collective* action' (Jeffrey Williams 1997:55). In the face of this individualizing 'romance of the intellectual' (Jeffrey Williams 1997), we can note that the

> legitimation of theories results more from a complex environmental interplay than from the intrinsic qualities of theories themselves. Theories cannot thus be considered in isolation, even if they are experienced through their own logic and in their own cultural realm (Lamont 1987:614–5).

This pits the social (how theories are received) and the individual (the brilliant star theorist) against one another. We could begin to argue against such a neat and tidy distinction between individual brilliance and collective action by suggesting that one of the effects of theory stardom is precisely that new collectivities or 'tribes' of Derrideans or Butlerites, say, come to gather around the work of individualized theorists (Becher and Trowler 2001). Star theorists' work can also be re-viewed as achieving pre-eminence not simply via sheer brilliance, but rather by mediating the values of theory culture back to itself (politics, originality, performance), just as general celebrities mediate social values and affects back to society. This introduces an apparent paradox into 'doing stardom' with cultural theory: such performativity both reinforces the individual and generates new affective-cognitive communities of 'second-order Derrideans . . . and Barthesians'(Agger 1992:163). These acolytes mimetically iterate the form and content of 'original writings'. But the lack of value generally accorded to such communities is evident in their secondary status; they are fallen or descended from the greatness of stars as originals and pioneers, being doomed to slavish or, at the very least, dependent citation. Theory stardom hence structurally enacts and imposes a 'two-tier system' (Robbins 1999 online) of haves and have-nots, masters and disciples, authentic individuals and non-authentic followers (Roustang 1982; Clément 1987). But to supposedly describe the 'secondariness' of Derrideans is also to performatively construct this fallen-ness, thereby recuperating and defending the theory star status quo. If the general, ubiquitous celebrity houses affect, and by so doing aids in the construction of new audience communities, then one of the values of theory stars could be their similar operation as affective incitements and 'housings'. Not simply affirming the individual, theory stars may go some way towards doing this, while also provoking and producing new social, academic networks, collectives and communal politics (Brodkey 1987:50).

The phenomenon of theory stardom has been criticised not only for its promotion of individualism, but also for its maintenance of hierarchies within theory culture. Richard Burt points out that stardom necessarily translates into 'inequitable academic distributions of symbolic and economic capital' (1998:124), meaning that reputations (symbolic capital) can be literally cashed in for economic capital (money) within the academic economy. High-earners are also feted and invited to speak at 'star-studded' events, occupying an elite position within theory culture, which is far from being a free and equitable exchange of pure ideas. Rather, it is a material culture within which not all academics' voices are equal, and where a very few are accorded far greater authority and prestige than the majority of participants.

This issue of stardom-as-repressive-hierarchy is especially problematic for cultural studies which prides itself on politicizing popular culture and fighting for all forms of cultural equity. Indeed, the question of stardom famously erupted at the 'Cultural Studies Now and In the Future' conference held at the University of Illinois in 1990. One of the founding fathers of cultural studies, Stuart Hall, had been speaking. A post-presentation questioner made the following point:

> [T]here is no scheduled place for a participant in this conference to say anything which is not to or from the podium. . . . In its structure, the conference most definitely privileges certain people, empowering them to speak while disempowering others. It . . . duplicates the traditional structures of power which practitioners of cultural studies . . . claim to be committed to subverting (Chasin in Hall 1992:293).

Stardom subordinates its academic Others, positioning them as disempowered knowledge workers rather than as valued theory-pioneers. Stars are licensed to speak for themselves and their constituencies, but non-stars are cast into the margins of theory culture. As Alexandra Chasin pointed out with regards to the Illinois conference, 'this . . . might have been an opportunity for self-criticism . . . for *asking the questions of ourselves that we ask theoretically about other institutions*' (in Hall 1992:293, my italics). Cultural theory fails, in this instance, to successfully direct itself at theory culture. The material conditions and hierarchical performances of scholarly identity are glossed over rather than being politicized and critiqued. While pop culture is exposed as political, theory culture is somehow exempted from this same challenge, in what might be called a textbook instance of non-accountable theory – theory fails to treat self and Other identically.

Although Alexandra Chasin's intervention as 'the voice of the [cultural studies] reader, self-represented' (Hartley 2003:163) does not directly use the term 'fan', subsequent commentaries on this 'audience eruption' (Pfister 1996:296) have suggested that what caused so much ire amongst non-stars at the Illinois conference was that they were 'positioned . . . as "fans" . . . meant to support a star-making (or star-polishing) machinery' (Pfister 1996:287). Joe Moran has repeated this claim, again placing the term 'fan' in scare quotes in order to partly destabilize it: 'the majority of conference delegates were being defined as passive "fans" of the celebrities on the podium, to the extent that only known and named people could participate' (2000:159).

As well as theory stardom setting itself above the academic Other-as-secondary-acolyte, theory culture also works performatively to set itself above the Other-as-fan. We might suppose that theory stardom would inevitably call into being a type of 'academic fandom'

(Lacey 2000:36), given that celebrity and fan appear to form a mutually constitutive binary. That is, to be a fan is to affectively focus upon fictional characters or mediated images of actual people. And to be a celebrity is to 'make a name' by having one's extended, virtual self become subject to such affective relations. However, fans of cultural theory seem to be almost always positioned elsewhere, this cultural identity being nervously placed in scare quotes – hence marked as questionable or improper – or attributed to other scholars. It is as if the label of 'theory fan' is radically inappropriate for serious academics. One can be a self-professed Derridean, Butlerite or Barthesian but being part of a star-based affective community does not, apparently, make one a fan of theory. Why should this fan identity pose such problems for cultural theorists?

As I have demonstrated so far, the matter of theory stardom has been discussed and critiqued in cultural theory. Such stardom is sometimes bemoaned as a commercialization of theory culture (Wernick 1991), and sometimes criticized for creating and sustaining a hierarchy of great names which is not conducive to the values of anti-individualistic collective action (Gilbert 2003a: 107). Whether desired, enacted, or attacked, stardom is nevertheless a way of dong something with cultural theory. It articulates an individualizing difference through the style, substance and mediation of theoretical work. Theory stardom thus works to sustain a range of belief-systems or ideologies: it self-presents theory culture as communally or collectively unified, at least in specific tribes of Derrideans, Deleuzians, Žižekians, and it supports a notion of the cultural theorist as autarchic. Autarchy is a term for the political state of self-governance and self-dependency. In other words, it is through theory stardom that cultural theory's dependence on an intertextual matrix, and on practices of citation, can be magically dissolved in favour of certain theorists being nominated and recognized as authentically 'themselves'. These stars stand as markers of pure, originary self-identity and autonomous individuality. They are frequently and common-sensically contrasted against scholarship's derivative, citational norms. Theory stars perform 'individualizing' and 'autonomizing' work for cultural theory: their value lies as much in 'performative acts of self-identification' (Cooper 2004:52) and 'intellectual privatization' (Donald Morton 2004:29) as in the content and substance of their theoretical-constative descriptions of the world.

As I've begun to intimate, theory fandom appears to represent even more of a problem for theory culture than the phenomenon of stardom. Unlike the star, the theory fan cannot readily be linked to values of autarchy and individualization. Instead, theory as a network of dependencies and citations seemingly becomes over-emphasized via any such fandom. Where the term 'fan' is used to describe a relationship to theory, this generally indicates an extremely negative portrayal, as in David Shumway's (1997:98) admonition that 'it would be better for . . . scholars, teachers, and students to stop being fans' of theory. Theory fans are frequently posited only in order to be symbolically annihilated, as in Pfister's (1996:287) and Moran's (2000:159) placing of the theory fan within an uneasy quarantine of scare quotes. I will examine and challenge this pattern of meaning – the theory-fan-as-scandalous – in what follows.

Theory fandom threatens to veer away from scholarly norms of rational, cognitive appreciation and move dangerously close to obsession and excessive emotionality. By virtue of being stereotyped as dangerously dependent, emotional and popular-cultural, rather than existing in the high-cultural realm of rational discrimination, the fan has either been expunged from theory culture, or re-admitted in very strictly defined ways. In the next section, I will consider why it may be important to focus more strongly on what it could mean, positively, to be a fan of theory. The language of fandom may seem to be miles away from reading and writing cultural theory, but I will suggest that this distance is not natural: it is an illusory and ideological effect of theory culture. And since cultural theory teaches us to be critical of our taken-for-granted starting points and common-sense ideas, we could begin by critiquing theory culture's own separation of theorist and fan. *Contra* Shumway (1997:98), we may then be able to argue that what cultural theory really needs is more fans.

Fan-worshipping and affecting

One of the problems cultural studies has faced is the issue of what actually constitutes a 'fan': what activities and practices can be taken to characterise the state of fandom? John Fiske has examined 'the relationship . . . of the fan to the more "normal" audience member', suggesting that 'the fan is an "excessive reader" who differs from the "ordinary" one in degree rather than kind' (1992:46). This slightly curious manoeuvre is probably intended to stress how fandom cannot be entirely opposed to non-fan/'ordinary' cultural consumption, but Fiske leaves the impression that there is something inherently extra-ordinary or abnormal about fan activities. Still, Fiske's aim is to define what is distinctive about being a fan: he achieves this by relating fandom to forms of productivity, arguing that unlike ordinary consumers, fans do not only make meanings from texts ('semiotic productivity'), they also make subculturally shared meanings ('enunciative productivity') and textual meanings of their own ('textual productivity' such as writing for fanzines: see Fiske 1992:37–9).

Fiske also stresses the knowledge that fans accumulate, using the term 'popular cultural capital' (1992:39) to describe how fans are highly literate and educated in relation to their favoured texts (see Hills 2002:50–8). A series of contrasts between fans and ordinary consumers has tended to structure scholarly definitions of fandom (see McKee 2002b:68). Indeed, Garry Crawford has argued that the distinction between excessive or ordinary consumption can also be mapped on to types of fandom, with academics tending to champion more extreme, spectacular types of fan practice, while excluding from discussion more mundane, everyday aspects of fandom:

> studies of fan cultures tend to focus upon the 'exceptional' rather than the 'mundane'. This has been true for most studies of media fan culture. For instance, . . . Jenkins (1992) . . . focuses primarily upon the activities and interests of the most dedicated and 'serious' of audiences . . . This has also been apparent within the majority of discussions of sports fans, and in . . . British sport research, which has tended to focus . . . on 'exceptional' . . . or the most 'dedicated' . . . types of supporters [hooligans or fanzine editors – MH] at the expense of more 'ordinary' fans (Crawford 2004:105).

Crawford suggests that this situation has to do with the ease with which exceptional fans can be recruited to take part in research projects, meaning that 'issues of access' lead researchers to focus on more dedicated fans (Crawford 2004:105–6). This type of distinction between forms of fandom has also been addressed in Jostein Gripsrud's work. Gripsrud distinguishes between proper fandom where 'an enthusiasm for some cultural object . . . takes on . . . a totalizing, defining role in people's lifestyles and identities' and 'forms and degrees of . . . appreciation and devotion which do . . . not necessarily merit the tag . . . "fandom" ' (2002:119).

Work in cultural studies has thus consistently stressed the distinctiveness of fandom (Jenkins 1992; Fiske 1992), as well as exploring different types of fandom (Hills 2002; Thomas 2002). Furthermore, given the passionate and engaged nature of almost all fan activities, this being particularly evident in Gripsrud's ' "proper" fandom', fans are one type of reader or audience where psychoanalytic theory has proved useful in understanding audiences' affective or emotional relationships with media texts. For example, psychoanalysis has allowed theorists to shed light on the ways in which some fans retain an object of fandom from childhood, carrying this through into their adult lives (see Harrington and Bielby 1995; Hills 2002). Furthermore, it is now commonplace for academic work to refute simplistic analyses of fan agency (or simplistic analyses of fans' commercial exploitation), meaning that Simone Murray's suggestion that 'scholarly study of media fandom is out of touch with the contemporary lineaments of the phenomenon it seeks to analyse' (2004b:21) is rather questionable. Instead of any pure valorization of fandom, fan identity has been seen as context- and situation-specific: 'Fandom is never . . . a neutral "expression" or a singular "referent"; its status and its performance shift across cultural sites' (Hills 2002:xii).

Given this, my interest here lies in the manner in which fandom has been generally ruled out, or (sub)culturally withheld, as a relevant term when scholars represent their consumption of cultural theory. Instead, Gripsrud's (2002:119) separation of 'proper' fandom and 'degrees of . . . appreciation and devotion' which do not quite merit the 'fan' label seems to partly capture how fandom has been warded off in relation to cultural theory and its supposed appreciation. I will argue here that this conceptual distinction – fandom versus appreciation – is not at all a neutral or natural reflection of cultural differences. Rather, it works to legitimate cultural theory as a form of high culture to be appreciated, thereby setting theorists above fans and their supposedly obsessive, all-consuming enthusiasms. And yet, the act of being a theorist can often be no less all-consuming, with cultural theory taking on a totalizing, defining role in scholar's identities:

> Anyone in academia, especially those who have written theses or dissertations, can attest to the emotional components of supposedly rational activity. A figure or topic can become the focal point of one's life; anything even remotely connected to one's research interests can have tremendous impact and obsessive appeal . . . Am I, then, a fan of . . . William James, John Dewey and Lewis Mumford? (Jensen 1992:21–2).

Reflecting on her cultural consumption as a scholar, Joli Jensen's answer is a qualified 'yes'. Being a fan of theorists is, she suggests, akin to being a fan of a sports team or TV show, but it is an attachment which has to be displayed in different ways. Rather than writing fan letters or reading fanzines, the academic writes 'review essays and appreciative quotation[s]' and reads fanzines 'in the scholarly versions – heavily footnoted biographies and eloquent critical appreciations' (1992:22). The scholar may also collect memorabilia relating to their academic interest, and defend their team of favoured theorists 'with respectable rowdiness (acerbic asides in scholarly articles) and acceptable violence (the controlled, intellectual aggression often witnessed in conference presentations)' (1992:22). Through this detailed comparison of fandom and academia, Jensen proposes that 'aficionado-hood is really disguised, and thereby legitimated, fandom. The pejorative connotations of fans and fandom prevent me from applying those terms to describe and explore my attachments' (1992:23).

Fleshing out many of Jensen's points through the study of a specific amateur scholarly community, Will Brooker argues that members of the Lewis Carroll Society (LCS) exhibit a range of 'fan traits' (2004:292) while producing a journal called *The Carrollian*, 'in many ways indistinguishable from . . . an academic journal' (2004:275). Brooker suggests that *The Carrollian*'s contents

> meet academic conventions of surveying the existing knowledge and producing
> new insights based on fresh reading or primary evidence; they use the
> conventions of formal expression, citation, and reference required by an
> academic journal . . . Undeniably 'scholarly' but not quite like a standard
> academic journal . . . produced with the passion, intensity and pedantry familiar
> from other fan cultures, but without the characteristics of unsystematic energy,
> blinkered single-mindedness and raw, untrained expression that fandom is
> supposed to display, *The Carrollian* straddles [the] two camps [of fandom and
> academia] (2004:275).

Brooker persuasively outlines how these amateur scholars and literary critics display characteristics of professional academia intermixed with fans' interests in community, arcana, debate, pilgrimage, performance and curatorship (2004:268–95). Although following the norms of trained literary appreciation of high culture, the LCS is 'driven only by the personal satisfaction and pleasure in the text that inspires "amateur" fandom' (Brooker 2004:275). Its literary criticism is immersed in what outsiders would perhaps see as 'piddlingly obscure detail and trivia' (2004:271), while Carrollian devotees feel a sense of 'protectiveness and defensiveness around the[ir] chosen text or icon' (2004:292). Yet this powerful blurring of the scholar and the fan in a type of 'scholarly fandom' (Lewis 2003:47–52), occurs without the institutional positioning of either group. That is, the LCS is not part of institutionalized, professionalized academia, and nor is it a self-professed fan club. By refusing and refuting such a term, its members devalue fandom as something stigmatized and belonging only to low or popular culture, while nevertheless still practising their literary criticism outside of official academic bounds. They thus share the professional academic's common sense notion, identified by Jensen (1992:23), that fandom is something 'pejorative', non-serious and trivial.

Seeking to occupy similar realms of high cultural value to the amateur LCS, professional academics may therefore also demur from considering their theory as fandom, wishing to avoid the stigma of the term 'fan'. Fans are systematically and culturally stereotyped as fanatics and obsessives; they are depicted in mass media representations as dysfunctional, out of touch with reality, and as fixated on pointless trivia (see Jenkins, 1992:9–16, for discussion of these stereotypes). The amateur/professional high culture of the LCS, and of cultural theory, evidently cannot countenance the possibility that their preoccupations might be represented, attacked or dismissed as fan trivia.

Having said this, one of the major developments in cultural theories of media fandom and consumption has been to challenge pathologizing fan stereotypes, arguing for a more positive view of fans as active and creative media audiences. Here, something is again performatively done with cultural theory: Jensen and Jenkins both consider how fans may be more like scholars than was previously thought. By doing so, they seek to confer some of academia's (sometimes insecure) legitimacy upon media fans. Henry Jenkins's *Textual Poachers* (1992), for instance, carefully portrays media fans in a very specific way; fans are said to take part in debate and discussion which 'resemble[s] a sort of idealized research seminar' (Michael 2000:120). There may be difficulties associated with the idea that fandom can be revalued by depicting it as a version of academia, not least of which is an implied assumption of scholarship's superiority to fandom (see Hills 2002:17–9). Regardless of such risks, cultural theory has not simply sought to say something constatively about fandom, it has also sought to intervene and act against stereotyped representations of fandom:

> [T]here has been something of a change in the critical fortunes of the fan. His or her activities have increasingly been seen by . . . academics as significant and meaningful in their own right . . . It is interesting in this respect that a number of academics, precisely the sort of people who in previous decades would strenuously have objected to being thought of as fans, will now in their writing about various forms of culture . . . happily proclaim their own fandom (Hutchings 2004:91).

Peter Hutchings identifies Henry Jenkins's work as emblematic of this shift within cultural studies and theory culture. It is important to recognise that not all professional academics are opposed to thinking of themselves as fans, and that this change has been brought about through cultural theory itself. Despite such helpful moves, we can still trace powerful limits and restrictions to the proclamation of academic-as-fan identities. As Jonathan Gray has put it, 'What, then, is "wrong" with fan studies? Or, rather . . . what important issues . . . are hiding in its shadow? For the problem lies in the path not taken . . .' (2003:68). And here is one such pathway: although many cultural studies' writers have professed their status as media or popular culture fans (Brooker 2000 and 2002; Hills 2002; Hutchings 2004; Jancovich 2000), they have *not* tended to directly link their academic and fan identities by self-identifying as fans of cultural theory. It may now be increasingly acceptable, if not expected, for professional scholars of popular culture to be fans of that culture, but 'doing cultural theory' is still defined as something outside and above 'being a fan'. Fandom's affects and the rationalities of cultural theory must seemingly be kept apart in order for cultural theory to be validated and legitimated. And yet the common-sense separation of media fandom – that which merits the label 'fan' – and theory fandom, which is rarely identified as such, makes little sense other than as a marker of academia's subcultural distinctiveness. Theory is itself a mediated, commercial product, just like the media texts that inspire fandom; it is consumed by its adherents in very similar ways to media fans' poaching from popular culture; and it produces its own associated celebrities and icons, as does media fandom (see Hills forthcoming). Performatively setting theory above popular culture, however, means that the language of theory fandom becomes disallowed. To think of academics as theory fans may strike many readers as plainly silly, absurd, and perhaps even an affront to the special, extraordinary status of authentic cultural theory. But considering the structural similarities between media fandom and theory consumption, it is difficult not to conclude that the structuring absence in the academy of something termed 'theory fandom' marks one ideological limit to what can be – or has been – done with cultural theory. And I want to argue that this limit, a cultural categorization that appears natural to its academic proponents, should be challenged in order to move towards more accountable theory, that is, theory which does not elevate the (academic) self over the (fan) Other, but instead applies equitable, common frameworks of understanding to both self and Other:

> I am interested in who we call a theorist, and what parts of culture we honour with the title of 'theory'. I am worried that we tend to think that academics and participants in what we used to call 'high culture' . . . are 'theorists'; while workers in popular forms of culture rarely receive that name (McKee 2002a:311).

McKee draws attention to the honouring function of being called a theorist, emphasizing that this carries an elevated status. Denying the term 'theorist' to non-academics, or to those working in pop culture, can therefore work to discursively separate and stratify these realms. *But who we label a 'fan' forms just as much a part of this hierarchy-sustaining process.* The natural-seeming scholarly separation of media fandom and theory appreciation (viewed as a non-fandom) supports cultural theorists' sense of themselves as set above fandom, and as 'more' than 'mere' fans. Although media fandom may have recently become an acceptable aspect of academic self-identity, as a result of new movements in cultural studies, theory fandom remains silenced and ruled out. Violating these keenly held categorizations is likely to provoke scorn from defenders of the contemporary status quo. For instance, scholar Barry Faulk argues that bringing the identities of cultural theorist and fan any closer together runs the risk of 'credentialing passion' and so 'confusing criticism with soul making' (2005:153). Faulk suggests that it is in bad faith for academics to parade fan status as a marker of their expertise, since this suggests that academic training is relatively unimportant and may thus 'discourage laypersons from understanding . . . the project of criticism, and perhaps from enlisting in the field and becoming a specialist' (2005:153). Though appearing to democratize cultural theory, and give a voice to marginalized (fan) Others outside the academy, any blurring of fan and theorist is instead, for Faulk, a step too far towards 'emotion and affect' and away from 'the virtues of critical reason' (2005:153). In this argument, fandom must be held at least partly at bay from the theorist's self-identity. To allow theorist and fan to become one and the same, so that the theorist can be thought of as a theory-fan, supposedly means the loss of cultural theory's status as rational critique.

A range of writers have (re)produced views of fandom which feed into this 'affect' versus 'reason' binary. Chris Atton argues that although 'the investigative work of fans can be as careful and as detailed as that of a professional historian' (2004:148), when fans write reviews of music scenes they nevertheless do so 'less as a set of critical essays, [and] more as a valorisation of the individual fan's taste and their place in the translocal community dedicated to their taste'. Fans are critical, to be sure, but this is 'mostly affective rather than argumentative' critique (2004:148). On this account, theory fandom could again only be an illegitimate expression within theory culture. It would threaten to displace scholarly, subcultural values of argument and communal criticism in favour of individual emotivism (Friedman and Squire 1998:14), where theory is good/bad because I like/don't like it.

Similarly, in his own review of the doorstopper *Cultural Studies*, Fredric Jameson notes that 'surely the most innovative treatment of the intellectual [here] . . . lies in the new model of the intellectual as "fan"' (1995:282). But Jameson goes on to suggest that fandom is not an entirely helpful model for intellectual practice because 'the transformation of the "people" [cultural theory should represent] into "fans"' (1995:283) has potentially negative consequences:

> [T]he first of these ['the people'] was a primary substance, calmly persisting in its essence, and exercising a powerful gravitational effect on . . . intellectuals . . . [However,] the new version ['fans'] opens up a hall of mirrors in which the 'people' itself longs to be a 'people' and be 'popular', feels its own . . . lack, longs for its own impossible stability, and narcissistically attempts, in a variety of rituals, to recuperate a being that never existed in the first place. That would . . . considerably dampen the enthusiasm of populist intellectuals for a condition not much better than their own (Jameson 1995:283).

Jameson therefore argues that fandom cannot offer a secure footing for cultural theory, since fans are – apparently unlike the democratic, political category of the people – a group who do not merely exist, but instead performatively enact their fan identities through their own rituals and narcissistic bids for identity (see also Sandvoss 2003:38–43). For Jameson, cultural theory can constatively reflect the real situations of the people, but risks losing itself in a hall of mirrors by presuming to reflect fan identities, with the subcultural constructedness of fan and academic identities stretching away to infinity. Theory and fandom may share a certain affinity, as Jameson implies, but to build cultural theory on this shared yet unstable ground risks immediately undermining its validity as Theory. Jameson's argument is an extremely curious one. For instance, there is little or no defence of the notion that the people can be equated with a 'primary substance', and there is also precious little defence of the notion that theory and fandom should be kept apart. Jameson's terms of debate seem to be almost entirely taken for granted, indicating the strength of scholarly doxa or common sense which does not require any defence, and can simply be asserted as if it is self-evidently true.

The sense of a theory culture doxa holding apart theory and fandom is further evident in acerbic asides such as Sharon O'Dair's in 'Stars, Tenure, and the Death of Ambition' (2000). O'Dair is discussing work by David Shumway when she notes that one particular essay 'places you and me [accredited academics – MH] in a relationship with Jacques Derrida that resembles a fifteen-year-old girl's relationship with Leonardo DiCaprio or Keanu Reeves' (2000:47). The disdain in this statement is all too evident. Firstly, O'Dair is drawing on a negative stereotype of fandom as a teenage phase. Secondly, fandom is gendered as a feminine and over-emotional attachment. And thirdly, this fandom is rendered as part of an improper, 'para-social' relationship. O'Dair therefore common-sensically positions the active, valued cultural theorist above the passive, devalued fan, drawing on a whole host of negative fan stereotypes:

> The fan has notoriously been regarded as a dupe, a passively blind receptor to corporate propaganda and establishment ideology, and an obsessive, strange social outcast. . . . [T]here has frequently been a gendered element to this pathologization. Behaviour perceived as fundamentally irrational, excessively emotional, foolish and passive has made the fan decisively feminine (Jonathan Gray 2003:67).

Again, it is assumed to be self-evidently or naturally the case that being a producer-consumer of cultural theory is not at all akin to being a media fan. For O'Dair, there can be no theory fans: the very suggestion that academics may be fans of theory is an affront to scholarly distinctions. By contrast, Catherine Liu appears to accept the existence of theory fans, suggesting that (post-)structuralist psychoanalyst Jacques Lacan created a circle of fans around his persona and his work: 'He . . . attracted to his person . . . a group of ardent followers who would represent the Lacanian movement' (2003:265). Liu argues that it was Lacan's very incomprehensibility which, in part, generated an aura around him:

> The magic that is beyond our grasp is also one of the material conditions of Lacan's aura. . . . audience members [for Lacan's seminars – M H] were captured by incomprehensibility, seeming to understand in order to stand in the auratic circle. Lacan . . . also put into practice . . . a kind of radical affirmation and permissiveness with regard to the fans who . . . were attracted (2003:267–8).

This permissiveness involved Lacan making himself available to whomsoever wished to see him. Charismatic performances of the incomprehensible shamanistic philosopher-analyst were hence combined with personal accessibility; followers were kept at a distance by Lacan's performative theory, but could seek to glimpse behind the scenes by actually meeting the man. This interplay between inciting absence and affirming presence is, of course, akin to the culture industry's promotional narratives of mediated stars, where consumers are encouraged to feel that they can find out about the real star behind their on-screen performances (Dyer 1991). Theory fandom may thus similarly emerge via theory culture's combination of personal appearances and mediated publication and promotion of names and their work. As Joanne Lacey has observed:

> Academic gossip about the private lives of theorists circulates, although not (as yet!) in the form of official publications . . . We may dress it up as something else, but the gossip enables us to access a 'real-life' realm [of favoured cultural theorists – M H] beyond the texts, (2000:48n7).

But Liu's observations of Lacan's textual mediation and real-life accessibility are not connected to any neutral admission of theory fandom; the fact that Jacques Lacan is described as having fans remains somewhat scandalous. We are told that Lacan's 'performance was a performance for those who enjoyed bathing in the enjoyment of understanding the incomprehensible' (2003:268). Hence, where cultural theory starts to generate fans it seemingly does so at the price of forfeiting any constative dimension. Instead, it becomes self-mystifying and perniciously cultish – a discourse that one belongs to, and subordinates one's rational self to, in order to feel a narcissistic sense of identification with the master theorist. The 'difficulty of Lacanian formulations lends itself to a kind of obsessional explication' (Liu 2003:265), as fan-like exegetes slavishly and obsessively repeat Lacanian formulae. Cultural theory is accused of going wrong here, of becoming reduced to formal hierarchies of in-group 'adepts' versus out-group 'agnostics'. In Liu's account, there is too much faith and not enough reason behind Lacan's 'aura' and his circle of fans: cultural theory is scandalously perverted from its properly rational course.

Alternatively, theory fandom can be acknowledged as a possibility but performed in ironic ways. This means simultaneously performing a fan identity and negatively stereotyping or devaluing fandom; the performer is protected from being interpreted simply and sincerely as a fan by their ironic stance. Such theory fandom becomes a kind of infelicitous performative which does not occur in the correct context, being carried out without 'the requisite feelings' (Austin 1976:40). Operating as a kind of 'faux-theory-fandom', this activity cites fandom's negative stereotypes in order to call attention to the theory star as someone improperly set above their academic colleagues (Butler 1997:49). Such a summoning-up of theory fandom also works as a partial attack on its supposed fan object, since it emphasizes and critiques academia's hierarchies. It is thus an act of cultural theory undertaken through the formal guise of fandom, but unfortunately it purchases its critique of theory stardom by iterating negative, pathologizing views of the fan. In *Notes from Underground: Zines and the Politics of Alternative Culture*, Stephen Duncombe (1997:109) recounts one such case of faux-theory-fandom, referring to the very same fanzine discussed in Wicke's (1994) work on celebrity feminism, *Judy!*. Taking a far more positive view of this than Judith Butler herself, Duncombe analyses *Judy!* as an instance of 'good-natured' humour:

> zine writers use laughter to assert control over a culture that is close to them, but impossibly distant at the same time [elevated beyond their reach – MH]. . . . Through gently teasing sexual fantasies about Butler, gossip on the personal exploits of celebrity academics, and quizzes like 'Are you a theory-fetishizing biscuit head?'. . . the authors effectively deflate celebrity academics and in doing so close – if . . . only symbolically – the gulf between them and their 'loser' status as graduate students and the elite world of the tenured superstar (1997:109).

Such a citation of fandom within the realms of theory can, at least, symbolically contest cultural theory's tendency to set itself above Others, highlighting and challenging this hierarchy. As Jennifer Wicke puts it: the 'author/publisher of *Judy!* [and its sexualized content – MH] craves celebrity, not Butler's body' (1994:771). To an extent, *Judy!* therefore partly enacts a levelling challenge to theory stardom and perhaps also partly fantasizes ascending its heights, yet it does these things by assuming that theory fandom is necessarily absurd, being capable of legibility only as a category-violating object of humour and/or horror (Carroll 2001). This 'scandalous' crossing of categorical boundaries (Jenkins 1992:16) attacks academic celebrity and prestige, but its border-crossing only makes sense as a transgression by recognising and so reproducing the proper boundary between theorist and fan. Playful transgression hence reinstates the very law that it supposedly breaks. Faux-theory-fandom still, ultimately, depends on an assumed separation of fan and theorist in order to produce its shocking effects: 'Transgressive behaviour . . . does not deny limits or boundaries, rather it exceeds them and so completes them. . . . The transgression is a component of the rule' (Jenks 2003:7; see also Wallen 1998:102).

The 'scholar-fandom' hybridity adopted by Henry Jenkins (1992), the anti-theory-fandom position (Faulk 2005; O'Dair 2000; Liu 2003), and faux-theory-fandom (*Judy!*) are all performative acts of cultural theory. Jenkins's work links fan and academic identities, though without integrating them in the figure of the theory fan, while academic doxa iterates negative fan stereotypes, and faux-fandom adopts and performs these stereotypes in order to further heighten the humorous and 'natural' absurdity of seriously considering academics to be theory fans. None of these positions, I want to suggest, adequately analyses structural similarities between fans and academics. And each of them, to varying degrees, performatively elevates scholarship above fandom, valorizing theory while either treating fandom as a dishonouring of theory's proper, rational status, or using theory's cultural value to transfer a hint of this to fan activities (as in Jenkins 1992; see Michael 2000).

R. L. Rutsky and Bradley Macdonald have stressed the performativity of cultural theory, noting that:

> Rather than judging cultural phenomena simply in terms of some pre-existing . . . theoretical direction, . . . we might do well to imagine a theory of cultural politics that would include diversion and unpredictability, that would emphasize its own ongoing performativity. Such a theory need not be seen merely as lacking direction or purpose. (2003:x).

However, this argument equates performativity with innovation, and with the tangential emergence of new ways of thinking and new ways of doing things. Considering previous theoretical approaches to fandom as performative, we need to note that while some cultural theory does indeed introduce unpredictable diversions and new directions (for example, Jenkins 1992), other equally performative theory iterates the already-said and the already-stereotyped in order to produce what it observes: namely, a gap between theorist and fan. Even this contrast between predictable and unpredictable theorizing does not entirely capture the situation with regards to fandom, since these variations occur within an overarching pattern or sameness – the structuring absence of theory fandom. Rutsky and Macdonald therefore prematurely reduce performativity to a valued marker of cultural change or drift, rather than considering that the performative *per se* is neither inherently good nor bad.

Although theory fandom has been recurrently and powerfully written out of theory culture, a handful of scholars have sought to approach the topic without prejudging it as absurd, or reproducing the common-sense doxa asserting that academia is naturally set above fandom. One such writer is Alan McKee, who considers the need to 'expand the definition of "fan" to include theoryheads' (2003b:128). McKee suggests:

> I would like to read books which explain not why Deleuze is a great philosopher, but 'why I love Deleuze', 'what Deleuze does for me'; for, after all, if we cannot even answer those questions, then how can we begin to ask the same things of fans of popular culture? Or lay any claim to understanding cultural consumption at all? (2003b:128).

The logic of McKee's point is compelling: it is striking to consider that cultural theory has much to say on the subject of why people consume popular culture – on what they do with it and get out of it – and yet has had incredibly little to say on the matter of consuming theory. If we restore an affective, emotional dimension to what is done with cultural theory then we can start to think about theory's pleasures without assuming in advance that emotion must automatically invalidate critical reason. Presumably certain cultural theory books are 'exciting . . . [being] the kind of scholarship that attracted and attracts bright . . . students' (Faulk 2005:143). So, to ignore the possibility and experience of theory fandom is to curiously negate the inspiring force of cultural theory's own aesthetics and arguments. Theory fandom, like media fandom, cannot just be a fixed iteration of fan identity, since at any contingent, unpredictable moment one can move into the experience and identity of a new fandom. This emergence often occurs without self-volition, as the self is opened to the 'textual other' (Pearce 1997), being transformed by this object (Bollas 1987:13–29 and 1993:33–46). Theory fandom, then, is transitive: it is a process of becoming which is partly captured by Alan Liu's term 'ethos': 'Ethos . . . is not in itself identity but the inchoate coming-to-be or basis of identity; it is identity at the point of emergence' (2004:71–2).

Theory fandom concerns the powerfully transformative experience of consuming cultural theory, an experience which can subsequently be routinized into card-carrying affiliation, whether as a Derridean, Lacanian, Winnicottian or Adornian. It is through the affective relations of theory fandom that cultural theory enters into the world, becoming more than just alien words on a page. And it is through experiencing such moments of an ethos that theorists-in-the-making feel the significance of cultural theory for and to their selves:

> By making certain things matter, people 'authorize' them to speak for them, not only as a spokesperson but as a surrogate voice . . . People give authority to that which they invest in; they let the objects of such investments speak for and in their stead (Grossberg 1992a:83–4).

To an extent, this makes theory fandom sound like media fandom: both are seemingly narcissistic or self-reflective (Sandvoss 2003:35–8). But theory fandom does not just reflect the prior self, it also changes this self-identity by giving rise to new identities and new cultural possibilities: 'affective empowerment involves the generation of energy and passion, the construction of possibility' (Grossberg 1992a:85). Theory fans therefore often seem to be passionately engaged with their favoured theorists' work, having a sense of cultural-political possibilities which this theory can help to produce. They may be dedicated feminists, having discovered that feminism is not a set of rules to be slavishly followed. As an emergent identity, feminism publicly reflects what matters to its theorists – for example, gender equality and fairness, indicating the good to be fought for. Or theory fans may be devoted Marxists, using the writings of Karl Marx and others to struggle to make a difference against capitalist systems and global exploitations of labour. Fans may, of course, also champion (post-)structuralist writers, or psychoanalytic gurus, always returning to and remaking their theoretical 'masters'' voices. What matters is that these theories matter to their devotees, who therefore read closely, creatively and passionately, and create theory as a living, affecting force in the world. Cultural theory affectively connects to its fans, who recognize a part of themselves in it. By doing so, it works to transform these fan-selves.

Relating

One rare example of a self-professed theory fan is Joanne Lacey, who analyses her own 'academic fandom' (2000:36) as a feminist, working-class scholar. Lacey recounts how:

> The discovery of *Landscape for a Good Woman* [by Carolyn Steedman] and *Schoolgirl Fictions* [by Valerie Walkerdine] were influential beyond my belief. Here, I could not only read about feeling out of place, but be offered conceptual frameworks for understanding and using feelings of dislocation. . . . I wrote Valerie Walkerdine fan letters; I cut out my own picture and pasted it on the cover of *Landscape for a Good Woman* (2000:43).

These admissions are certainly unusual, and it may be the case that relatively few academics have had such obviously, directly fan-like experiences of theory. But Lacey's account nevertheless carries structural features such as a 'discovery' of theory which influences her 'beyond . . . belief'. Self-reflection – reading about her own experiences mediated in and through theory – gives rise to an inspiring self-transformation. This transformative encounter with theory strongly resembles media fans' 'becoming a fan' stories (Hills 2002:6–7). Here too fandom emerges unexpectedly and transformatively. It is a kind of aesthetic discovery which speaks to the self. Fandom – whether media-related or theory-based – thus appears to be entered into involuntarily, cognitively and affectively, as a kind of 'aleatory object':

> Objects . . . often arrive by chance . . . We have not, as it were, selected the aleatory object to express an idiom of self. Instead, we are played upon by the inspiring arrival of the unselected, which often yields a very special type of pleasure – that of surprise. It opens us up, liberating an area like a key fitting a lock. In such moments we can say that objects use us (Bollas 1993:37).

Reflecting on her becoming a fan of academic work, Lacey notes how her 'confessions feel uncomfortable and immature. But such feelings of discomfort link in interesting ways to some of the existing . . . work on fandom as a kind of pathology' (2000:43). It is undoubtedly difficult for her (and other academics) to profess theory fandom, since this gesture risks the scholarly self being devalued as an over-emotional fan rather than being morally valued as a proper critical theorist. Lacey suggests that as well as theory fandom being disavowed and rendered structurally absent in the academy, it is also frequently disguised or played down:

> What is interesting about the ways in which academics tend to discuss their relationships to favoured texts is that . . . desire is written out of the equation in favour of respect and admiration, feelings which are much more acceptable in the academy (2000:43).

It may, however, be more acceptable for affective fan-text relations to be confessed within feminism, given the established presence of more personal writing styles here (see Wolff 1995 and Wise 1990). Indeed, the feminist scholars that Lacey confesses to being an academic fan of – Steedman and Walkerdine – have both written themselves into their cultural theory in productive and highly personalized ways. Feminism has been especially attentive to the affective dimensions of theory-production, leading Lyn Thomas to suggest that '[a]cademic feminism is perhaps one of the few aspects of feminist identities or subcultures which *has* been explored' (2002:11; see also Brunsdon 1991). This suggests that scholars outside feminism may be more resistant to voicing theory fandom, for fear of reducing theory's appreciation to

> private aspects of . . . [an] . . . individual encounter [with a text] . . . and the attempt to ground the profession [of cultural theory] in a realm of transcendence and miracle that resists full articulation or rational justification (Faulk 2005:151).

Barry Faulk also expresses the concern that professing theory fandom may become a prescriptive norm, causing 'thousands of graduate students' to produce 'rote recitations of professions of . . . zeal' (2005:152). Yet this common-sense objection to allowing a significant place for transformative affect and relationality within theory culture rings somewhat hollow. We might ask why it is that relations to cultural theory should always be supposedly fully rational or justifiable in such terms. What is lost if theory is viewed as rational *and* emotional, as an expression of logical self-mastery *and* an articulation of passionate self-absence or self-transformation? Why is emotion felt to degrade theory's cultural life? And we may well ponder how Faulk's feared 'rote recitation' would differ from the current situation, given that graduate students are still generally required to suppress their enthusiasms and passions for specific theories – their private reasons for relating to certain theories and not others – while many undergraduates may find even the notion of being passionate about cultural theory an extremely odd idea. Why should affect be restricted to the private and fixed outside of cultural theory?

Against such arguments and assumptions, I want to suggest that it is important not to marginalize theory fandom, since it is one of the most crucial things that professional scholars and amateur apprentice theorists do with theory. Without such moments of discovery, cultural theory can indeed seem like an imposition rather than something that relates to one's own concerns and 'mattering maps'. Viewed as resolutely rational and logical, rather than as a source of self-relating and self-transforming aesthetic experience, cultural theory becomes dangerously pre-judged and misrecognized as alien to the consuming self. Cultural theorists may purchase a type of masculinist authority and objectivity by writing out their theory fandom, but at the same time this manoeuvre makes theory into something cut apart from, and set above, its readers' or consumers' experiences and feelings.

By contrast, 'affective reflexivity' (Hills 2002:183–4), broadly speaking the act of reflecting upon our emotional states, does not just hold open the possibility of allowing us to think about our attachments to media texts. It also opens up the possibility of thinking about fan attachments to theory, making these a valid part of the self's repertoire of cultural investments, and part of everyday lived experience for theory's practitioners and students (who may experience widely varying affects of frustration and inspiration, as well as the dull compulsion to get a grade). Extending affective reflexivity into theory fandom as well as media fandom, I would note the following: like Lacey (2000), I eventually met and worked with a number of academics whose written work I had first idealized as an academic fan. Though it may seem odd, I was undoubtedly a fan of Henry Jenkins's *Textual Poachers*, as well as John Tulloch and Manuel Alvarado's *Doctor Who: The Unfolding Text* (1983) and Tulloch and Jenkins's *Science Fiction Audiences* (1995). These books were never just academic studies to me, they also formed a part of my fan collection of *Doctor Who*-related merchandise. And via a contagion of affect, my *Doctor Who* fandom carried over into a fandom of these academic writers.

Having confessed this much, why might I also have become a fan of theorists such as the psychoanalyst Donald Woods Winnicott? Unlike Henry Jenkins and John Tulloch, Winnicott never directly wrote about media fans or *Doctor Who*, and unlike those aforementioned scholars, I never got the chance to meet or work with him – he died in the year of my birth, 1971. Nevertheless, there are still academic affects and commitments at play here, as well as cognitive engagements. Arguments I have offered for the use of Winnicottian work in fan studies (Hills 2002) are, after all, not only distanced, detached or rational; they also emerge in relation to my embodied, biographical self. I first encountered Winnicott's work, for example, in media/cultural theory produced by one of my undergraduate tutors at Sussex University, Professor Roger Silverstone, who later became my PhD supervisor. In part, my use of Winnicott – while it was also related to broader shifts in the field of cultural theory – therefore allowed for an imagined connection to an idealized, paternal and mentoring figure whom I have undoubtedly experienced as a playful and good enough source of academic inspiration. Winnicott's appeal for me is over-determined in other ways: the signifiers D. W. (Winnicott's initials) remind me, rather obsessively perhaps, of the TV series I have loved all my life, *Doctor Who*. And the over-determination of my attachment to Winnicott is further compounded by the fact that my mother, as a trainee teacher, was herself taught Winnicott's work. When she first learnt that I was beginning to draw on this theory in my doctorate, she kindly presented me with one of her old Winnicott books (which was coincidentally published by Pelican, just like many of the founding texts of cultural studies). The figure of Winnicott, and his theory of mothering, therefore became part of a mother-son gift and a communication of care. Winnicott's work is for me not simply a logical matter of psychoanalytic theory: it has also come to exist as a maternal gift, an inheritance from academic mentor to disciple, and an affectively laden signifier associated with the popular-cultural text I have most centrally been a fan of across my biography. This is why I love Winnicott.

Michael O'Shaughnessy argues that audiences 'use texts as a mirror for themselves' by projecting aspects of the self into their keenly favoured or hated texts (1999:60). Although writing in a sociological rather than psychoanalytic vein, Cornel Sandvoss has similarly suggested that:

> In fandom we extend ourselves . . . into the world through the way we consume and appropriate mass media [or niche media – MH] (and their content). . . . The object of fandom is therefore a reflection of the fan. What fans are fascinated by is their own image, an extension of themselves. . . . The notion of fandom as an extension of self implies that fandom is based on the fan's projection (2003:39).

If this is so, then cultural theorists may also project aspects of themselves into their favoured theorists, and extend or relate their sense of self to specific theories. For me, Winnicott carries a sense of the mediator, the figure who didn't want to upset the psychoanalytic apple cart by founding a school, but who instead sought to balance and placate fiercely rival (Freudian and Kleinian) schools. Winnicott is powerfully linked with a sense of independence through this (being part of the so-called Independent School). By noting these points, I value my own desired independence as well as a desire not to be swallowed up by a school of thought or community.

Why has cultural theory become so important to me?

- Perhaps because I have always been defined across my biography as somebody who did well at school and in education, and so this success offered certain satisfactions and attentions. Becoming a cultural theorist in my adult life has therefore enabled me to build on emotional patterns, and self-esteem, established across my childhood and adolescence.

- Perhaps because Theory allows me to experience a textualized agency akin to that of media fans selectively interpreting their favoured texts. In a sense, being a media fan may have prepared me for the textual focus and close reading of scholarship, making academia seem less alien to me than it must to many students.

- Perhaps because Theory offers a way of belonging to an academic community that is nevertheless highly individualistic. This resonates with the subculturalist's and the fan's pursuit of 'distinctive individuality' (Muggleton 2000:63), working to secure a powerful sense of group identity ('us' versus 'them') but also allowing for a desired individuation.

To be sure, theory fandom cannot be willed into being or instrumentally pursued. But the likelihood of its arrival might be hastened if we seek to read and write theory relating to, or even directly challenging, our own concerns, tastes, politics and pre-existent popular-cultural fandoms. It is only by finding and dwelling on what speaks to the self, either affirmatively or as a provocation, that cultural theory can be felt as most vibrantly productive. The difficulty is that knowledge-production, whether as a professional or a student, tends to crowd out theory fandom by putting us all under pressures to read, write and think compliantly. Rather than tracing or celebrating resistance and agency in cultural others, it may be as well for cultural theorists, at all career points, to seek to resist forces of theory-compliance which say 'you must do it this way' or 'you must believe this'. Cultural theory in its more 'adventurous approach' (Williams 2004:8) may be inherently riskier, but is also likely to be more rewarding in terms of supporting and sustaining personal creativity within institutional or communal settings. And it is only by considering what creative possibilities may 'brood . . . within knowledge work' (Liu 2004:72) that we can remake ourselves and our theories. None of this can be done monolithically or instantaneously, and 'small ways that you can explore creative, slightly novel elements in your work' (Williams 2004:8) can be a starting point. And it remains the case that one small creativity may be precisely to challenge the structuring absence of theory fandom in scholarly doxa, and to begin to think of doing things with cultural theory as a fan rather than dreaming of being a star theorist.

In this chapter, I have argued that cultural theory tends to be performatively positioned above a series of Others in the normative practices of theory culture. Specific academics are singled out as stars or celebrities and set above their colleagues, while more generally, the doing of cultural theory is itself set above 'mere' fandom. The celebrity-function is a powerfully individualizing force within theory culture, as well as affirming theory's assumed power to make a rationalistic, argumentative difference. Theory stars are hence esteemed for the ways in which they mirror the values of theory culture, exaggeratedly displaying what is perceived to be good cultural theory – usually, original and influential work. Stars are produced by social and communal relations of academia, but like any fetishized product, they tend to be mis-recognised as effecting personal 'charisma' (Liu 2003) and scholarly 'brilliance'. The hierarchies implied by theory stars have been critiqued in cultural theory/studies, indicating its politicizing commitment to values of equality and community. Despite such criticisms, the celebrity-function has continued to hold sway in contemporary cultural theory, making this a curiously ambivalent zone of anti- and pro-individualism.

While scholarly subcultural celebrities are useful to and for cultural theory, theory fans are far more problematic. Here, the power and agency of the 'individualising' star are threatened by the figure of the fan, and by negative stereotypes of excessive emotion and non-autarchic dependence. In contrast to the prevalence of theory stars, who one might reasonably assume would have their own fans, there would appear to be a marked absence of theory fans in theory culture. This devalued identity is generally written out in favour of rationalist scholarly self-representations. Cultural theorists thus falsify their own affective experiences of discovering theory, and their own emotional commitments to theory, also denying such emotional expressions and articulations to students and apprentice theorists, and unhelpfully portraying theory as an over-rationalised machine of pure logic or 'critical' cognition. Perhaps theory culture would benefit from having a lot fewer stars and a lot more fans, thereby beginning to shift its philosophical and spatial imagery from one of being cognitively 'set above' to being affectively 'set in relation with'.

▶ Conclusion

Performing Cultural Theory

Across this book I have argued for the need to approach cultural theory as something 'performative' as well as 'constative'. While many textbooks take as their starting point the notion of introducing what theory constatively *says* – as if its language is an invisible mediator for pure thought – my own point of departure has been to consistently emphasize what theory performatively *does*.

It is often theory's detractors who claim that theory does things rather than just describing things, suggesting, for example, that it reads too much into texts. But the charge that cultural theory acts on its objects of study is one which restrictively views performativity as failed objectivity. Alternatively, cultural theory's charge sheet sometimes reads 'uses too much jargon', again supposedly failing to make itself into a plain, descriptive mirror for reality, this time by too obviously engaging in concept-formation and word-play. Or, theory is allegedly trapped in its ivory tower, the implication here being that it is fatally cut adrift from properly and constatively describing the world, instead getting caught up in self-referential navel-gazing. All these moralizing critiques rely on aligning the constative with the natural and the good, while demonizing the performative as artificial and bad.

It should be evident that I do not equate discussing cultural theory as performative with any such derogation of theory. Performativity is, in fact, not at all the same thing as failed objectivity, whether via jargonizing or losing touch with the real. My use of the term does not subscribe to, nor seek to reproduce, 'the stigma all performative discourse might be seen to share – if by degree' (Salamensky 2001:19). While constative discourse innocently describes the world, performative discourse tends to be stigmatised for the way in which it performs in the world, sometimes seeming unreal or 'stagey'. I have used 'performativity' non-judgementally here to highlight the more generalized and non-theatrical performances of cultural theory, such as the performing of a reading, or the way that theorists perform their subcultural distinctiveness: 'This involves not only learning how to read and write technically . . . but also how to live a theoretical life defined by one's affiliations to certain sacred texts and subcultures clearly set apart from intellectual business-as-usual' (Agger 1992:188; see also Litvak 1997:2).

Partly affiliating myself with Austinian theory, I have suggested that cultural theory does things like setting its passionate engagements with texts 'above' mere fandom (Chapter Seven). Cultural theory also does things like politicizing pop culture (Chapter Six): a performative act which creates even while it claims to observe, making culture a site for political struggle or activism. Cultural theorists also perform the work of defining: shaping what can count as culture (Chapter One) and theory (Chapter Two). Defining culture has proved to be no easy task, but cultural studies has nevertheless performatively extended the range of what is included under this term, contesting versions of 'capital C Culture' which restrict this sacralising distinction to high culture.

After introducing a number of theories of culture in Chapter One, I argued for a notion of culture as 'textualized agency', meaning that culture can be considered as whatever people do with and through texts. This is not always a matter of making meaning as structuralists would have it, nor is it always making ordinary as culturalists would argue. It can be both of these things, as well as being 'cultic' in Halton's (1992) sense, and 'ordering' in the manner suggested by (post-)structuralists Kendall and Wickham (2001). Choosing between the versions of culture put forward by different schools of thought is unhelpful since it makes our definition a badge of belonging to one or another academic sub-subculture. Instead, I argued for a definition of culture broad enough to move beyond common-sense versions of 'culture' = painting/art/theatre, and hopefully still precise enough to avoid critical accusations that culture is entirely dissolved into textuality or sociality.

Defining culture as textualized agency gave me a way into discussing cultural theory precisely as theory. Rather than simply introducing a range of approaches to culture, something which tends to treat theory as an idealized vehicle or conveyor belt for forms of thought, in Chapter Two I sought to evaluate the attributes of Theory. After all, cultural theory is itself a type of textualized agency: it involves doing things with texts, whether these are texts of audience talk, texts posted online, texts written and circulated as media fictions, or scholarly books and articles treated as an 'intertextual matrix' to be navigated. Considering cultural theory as a type of institutionally bound culture rather than as a magical force outside of materiality and the world, I have argued that it is equally important to analyse cultural theory and 'theory culture'.

Theory culture – doing things with texts – primarily involves ways of reading and writing, and I examined these in Part Two, along with constatively introducing key theories of reading (Hall 1980 and De Certeau 1988) and writing (Ong 1982 and Derrida 1976). Despite the organizational and analytical device of separating out reading and writing, I suggested in Chapter Five that these activities are inseparable and dynamically related components of theory culture, since this always involves 'writing reading' (Sage 1998) at different 'career points' (Crawford 2004).

Although this book has not been a 'how to' guide in the sense of being a prescriptive primer in 'how to use cultural theory' (see Inglis 1993:227–48; du Gay et al 1997; A. Gray 2003; Stokes 2003; Williams 2004), in Chapters Four and Five I nevertheless sketched out a series of ways for apprentice theorists to conduct the effective reading and writing of cultural theory. Treating cultural theory as performative means considering both what that theory does – how it constructs and affects the world – and also what apprentice, amateur and professional theorists can do with theory. 'Strategically-tactically' reading theory, and creatively (re-)writing it (see Chapters Four to Six), brings cultural theory down to earth, making it no longer an alien thing whose dead words are distant

from our political and personal 'mattering maps' (Grossberg 1992b). As Cristopher Nash
has remarked:

> One of the by-products of many of our recent theories' proper exhortation that
> we stop settling easily on what utterances seem to 'say' (constatively) is the
> acute realization that we must start looking more closely at what utterances
> (performatively) 'do'. Each thing said is someone's model of how to behave: of
> the kinds of things to say to ourselves, and to each other, of what comes first,
> what comes last, what doesn't matter and what shouldn't be said or thought at
> all (2001:33).

Cultural theory is one way of articulating what is felt and thought to matter. It intently values
and devalues, but these value claims can be remade by new generations of theorists. Indeed, a
number of writers have linked the very rise of cultural studies/theory to generational changes:

> The younger scholars who have turned so spontaneously and massively to
> cultural studies are the first generation of university teachers and critics who
> were brought up with television . . . Many of them as children and teenagers
> spent as much time watching television or listening to popular music as reading
> books . . . It is not surprising that young scholars should want to study what has
> to a considerable degree made them what they are (Miller 1998:60; see also
> Agger 1992:7).

Rather than viewing cultural theory/studies as alien and forbidding, we can think of it as
capturing what matters to generations brought up in a 'media world' (Bird 2003), where 'the
strong tide of interest running through a generation in the style and preoccupations of
Cultural Studies . . . is evidence of the subject's larger timeliness' (Inglis 1993:229). On this
account, one of the things that readers and writers do with cultural theory is, quite simply, to
express and systematically re-articulate their very own 'mattering maps' of cultural
consumption. Of course, this doesn't sound as morally heroic as cultural theory viewed as a
vehicle for political activism (Philo and Miller 2001), but these are hardly either/or options.
Expressing one's love of specific cultural forms via cultural theory can challenge
non-theoretical moralities and stereotyped representations of media consumption (see, for
example, Jenkins 1992 and Brunsdon 2000).

Cultural theory is typically an act of engagement with the here and now, or at least with
what matters to people. And this, perhaps, is what makes it threatening to those who should
constitute its new constituencies: it seems to replace 'lay theories' and 'lay expertise' with old-
fashioned expert knowledge. Surely consumers already know what they are doing when they
watch films, read magazines or play video games? They don't need cultural theory to explain
anything, because they are already vernacular experts 'in' culture (McLaughlin 1996; McKee
2004). However, such opposition mistakes what can be done with cultural theory, sensing it
to be an over-rationalizing imposition (Real 2001:176), or a performance of 'failed
objectivity'. Such withdrawals from the terrain of cultural theory/studies fail to see how this
theory's concerns have been amassed through the participation of generations of scholars
aiming to understand and change the contemporary world, and themselves (Barcan 2003).

In other words, rather than viewing cultural theory as a distant, alien and academic machine, we can see it instead as a far more proximate recruitment drive. It appeals to students, seeking to inspire them into action within (and beyond) its 'participatory culture' (Jenkins 1992). This 'desire called cultural studies' (Jameson 1995:251) wants to persuade, transform, interest and affect its audiences. It is performative through and through. Its detractors may, in fact, have correctly identified this desire to recruit, wishing to conservatively defend their pre-established cultural identities against cultural theory's transformative acts.

Cultural theory/studies has set itself apart from, and above, a variety of Others. Despite this gesture of detachment, it remains powerfully made up of the very Others that it arranges itself against (especially fans and forms of popular culture). This fact is evident through cultural studies' recruitment of students, through its inevitable intersections with commercial publishing, and through its intertextual interactions with popular narrative and popular culture. The training of academics does not definitively hold at bay these 'Other' identities and affects, just as the 'making of readings' within accredited academic interpretive communities (feminist, deconstructive, structuralist) can never entirely displace personalized, memorialized 'reading processes' (Pearce 1997). Cultural theory is necessarily permeable, rather than fully being the kind of institution-cum-fortress envisaged by de Certeau (1988) in his theory of 'powerful' strategies.

It may be that academics are 'as unwilling as others to study the organization of their social world. They don't want their secrets exposed or their favorite myths revealed as fairy tales' (Becker 1986:128). Carrying out a 'cultural studies of cultural studies' (Hall 2002:111), however, means highlighting how what scholars say (cultural theory as a product or an idealized set of transcendent thoughts) doesn't always neatly line up with what they do (theory culture as a process of materially working with and on commercial texts). Seeking to construct itself as authentically apart from a world to be studied, for example, cultural theory can never quite be authentically detached enough (Striphas 1998:465). This suggests that 'performative contradiction', an ironic counterpoint between language's performative and constative dimensions, marks cultural theory in a variety of ways, as theorists' 'actions . . . contradict [their] statements' (Stones 1996:46).

'Performative contradiction' is often used as a term with which scholars seek to undermine their rivals' arguments. Akin to non-academics' equation of performativity with failed objectivity, this is another limited and stigmatizing perspective on the performative. When scholars divine such contradictions in others' work, they are invariably attempting to demolish, render illegitimate or supplant schools of thought which they oppose. Classic examples of this include:

1. Attacks on (post-)structuralist thought for constatively challenging the possibility of fixed meanings and interpretations while its theorists and writers performatively assume their arguments should be properly interpreted (see Habermas 1990).

2. Objections that much critical (anti-capitalist) cultural theory constatively describes ideology as an invisible, insidious, omnipresent force persuading us how to naturally think, but then performatively unveils this ideology in specific cultural sites, hence implying that the critic is 'outside' ideology (see Fiske 1990:90).

3. Accusations that theorists constatively describing 'grand narratives' as a thing of the past (over-arching ways of making sense of the world, such as communism or psychoanalysis) performatively create a new grand narrative in the shape of their own theory (Branston and Stafford 2003:391; Nash 2001:3).

4. Opposition to what are termed 'constructivist' arguments in cultural theory. Here, theorists argue that the cultural world and its meanings, such as gender identities, are linguistically constructed rather than being essentially or naturally true (for example, Butler 1999; see Belsey 2005:10–13). However, this assumes that theorists' own statements can remain as acts of truth-telling, existing outside the realms of construction (see Bordwell 1989:13). What is theoretically done may therefore be in performative contradiction with what is said.

5. Allegations that while cultural studies/theory constatively challenges forces of capital, many of its concepts are, performatively, generalized and 'dereferentialized' terms which themselves circulate as part of global capital. Such abstracted theory is not tied to any one locale or its context, being open to 'franchising' and transnationalization (Readings 1996:17 and 43; Osborne 2000:17; Kraniauskas 1998).

6. Observations that some cultural theorists are constatively pessimistic about possibilities for progressive cultural change (any move towards greater democracy and equity), yet performatively optimistic, so that their teaching is premised on the idea that it is possible to make a difference against systems of cultural power (see Chabot Davis 2004:406).

This last example, raising the matter of what is done with cultural theory in its teaching, leads into a further couple of 'performative contradictions' with a specific bearing on the themes and interests of this book:

7. Constatively, theorists might describe 'theoretical point number 1 [as:] Nothing should be accepted at face value; everything is suspect' (Nealon and Searls Giroux 2003:6). However, when these theorists go on to performatively challenge notions such as 'the unique individual' (2003:43), their own acts of cultural theory are not included under the slogan 'everything is suspect', being exempted from 'theory rule number 1' (2003:10).

8. Constatively, the writer of a guide on *How to get a 2:1 in Media, Communication and Cultural Studies* might state that his book is 'not really intended for students . . . who simply want to get a degree . . . It has not been written to enable a student to take the easiest road to satisfying assessment criteria' (Williams 2004:8). However, this statement doesn't alter the fact that what the writer is doing is making available 'many checklists and guidelines which, if applied mechanically, ought to lead to reasonable results' (2004:8). Constatively, this scholar is strongly opposed to 'instrumental' study (2004:7). Yet performatively, his text – not least in its title – is less clearly anti-instrumentalist.

I want to argue that none of these examples of performative contradiction should immediately be considered as failures of cultural theory, where such theory becomes 'self-refuting' (Bordwell 1996:13) or, at the very least, 'particularly ironic' (Chabot Davis 2004:406). To view performatives as somehow invalidating constatives is to take a strictly logical view of cultural theory, where internal self-consistency is valued above all else. Instead, thinking positively (but still critically) about what cultural theory does as well as what it says can lead us to consider the situatedness of cultural theory – emphasizing its own contexts, aims and affective engagements within theory culture.

Many of the attacks on theory for its alleged contradictoriness, such as the first four points in my list above, involve theorists seemingly absenting themselves from what are otherwise said to be 'general' cultural conditions. This performative detachment does not, however, inherently invalidate what is stated or argued for. Rather, it indicates theory culture's tendency to bracket itself apart from what is being studied, while still not claiming any pure or absolute objectivity. This separation of theory into an Other sphere can be recognised and challenged (see Chapters Six and Seven), since as a self-representation it does not always best serve the legitimation of cultural theory. Accepting a more engaged, passionate, and even partisan academic self-identity, rather than seeming to claim 'necessary' objectivity (Hall 1994:266), may be more helpful:

> The practice of cultural studies in the United States, I believe, bears some responsibility for perpetuating this image of scholars . . . somehow above the game, or at least operating at a safe remove from the objects they scrutinize . . . In other words . . . we failed to make our interest in – and passion for – art and judgment known to the public outside the academy. Theorizing representations of all kinds, we neglected . . . to attend to how theorists of representation were represented (Faulk 2005:142).

It is only by noting what cultural theorists actually do with theory, and how certain factions use it within 'self-presentation[s]' as 'hyperprofessional specialists immune to the blandishments of the culture they inhabit' (Faulk 2005:142), that we can perhaps usefully complicate such claims. Accusing theorists of performatively contradicting themselves, on the other hand, either leaves myths of 'necessary' objectivity intact, or works to devalue specific theories rather than shifting the grounds of debate to consider what theorists are aiming, politically, to achieve via cultural theory.

The fifth criticism, meanwhile, involves a further version of cultural theory's alleged 'inauthenticity', reflecting on the commercial contexts within which theory culture operates. Gaining a wide, transnational reach hardly automatically invalidates cultural theory. On the contrary, finding new readerships is arguably one helpful aspect of theory culture's commercialization (see Chapter Five). Again, this leads us to think about cultural theory's contexts rather than de-materializing these and treating theory as 'confined or defined in schools and movements', and hence as something 'separated from what people do' (Nealon and Searls Giroux 2003:3 and 7).

The sixth and seventh criticisms also emphasize the teaching scene that theory frequently operates within. These points stress how doing cultural theory is never simply a matter of performing cognitive mastery. Beyond this, theory is marked by desire. It carries desire on the teacher's part to affectively move, inspire and transform their students, and a potential desire on the part of students to become part of theory culture's in-group, claiming new powers to act on the world: 'Understanding that eros is a force that enhances our . . . effort to be self-actualising . . . enables both professors and students to use such energy in a classroom setting in ways that invigorate discussion and excite the critical imagination' (hooks 1997:77). And as Nealon and Searls Giroux write: 'students . . . need theory precisely because it does some work for . . . [them] . . . and, with any luck at all, it does some work *on* [them]' (2003:7). Cultural theory is traversed by empathy: theorists tends to identify with marginalized groups in culture, and students' emotional engagements can act as 'vehicle[s] of political learning' (Berezin 2001:93; Ahmed 2004:171). As Fred Inglis remarks, there is a story here, one of 'how Cultural Studies will make you good' (1993:229).

To approach cultural theory simply as a constative reflection is to miss the implications of its 'passionate politics' (Goodwin et al 2001). The affective reflexivity of cultural studies' amateurs and professionals, their interestedness in cultural interests, goes missing whenever performative contradiction is rather simplistically alleged to destroy theoretical statements. For instance, returning to the sixth criticism above – rather than 'white anti-racist scholars' (Chabot Davis 2004:406) contradicting themselves by professing pessimistic chances for cultural change while optimistically teaching anti-racist cultural studies, they may be partly caricaturing cultural systems of power in an attempt to provoke affective reactions in apprentice theorists. In other words, characterizing racism or sexism as powerfully monolithic and immoral systems can serve as sensationalizing 'scare stories' and incitements to outrage, perhaps even activism. Theory-as-activism requires clear moral co-ordinates; it calls up legible tales of good and evil in order to legitimate its own investments and work towards affective contagion (Wallen 1998:107). Marxism, feminism and psychoanalysis all operate powerfully in this vein, nominating evils of capitalism, patriarchy and repression (see Hills 2005:145–60 on 'theory horror').

And taking a second look at the seventh criticism, we can suggest that positing a 'theory rule number 1: Everything is suspect' (Nealon and Searls Giroux 2003:10), but then leaving the results of consciousness-raising outside the rule is understandable not as a lapse in pure logic, but rather as a disjunction between political aims ('be enlightened') and self-consistency ('what you now believe is as suspect as what you used to believe, since everything is suspect'). Should the cultural theorist display pure logic at the cost of undermining their 'passionate politics'? This mistakes the force and affective relations of cultural theory, assuming that theory should only be a value-free, constative description. In any case, the performativity of cultural theory cannot be switched off: theory necessarily presupposes a relation to a readership, and so necessarily acts on the world.

Even the eighth criticism above can be reread not as a logical fault, but rather as a sign of tensions between commercial culture and theory culture. Williams is anxious not to be seen as rewarding instrumental student work, but this scholarly self-representation does not entirely resonate with the commercial logic behind publishing a book on 'how to get a 2:1'. The title assumes that this target is most attractive to most students. Rather than accusing the author of 'selling out', we could instead use this multivocality to again ponder the material contexts of theory culture, and how it interacts with apparent Others such as commercialism (Chapter Five).

Focusing on performative contradictions as much as on performativity *per se* can reveal just how things are done with cultural theory. We can see how students are persuaded or affected, how publishers are placated or appealed to, and how fellow scholars and their work are attacked. It is unsurprising that contradictions sometimes emerge between what is said and what is done, given that cultural theory seeks to affect such different constituencies occupying such different career points within the amateur-professional continuum of theory culture.

Approaching cultural theory in the way I have done throughout this book may seem self-referential or narcissistic to some. But to take theory culture's self-representations at face value is, I think, to fail to pursue accountable theory (Couldry 2000:126) in which self and other, the academic-consumer as much as the fan-consumer (Hills 2002), are equably and similarly theorized. Introducing cultural theory constatively serves to mystify theory as an alien domain generated by an intellectual elite. It dematerializes theory's textualized agency, its language and its cultural contexts, making it into great, transcendent thoughts that are somehow magically captured on the page. If readers of *How To Do Things* . . . do only two things with cultural theory as a result of consuming this text, I very much hope that they start to feel confident enough to challenge theory, and that they begin to creatively make it tell stories that reflect or mediate their experiences. If cultural theory is to remain the vibrant enterprise that it has been from at least the late 1960s onwards, it will have to work through the interests, passions and politics of the 'Net generation' of the noughties, much as it already has done for the baby-boomer 'TV generation'.

Cultural theory isn't reducible to lists of great writers. It isn't just glossaries or dictionaries of great concepts either (see Giroux 1997:240 – the quote which acts a prologue to this study). Learning 'names or movements' (Nealon and Searls Giroux 2003:7) is a predominantly constative approach, one which seeks to describe cultural theory. But when treated as essentially performative, and viewed within theory culture, cultural theory can instead be considered as ways of doing things with preceding theories. It is about making a difference by making thought different, and about making do with the conceptual building-bricks left for us by other theory 'poachers' turned 'gamekeepers', or 'enthusiasts' turned 'professionals'. After all, cultural theory's very own stars and fans (Chapter Seven) were all once beginners in the Theory trade, glimpsing their interests and 'mattering maps' represented theoretically for the first time. That being so, and since I began Chapter One by noting that cultural theory/studies textbooks all too often start with citations of Raymond Williams and his creed that 'culture is ordinary', I'll conclude with a less orthodox reminder: 'cultural . . . theorists are ordinary' too (Faulk 2005:143).

Bibliography

Abbott, A. (2001) *Chaos of Disciplines*. Chicago: University of Chicago Press.

Abercrombie, N. and Longhurst, B. (1998) *Audiences: A Sociological Theory of Performance and Imagination*. London: Sage.

Adam, B. and Allan, S. (1995) 'Theorizing Culture: An Introduction', in B. Adam and S. Allan (eds), *Theorizing Culture: An Interdisciplinary Critique After Postmodernism*. London: UCL Press, pp. xiii–xvii.

Adorno, T. (1991) *The Culture Industry: Selected Essays on Mass Culture*. London: Routledge.

Agger, B. (1989) *Fast Capitalism: A Critical Theory of Significance*. Urbana and Chicago: University of Illinois Press.

———(1990) *The Decline of Discourse: Reading, Writing and Resistance in Postmodern Capitalism*. London: Falmer Press.

———(1992) *Cultural Studies as Critical Theory*. London: Falmer Press.

Ahearne, J. (1995) *Michel de Certeau: Interpretation and its Other*. Cambridge: Polity Press.

Ahmed, S. (2004) *The Cultural Politics of Emotion*. Edinburgh: Edinburgh University Press.

Alasuutari, P. (1995) *Researching Culture: Qualitative Method and Cultural Studies*. London: Sage.

———(1998) *An Invitation to Social Research*. London: Sage.

Alexander, J. C. (1992) 'The Promise of a Cultural Sociology: Technological Discourse and the Sacred and Profane Information Machine', in R. Münch and N. J. Smelser (eds), *Theory of Culture*. Berkeley: University of California Press, pp. 293–323.

Althusser, L. and Balibar, E. (1970) *Reading Capital*. London: New Left Books.

Altman, R. (1999) *Film/Genre*. London: BFI Publishing.

Andrejevic, M. (2004) *Reality TV: The Work of Being Watched*. Rowman and Littlefield, Lanham, Maryland.

Ang, I. (1991) 'Wanted: Audiences. On the Politics of Empirical Audience Studies', in E. Seiter, H. Borchers, G. Kreutzner and E.-M. Warth (eds), *Remote Control: Television, Audiences and Cultural Power*. London and New York: Routledge, pp. 96–115.

———(1996) *Living Room Wars: Rethinking Media Audiences for a Postmodern World*. London and New York: Routledge.

———(2005) 'Who Needs Cultural Research?', in P. Leistyna (ed.), *Cultural Studies: From Theory to Action*. Oxford: Blackwell Publishing, pp. 477–83.

Archer, M. (1996) *Culture and Agency: The Place of Culture in Social Theory, Revised Edition*. Cambridge: Cambridge University Press.

Aronowitz, S. (1994) *Dead Artists, Live Theories, and Other Cultural Problems*. New York and London: Routledge.

Atkinson, M. (1998) *The Secret Marriage of Sherlock Holmes and Other Eccentric Readings*. Ann Arbor: University of Michigan Press.

Atkinson, P. (1990) *The Ethnographic Imagination: Textual Constructions of Reality*. London: Routledge.

Atton, C. (2004) *An Alternative Internet*. Edinburgh: Edinburgh University Press.

Augé, M. (1999) *An Anthropology for Contemporaneous Worlds*. Stanford: Stanford University Press.

Austin, J. L. (1976) *How To Do Things With Words*. Oxford and New York: Oxford University Press.

———(1979) *Philosophical Papers: Third Edition*. Oxford: Clarendon Press.

Back, L. (1998) 'Reading and Writing Research', in C. Seale (ed.), *Researching Society and Culture*. London: Sage, pp. 285–96.

Badmington, N. (2004) *Alien Chic: Posthumanism and the Other Within*. London and New York: Routledge.

Barcan, R. (2003) 'The Idleness of Academics: Reflections on the Usefulness of Cultural Studies', in *Continuum*, 17 (4), pp. 363–78.

Barker, M. and Beezer, A. (1992) 'Introduction: What's in a Text?', in M. Barker and A. Beezer (eds), *Reading Into Cultural Studies*. London and New York: Routledge, pp. 1–20.

Barker, M. with Austin, T. (2000) *From* Antz *to* Titanic*: Reinventing Film Analysis*. London: Pluto Press.

Barker, M. with Petley, J. (2001) 'On the Problems of Being a "Trendy Travesty"', in M. Barker and J. Petley (eds), *Ill Effects: The Media/Violence Debate*. London and New York: Routledge, pp. 202–24.

Barrett, M. (1999) *Imagination in Theory: Essays on Writing and Culture*. Cambridge: Polity Press.

Barthes, R. (1974) *S/Z: An Essay*. New York: Hill and Wang.

———(1977) *Image-Music-Text*. London: Fontana.

———(1981) *Camera Lucida*. New York: Hill and Wang.

———(1983) *The Fashion System*. New York: Hill and Wang.

Baudrillard, J. (1996) *The System of Objects*. London: Verso.

Becher, T. and Trowler, P. R. (2001) *Academic Tribes and Territories: Second Edition*. Buckingham: Open University Press.

Becker, H. S. (with a chapter by Richards, P.) (1986) *Writing for Social Scientists*. Chicago: University of Chicago Press.

Beezer, A. (1992) 'Dick Hebdige, *Subculture: The Meaning of Style*', in M. Barker and A. Beezer (eds), *Reading Into Cultural Studies*. London and New York: Routledge, pp. 101–18.

Belghazi, T. (1995) 'Cultural Studies, the University and the Question of Borders', in B. Adam and S. Allan (eds), *Theorizing Culture: An Interdisciplinary Critique After Postmodernism*. London: UCL Press, pp. 165–73.

Bell, V. (1999) 'Performativity and Belonging: An Introduction', in V. Bell (ed.), *Performativity and Belonging*. London: Sage, pp. 1–10.

Bell, V. and Butler, J. (1999) 'On Speech, Race and Melancholia: An Interview with J. Butler', in V. Bell (ed.), *Performativity and Belonging*. London: Sage, pp. 163–74.

Bellamy, R. (1997) 'The Intellectual as Social Critic: A. Gramsci and M. Walzer', in J. Jennings and A. Kemp-Welch (eds), *Intellectuals in Politics*. London and New York: Routledge, pp. 25–44.

Belsey, C. (2005) *Culture and the Real*. London and New York: Routledge.

Benjamin, W. (1992) *Illuminations*. London: Fontana.

Bennett, A. (1999) 'Subcultures or Neo-Tribes? Rethinking the Relationship Between Youth, Style and Musical Taste', in *Sociology*, 33 (3) pp. 599–617.

———(2000) *Popular Music and Youth Culture*. London: Macmillan.

Bennett, T. (1998) *Culture: A Reformer's Science*, London: Sage.

Bennett, A. and Kahn-Harris, K. (2004) 'Introduction', in A. Bennett and K. Kahn-Harris (eds), *After Subculture: Critical Studies in Contemporary Youth Culture*. London: Palgrave-Macmillan, pp. 1–18.

Bennett, T. and Woollacott, J. (1987) *Bond and Beyond*. London: Macmillan.

Bennington, G. (1999) 'Inter', in M. McQuillan, G. MacDonald, R. Purves and S. Thomson (eds), *Post-Theory: New Directions in Criticism*. Edinburgh: Edinburgh University Press, pp. 103–19.

Berezin, M. (2001) 'Emotions and Political Identity: Mobilizing Affection for the Polity', in J. Goodwin, J. M. Jasper and F. Polletta (eds), *Passionate Politics: Emotions and Social Movements*. Chicago and London: University of Chicago Press, pp. 83–98.

Bhabha, H. K. (1994) *The Location of Culture*. London and New York: Routledge.

Birchall, C. (1999) 'Alt.Conspiracy.Princess-Diana: The Conspiracy of Discourse', in *New Formations*, No. 36: pp. 125–40.

Bird, S. E. (2003) *The Audience in Everyday Life: Living in a Media World*. New York and London: Routledge.

Bollas, C. (1987) *The Shadow of the Object*. London: Free Association Books.

———(1993) *Being a Character: Psychoanalysis and Self Experience*. London: Routledge.

Boorstin, D. J. (1963) *The Image or What Happened to the American Dream*. London: Penguin.

Bordwell, D. (1989) *Making Meaning: Inference and Rhetoric in the Interpretation of Cinema*. Massachusetts: Harvard University Press.

———(1996) 'Contemporary Film Studies and the Vicissitudes of Grand Theory', in D. Bordwell and N. Carroll (eds), *Post-Theory: Reconstructing Film Studies*, Wisconsin: University of Wisconsin Press, pp. 3–36.

Bordwell, D. and Carroll, N. (eds) (1996) *Post-Theory: Reconstructing Film Studies*. Wisconsin: University of Wisconsin Press.

Bourdieu, P. (1986) *Distinction*. London: Routledge.

———(1988) *Homo Academicus*. Cambridge: Polity Press.

———(2000) *Pascalian Meditations*. Cambridge: Polity Press.

Bourdieu, P., Passeron, J.-C. and De Saint Martin, M. (1994) *Academic Discourse*. Cambridge: Polity Press.

Branston, G. (2000) 'Why Theory?', in C. Gledhill and L. Williams (eds), *Reinventing Film Studies*. London: Arnold, pp. 18–33.

Branston, G. and Stafford, R. (2003) *The Media Student's Book – Third Edition*. London and New York: Routledge.

Braudy, L. (1986) *The Frenzy of Renown: Fame and Its History*. Oxford: Oxford University Press.

Brenner, G. (2004) *Performative Criticism: Experiments in Reader Response*. New York: SUNY Press.

Brew, A. (2001) *The Nature of Research: Inquiry in Academic Contexts*. London and New York: Routledge-Falmer.

Brodkey, L. (1987) *Academic Writing as Social Practice*. Philadelphia: Temple University Press.

Brooker, P. (2003) *A Glossary of Cultural Theory: Second Edition*. London: Arnold.

Brooker, W. (1998) 'Under Construction: Cultural Studies in Cyberspace', in the *International Journal of Cultural Studies*, 1 (3), pp. 415–24.

——(2000) *Batman Unmasked: Analysing a Cultural Icon*. London: Continuum.

——(2002) *Using the Force: Creativity, Community and* Star Wars *Fans*. New York and London: Continuum.

——(2004) *Alice's Adventures: Lewis Carroll in Popular Culture*. New York and London: Continuum.

Brunsdon, C. (1991) 'Pedagogies of the Feminine: Feminist Teaching and Women's Genres', in *Screen*, 32 (4), pp. 364–81.

——(2000) *The Feminist, the Housewife, and the Soap Opera*. Oxford: Clarendon Press.

Buchanan, I. (1999) 'Deleuze and Cultural Studies', in I. Buchanan (ed.), *A Deleuzian Century?*. Durham and London: Duke University Press, pp. 103–17.

——(2000a) *Michel de Certeau: Cultural Theorist*. London: Sage.

——(2000b) *Deleuzism: A Metacommentary*. Edinburgh: Edinburgh University Press.

Buckingham, D. (1993) 'Conclusion: Re-reading Audiences', in D. Buckingham (ed.), *Reading Audiences: Young People and the Media*. Manchester: Manchester University Press, pp. 202–18.

Bukatman, S. (1994) 'X-Bodies (the Torment of the Mutant Superhero)', in R. Sappington and T. Stallings (eds), *Uncontrollable Bodies: Testimonies of Identity and Culture*. Seattle: Bay Press, pp. 93–129.

Burke, S. (1998) *The Death and Return of the Author: Second Edition*. Edinburgh: Edinburgh University Press.

Burkitt, I. (1999) *Bodies of Thought*. London: Sage.

Burt, R. (1998) *Unspeakable Shaxxxspeares*. London: Macmillan.

Butler, J. (1993) *Bodies That Matter: On the Discursive Limits of 'Sex'*. New York and London: Routledge.

——(1997) *Excitable Speech: A Politics of the Performative*. New York and London: Routledge.

——(1999 [1990]) *Gender Trouble: Feminism and the Subversion of Identity (10th Anniversary Edition)*. New York and London: Routledge.

——(2003) 'Values of Difficulty', in J. Culler and K. Lamb (eds), *Just Being Difficult? Academic Writing in the Public Arena*. Stanford: Stanford University Press, pp. 199–215.

Butler, R. (2005) *Slavoj Žižek: Live Theory*. New York and London: Continuum.

Buxton, D. (1990) *From* The Avengers *to* Miami Vice*: Form and Ideology in Television Series*. Manchester: Manchester University Press.

Calinescu, M. (1993) *Rereading*. New Haven: Yale University Press.

Carrington, B. (2001) 'Decentering the Centre: Cultural Studies in Britain and its Legacy', in T. Miller (ed.), *A Companion to Cultural Studies*. Oxford: Blackwell Publishing, pp. 275–97.

Carroll, N. (1996) 'Prospects for Film Theory: A Personal Assessment', in D. Bordwell and N. Carroll (eds), *Post-Theory: Reconstructing Film Studies*. Wisconsin: University of Wisconsin Press, pp. 37–68.

——(2001) 'Horror and Humor', in *Beyond Aesthetics: Philosophical Essays*. Cambridge and New York: Cambridge University Press, pp. 235–54.

Chabot Davis, K. (2004) 'Oprah's Book Club and the Politics of Cross-Racial Empathy', in *International Journal of Cultural Studies*, 7 (4), pp. 399–419.

Chaney, D. (1994) *The Cultural Turn*. London and New York: Routledge.

Chaney, D. (2004) 'Fragmented Culture and Subcultures', in A. Bennett and K. Kahn-Harris (eds), *After Subculture: Critical Studies in Contemporary Youth Culture*. London: Palgrave-Macmillan, pp. 36–48.

Chartier, R. (1995) *Forms and Meanings: Texts, Performances, and Audiences from Codex to Computer*. Philadelphia: University of Pennsylvania Press.

Cherland, M. R. (1994) *Private Practices: Girls Reading Fiction and Constructing Identity*. London: Taylor and Francis.

Chow, R. (2003) 'The Resistance of Theory; or, The Worth of Agony', in J. Culler and K. Lamb (eds), *Just Being Difficult? Academic Writing in the Public Arena*. Stanford: Stanford University Press, pp. 95–105.

Clarke, G. (1990) 'Defending Ski-Jumpers: A Critique of Theories of Youth Subcultures', in S. Frith and A. Goodwin (eds), *On Record: Rock, Pop and the Written Word*. London: Routledge, pp. 81–96.

Clarke, J. (1976) 'Style', in S. Hall and T. Jefferson (eds), *Resistance Through Rituals: Youth Subcultures in Post-war Britain*. London: Hutchinson, pp. 175–91.

Clarke, J., Hall, S., Jefferson, T. and Roberts, B. (1976) 'Subcultures, Cultures and Class: A Theoretical Overview', in S. Hall and T. Jefferson (eds), *Resistance Through Rituals: Youth Subcultures in Post-war Britain*. London: Hutchinson, pp. 9–74.

Clément, C. (1987) *The Weary Sons of Freud*. London: Verso.

Clifford, J. and Marcus, G. E. (eds) (1986) *Writing Culture: The Poetics and Politics of Ethnography*. Berkeley: University of California Press.

Cohen, P. (1972) *Subcultural Conflict and Working Class Community: Working Papers in Cultural Studies 2*. CCCS, Birmingham.

Collins, R. (2000) *The Sociology of Philosophies*. Massachusetts: Harvard University Press.

Cooper, A. (2004) 'Appropriate Nineteenth-Century Texts? Questions Concerning the Popular Culture of Theory', in I. Callus and S. Herbrechter (eds), *Critical Studies: Post-Theory, Culture, Criticism*. Amsterdam and New York: Rodopi, pp. 49–74.

Couldry, N. (2000) *Inside Culture: Re-imagining the Method of Cultural Studies*. London: Sage.

———(2003) *Media Rituals: A Critical Approach*. London and New York: Routledge.

Craib, I. (1992) *Anthony Giddens*. London and New York: Routledge.

———(1998) *Experiencing Identity*. London: Sage.

Cranny-Francis, A., Waring, W., Stavropoulos, P. and Kirby, J. (2003) *Gender Studies: Terms and Debates*. London: Palgrave-Macmillan.

Crawford, G. (2003) 'The Career of the Sport Supporter: The Case of the Manchester Storm', in *Sociology*, 37 (2), pp. 219–37.

———(2004) *Consuming Sport: Fans, Sport and Culture*. London and New York: Routledge.

Crème, P. and Lea, M. R. (1997) *Writing at University: A Guide for Students*. Buckingham: Open University Press.

Culler, J. (2000) 'The Literary in Theory', in J. Butler, J. Guillory and K. Thomas (eds), *What's Left of Theory?* New York and London: Routledge, pp. 273–92.

———(2003) 'Bad Writing and Good Philosophy', in J. Culler and K. Lamb (eds), *Just Being Difficult? Academic Writing in the Public Arena*. Stanford: Stanford University Press, pp. 43–57.

Culler, J. C. and Lamb, K. (eds) (2003) *Just Being Difficult? Academic Writing in the Public Arena*. Stanford: Stanford University Press.

Cunningham, V. (2002) *Reading After Theory*. Oxford: Blackwell Publishing.

Dacre, A. (1998) 'Predator 3, or, The Cultural Logic of Late Capitalism', in *The UTS Review*, 4 (2), pp. 1–13.

Davies, I. (1995) *Cultural Studies and Beyond: Fragments of Empire*. London and New York: Routledge.

Davis, C. (2001) 'Althusser on Reading and Self-reading', in *Textual Practice*, 15 (2), pp. 299–316.

Davis, H. (2004) *Understanding Stuart Hall*. London: Sage.

Debray, R. (2000) *Transmitting Culture*. New York: Columbia University Press.

De Certeau, M. (1988) *The Practice of Everyday Life*. Berkeley and London: University of California Press.

Derrida, J. (1976) *Of Grammatology*. Baltimore and London: Johns Hopkins University Press.

———(1978) *Writing and Difference*. London: Routledge and Kegan Paul.

———(1988) *Limited Inc*. Evanston: Northwestern University Press.

———(1992) 'Mochlos; or, The Conflict of the Faculties', in R. Rand (ed.), *Logomachia: The Conflict of the Faculties*. Lincoln and London: University of Nebraska Press, pp. 3–34.

———(2003) 'Following Theory', in M. Payne and J. Schad (eds), *life.after.theory*. London and New York: Continuum, pp. 1–51.

Dollimore, J. (2001) *Sex, Literature and Censorship*. Cambridge: Polity Press.

Donoghue, D. (1998) *The Practice of Reading*. New Haven and London: Yale University Press.

Driscoll, C. (2001) 'The Moving Ground: Locating Everyday Life', in *South Atlantic Quarterly*, 100 (2), pp. 381–98.

Du Bois, W. E. B. (1903) *The Souls of Black Folks*. A. C. McClurg, Chicago.

Duffett, M. (2004) 'Matt Hills, *Fan Cultures*', in *European Journal of Cultural Studies*, 7 (2), pp. 255–8.

Du Gay, P., Hall, S., Janes, L., Mackay, H. and Negus, K. (1997) *Doing Cultural Studies: The Story of the Sony Walkman*. London: Sage.

Duncombe, S. (1997) *Notes from Underground: Zines and the Politics of Alternative Culture*. London: Verso.

During, S. (1994) 'Introduction', in S. During (ed.), *The Cultural Studies Reader*. London and New York: Routledge, pp. 1–25.

Dyer, R. (1979) *Stars*. London: BFI Publishing.

———(1986) *Heavenly Bodies: Film Stars and Society*. London: BFI Publishing.

———(1991) '*A Star is Born* and the Construction of Authenticity', in C. Gledhill (ed.), *Stardom: Industry of Desire*. London: Routledge, pp. 132–40.

Eagleton, T. (2000) *The Idea of Culture*. Oxford: Blackwell Publishing.

———(2003) *After Theory*. London: Allen Lane.

Edmunds, J. and Turner, B. S. (2002) *Generations, Culture and Society*. Buckingham: Open University Press.

Edmundson, M. (1997) *Nightmare on Main Street: Angels, Sadomasochism, and the Culture of Gothic*. Cambridge, Massachusetts: Harvard University Press.

Ekegren, P. (1999) *The Reading of Theoretical Texts: A Critique of Criticism in the Social Sciences*. London and New York: Routledge.

Elliott, P. (1973) *Making of a Television Series: A Case Study in the Sociology of Culture*. London: Constable.

Elliott, A. and Turner, B. S. (eds) (2001) *Profiles in Contemporary Social Theory*. London: Sage.

Evans, M. (2004) *Killing Thinking: The Death of the Universities*. London and New York: Continuum.

Fairbairn, G. J. and Fairbairn, S. A. (2001) *Reading At University: A Guide for Students*. Buckingham: Open University Press.

Fairbairn, G. J. and Winch, C. (1996) *Reading, Writing and Reasoning: A Guide for Students: Second Edition*. Maidenhead: Open University Press.

Farrell, M. P. (2001) *Collaborative Circles: Friendship Dynamics and Creative Work*. Chicago: University of Chicago Press.

Faulk, B. (2005) 'Cultural Studies and the New Populism', in M. Bérubé (ed.), *The Aesthetics of Cultural Studies*. Oxford: Blackwell Publishing, pp. 140–55.

Femia, J. V. (1987) *Gramsci's Political Thought*. Oxford: Clarendon Press.

Fenster, M. (1999) *Conspiracy Theories*. Minneapolis: University of Minnesota Press.

Fish, S. (1980) *Is There A Text In This Class? The Authority of Interpretive Communities*. Massachusetts and London: Harvard University Press.

Fiske, J. (1987) *Television Culture*. London: Methuen.

———(1989) *Understanding Popular Culture*. London: Unwin Hyman.

———(1990) 'Ethnosemiotics: Some Personal and Theoretical Reflections', in *Cultural Studies*, 4 (1) pp. 85–99.

———(1992) 'The Cultural Economy of Fandom', in L. A. Lewis (ed.), *The Adoring Audience*. New York and London: Routledge, pp. 30–49.

Foucault, M. (1967) *Madness and Civilisation: A History of Insanity in the Age of Reason*. London: Tavistock Publications.

———(1970) *The Order of Things: An Archaeology of the Human Sciences*. London: Tavistock Publications.

———(1977) *Discipline and Punish: The Birth of the Prison*. London: Allen Lane.

———(1979) 'What is an Author?' in *Screen*, 20 (1), pp. 13–33.

———(1986) *The History of Sexuality Vol. 3: The Care of the Self*. New York: Pantheon Books.

Fraiman, S. (2003) *Cool Men and the Second Sex*. New York: Columbia University Press.

Friedman, E. G. and Squire, C. (1998) *Morality USA*. Minneapolis: University of Minnesota Press.

Frith, S. (1991) 'The Good, the Bad, and the Indifferent: Defending Popular Culture from the Populists', in *Diacritics*, 21 (4) pp. 102–15.

Frow, J. (1995) *Cultural Studies and Cultural Value*. Oxford: Clarendon Press.

Fuery, P. and Mansfield, N. (2000) *Cultural Studies and Critical Theory: Second Edition*. Oxford: Oxford University Press.

Furedi, F. (2004) *Where Have All the Intellectuals Gone? Confronting 21st Century Philistinism*. London and New York: Continuum.

Galef, D. (1998) 'Observations on Rereading', in D. Galef (ed.), *Second Thoughts: A Focus on Rereading*. Detriot: Wayne State University Press, pp. 17–33.

Game, A. and Metcalfe, A. (1996) *Passionate Sociology*. London: Sage.

Gamson, J. (1994) *Claims to Fame: Celebrity in Contemporary America*. California and London: University of California Press.

Garber, M. (2001) *Academic Instincts*. Princeton and Oxford: Princeton University Press.

Garnham, N. (2000) *Emancipation, the Media, and Modernity: Arguments about the Media and Social Theory*. Oxford: Oxford University Press.

Genette, G. (1997) *Paratexts: Thresholds of Interpretation*. Cambridge: Cambridge University Press.

Geraghty, C. (2003) 'Aesthetics and Quality in Popular Television Drama', in *International Journal of Cultural Studies*, 6 (1), pp. 25–45.

Gergen, K. J. (1991) *The Saturated Self*. New York: Basic Books.

Germano, W. (2001) *Getting It Published: A Guide for Scholars and Anyone Else Serious about Serious Books*. Chicago: University of Chicago Press.

Giddens, A. (1979) *Central Problems in Social Theory*. London: Macmillan.

———(1984) *The Constitution of Society*. Cambridge: Polity Press.

Gilbert, J. (2003a) 'Small Faces: The Tyranny of Celebrity in Post-Oedipal Culture', in *Mediactive*, Issue 2, pp. 86–109.

———(2003b) 'Friends and Enemies: Which Side is Cultural Studies On?', in Paul Bowman (ed.), *Interrogating Cultural Studies: Theory, Politics and Practice*. London: Pluto Press, pp. 145–61.

Giles, D. (2000) *Illusions of Immortality: A Psychology of Fame and Celebrity*. London: Macmillan.

Giles, J. and Middleton, T. (1999) *Studying Culture: A Practical Introduction*. Oxford: Blackwell Publishing.

Gilroy, P., Grossberg, L. and McRobbie, A. (eds) (2000) *Without Guarantees: In Honour of Stuart Hall*. London: Verso.

Giroux, H. A. (1997) 'Is There a Place for Cultural Studies in Colleges of Education?', in H. A. Giroux and P. Shannon (eds), *Education and Cultural Studies*. New York and London: Routledge, pp. 231–47.

Gledhill, C. and Williams, L. (eds) (2000) *Reinventing Film Studies*. London: Arnold.

Glynn, K. (2000) *Tabloid Culture: Trash Taste, Popular Power, and the Transformation of American Television*. Durham and London: Duke University Press.

Goodchild, P. (1996) *Deleuze and Guattari: An Introduction to the Politics of Desire*. London: Sage.

Goodwin, J., Jasper, J. M. and Polletta, F. (eds) (2001) *Passionate Politics: Emotions and Social Movements*. Chicago and London: University of Chicago Press.

Gramsci, A. (1971) *Selections from the Prison Notebooks*. London: Lawrence and Wishart.

Gray, A. (2003) *Research Practice for Cultural Studies*. London: Sage.

Gray, J. (2003) 'New Audiences, New Textualities: Anti-fans and Non-fans', in *International Journal of Cultural Studies*, 6 (1), pp. 64–81.

———(forthcoming) *Watching With The Simpsons: Television, Parody and Intertextuality*. London and New York: Routledge.

Green, M. (1997) 'Working Practices', in J. McGuigan (ed.), *Cultural Methodologies*. London: Sage, pp. 193–209.

———(2000) 'Your Own Work: Research, Interviews, Writing in Media Studies', in Dan Fleming (ed.), *Formations: A 21st-century Media Studies Textbook*. Manchester and New York: Manchester University Press, pp. 303–308, 314–20.

Greene, R. and Vernezze, P. (2004) The Sopranos *and Philosophy: I Kill Therefore I Am*. Chicago and Illinois: Open Court Publishing.

Greig, M. (2004) 'Habermas and the Holy Grail of Reason: *The Philosophical Discourse of Modernity* between Theatre and Theory', in *Social Semiotics*, 14 (2), pp. 215–32.

Gripsrud, J. (2002) 'Fans, Viewers and Television Theory', in P. Le Guern (ed.), *Les Cultes Médiatiques*. Rennes: Presses Universitaires De Rennes, pp. 113–31.

Grossberg, L. (1992a) *We Gotta Get Out of This Place*. London: Routledge.

———(1992b) 'Is There a Fan in the House? The Affective Sensibility of Fandom', in L. A. Lewis (ed.), *The Adoring Audience*. London: Routledge, pp. 50–65.

———(1996) 'Toward a Genealogy of the State of Cultural Studies', in C. Nelson and D. P. Gaonkar (eds), *Disciplinarity and Dissent in Cultural Studies*. New York and London: Routledge, pp. 131–47.

———(1997a) *Bringing It All Back Home: Essays on Cultural Studies*. Durham: Duke University Press.

———(1997b) *Dancing in Spite of Myself: Essays on Popular Culture*. Durham: Duke University Press.

Gurevitch, M. and Scannell, P. (2003) 'Canonization Achieved? Stuart Hall's "Encoding/Decoding"', in E. Katz, J. D. Peters, T. Liebes and A. Orloff (eds), *Canonic Texts in Media Research*. Cambridge: Polity Press, pp. 231–47.

Habermas, J. (1990) *The Philosophical Discourse of Modernity*. Cambridge: Polity Press.

Hall, G. (2002) *Culture in Bits*. London and New York: Continuum.

Hall, S. (1973) *Encoding and Decoding in the Media Discourse: Stencilled Paper 7*. CCCS, Birmingham.

———(1980) 'Encoding/Decoding', in S. Hall, D. Hobson, A. Lowe and P. Willis (eds), *Culture, Media, Language*. London: Hutchinson, pp. 128–38.

———(1992) 'Cultural Studies and its Theoretical Legacies', in L. Grossberg, C. Nelson and P. Treichler (eds), *Cultural Studies*. New York and London: Routledge, pp. 277–94.

———(1994) 'Reflections upon the Encoding/Decoding Model: An Interview with S. Hall', in J. Cruz and J. Lewis (eds), *Viewing, Reading, Listening: Audiences and Cultural Reception*. Colorado: Westview Press, Boulder, pp. 253–74.

———(1996) 'Cultural Studies: Two Paradigms', in J. Storey (ed.), *What Is Cultural Studies?*. London: Arnold, pp. 31–48.

Hall, S. and Jefferson, T. (eds) (1976) *Resistance Through Rituals: Youth Subcultures in Post-war Britain*. London: Hutchinson.

Halton, E. (1992) 'The Cultic Roots of Culture', in R. Münch and N. J. Smelser (eds), *Theory of Culture*. Berkeley: University of California Press, pp. 29–63.

Hammersley, M. (1998) *Reading Ethnographic Research, Second Edition*. London and New York: Longman.

Hanley, R. (1997) *The Metaphysics of* Star Trek. New York: Basic Books.

Harrington, C. L. and Bielby, D. D. (1995) *Soap Fans: Pursuing Pleasure and Making Meaning in Everyday Life*. Philadelphia: Temple University Press.

Harris, D. (1992) *From Class Struggle to the Politics of Pleasure: The Effects of Gramscianism on Cultural Studies*. London and New York: Routledge.

Hartley, J. (1999) ' "Text" and "Audience": One and the Same? Methodological Tensions in Media Research', in *Textual Practice*, 13 (3), pp. 487–508.

———(2002) *Communication, Cultural and Media Studies: The Key Concepts, Third Edition*. London and New York: Routledge.

———(2003) *A Short History of Cultural Studies*. London: Sage.

———(2004) 'The "Value Chain of Meaning" and the New Economy', in *International Journal of Cultural Studies*, 7 (2), pp. 129–41.

Hebdige, D. (1976) 'The Meaning of Mod', in S. Hall and T. Jefferson (eds), *Resistance Through Rituals: Youth Subcultures in Post-war Britain*. London: Hutchinson, pp. 87–96.

———(1979) *Subculture: The Meaning of Style*. London: Methuen.

Herman, P. C. (2000) 'Introduction: '60s Theory/'90s Practice', in P. C. Herman (ed.), *Day Late, Dollar Short: The Next Generation and the New Academy*. New York: SUNY Press, pp. 1–23.

Hermes, J. (1995) *Reading Women's Magazines*. Cambridge: Polity Press.

———(1999) 'Media Figures in Identity Construction', in P. Alasuutari (ed.), *Rethinking the Media Audience*. London: Sage, pp. 69–85.

Hermes, J., Gray, A. and Alasuutari, P. (2004) 'Editors' Introduction', in *European Journal of Cultural Studies*, 7 (2), pp. 131–4.

Highmore, B. (2002) *Everyday Life and Cultural Theory: An Introduction*. London and New York: Routledge.

Hills, M. (1999) 'The "Common Sense" of Cultural Studies', in *Diegesis*, No. 5, pp. 6–15.

———(2002) *Fan Cultures*. London and New York: Routledge.

———(2003) 'Recognition in the Eyes of the Relevant Beholder: Representing "Subcultural Celebrity" and Cult TV Fan Cultures', in *Mediactive*, Issue 2, pp. 59–73.

———(2004) 'Doing Things with Theory: From Freud's Worst Nightmare to (Disciplinary) Dreams of Horror's Cultural Value', in S. J. Schneider (ed.), *Horror Film and Psychoanalysis: Freud's Worst Nightmare*. Cambridge: Cambridge University Press, pp. 205–21.

———(2005) *The Pleasures of Horror*. London and New York: Continuum.

———(forthcoming) 'Academic Textual Poachers: *Blade Runner* as Cult Canonical Movie', in W. Brooker (ed.), *The Blade Runner Experience*. London and New York: Wallflower Press.

Hodkinson, P. (2002) *Goth: Identity, Style and Subculture*. Oxford and New York: Berg.

———(2004) 'The Goth Scene and (Sub)Cultural Substance', in A. Bennett and K. Kahn-Harris (eds), *After Subculture: Critical Studies in Contemporary Youth Culture*. London: Palgrave-Macmillan, pp. 135–47.

Hollows, J. (2003) 'The Masculinity of Cult', in M. Jancovich, A. L. Reboll, J. Stringer and A. Willis (eds), *Defining Cult Movies: The Cultural Politics of Oppositional Taste*. Manchester: Manchester University Press, pp. 35–53.

Hooks, B. (1997) 'Eros, Eroticism, and the Pedagogical Process', in A. McRobbie (ed.), *Back to Reality? Social Experience and Cultural Studies*. Manchester: Manchester University Press, pp. 74–80.

Hopper, S. (1995) 'Reflexivity in Academic Culture', in B. Adam and S. Allan (eds), *Theorizing Culture: An Interdisciplinary Critique After Postmodernism*. London: UCL Press, pp. 58–69.

Horkheimer, M. and Adorno, T. (1973) *Dialectic of Enlightenment*. London: Allen Lane.

Hutchings, P. (2004) *The Horror Film*. Essex: Pearson Education Limited, Harlow.

Hutnyk, J. (2004) *Bad Marxism: Capitalism and Cultural Studies*. London and Ann Arbor: Pluto Press.

Inglis, F. (1990) *Media Theory: An Introduction*. Oxford: Blackwell Publishing.

———(1993) *Cultural Studies*. Oxford: Blackwell Publishing.

———(2004) *Culture*. Cambridge: Polity Press.

Irwin, W. (ed.) (2002) The Matrix *and Philosophy: Welcome to the Desert of the Real*. Chicago and Illinois: Open Court Publishing.

Jackson, H. J. (2001) *Marginalia: Readers Writing in Books*. New Haven and London: Yale University Press.

Jackson, P., Lowe, M., Miller, D. and Mort, F. (eds), *Commercial Cultures: Economies, Practices, Spaces*. Oxford: Berg.

Jacoby, R. (1987) *The Last Intellectuals: American Culture in the Age of Academe*. New York: Basic Books.

———(1989) 'The Decline of American Intellectuals', in I. Angus and S. Jhally (eds), *Cultural Politics in Contemporary America*. New York and London: Routledge, pp. 271–81.

Jagodzinski, J. (2004) *Youth Fantasies: The Perverse Landscape of the Media*. London: Palgrave-Macmillan.

Jameson, F. (1995) 'On Cultural Studies', in J. Rajchman (ed.), *The Identity in Question*. London: Routledge, pp. 251–95.

Jancovich, M. (2000) ' "A Real Shocker": Authenticity, Genre and the Struggle for Distinction', in *Continuum*, 14 (1), pp. 23–35.

———(2002) 'General Introduction', in M. Jancovich (ed.), *Horror, The Film Reader*. London and New York: Routledge, pp. 1–19.

Jarvis, S. (1998) *Adorno: A Critical Introduction*. Cambridge: Polity Press.

Jay, M. (1973) *The Dialectical Imagination: A History of the Frankfurt School and the Institute of Social Research 1923–50*. London: Heineman.

Jenkins, H. (1992) *Textual Poachers*. New York and London: Routledge.

Jenkins, H., McPherson, T. and Shattuc, J. (2002) 'The Culture That Sticks to Your Skin: A Manifesto for a New Cultural Studies', in H. Jenkins, T. McPherson and J. Shattuc (eds), *Hop on Pop: The Politics and Pleasures of Popular Culture*. Durham and London: Duke University Press, pp. 3–42.

Jenks, C. (1993) *Culture*. London and New York: Routledge.

———(2003) *Transgression*. London and New York: Routledge.

———(2005) *Subculture: The Fragmentation of the Social*. London: Sage.

Jensen, J. (1992) 'Fandom as Pathology: The Consequences of Characterization', in L. A. Lewis (ed.), *The Adoring Audience*. New York and London: Routledge, pp. 9–29.

Jhally, S. and Lewis, J. (1992) *Enlightened Racism: The Cosby Show, Audiences, and the Myth of the American Dream*. Colorado: Westview Press, Boulder.

Johnson, R. (1996) 'What is Cultural Studies Anyway?', in J. Storey (ed.), *What Is Cultural Studies?*. London: Arnold, pp. 75–114.

Johnson, R., Chambers, D., Raghuram, P. and Tincknell, E. (2004) *The Practice of Cultural Studies*. London: Sage.

Karner, C. (2004) 'Theorising Power and Resistance among "Travellers" ', in *Social Semiotics*, 14 (3), pp. 249–71.

Katz, E., Peters, J. D., Liebes, T. and Orloff, A. (eds) (2003) *Canonic Texts in Media Research*. Cambridge: Polity Press.

Kendall, G. and Wickham, G. (2001) *Understanding Culture: Cultural Studies, Order, Ordering*. London: Sage.

Kennedy, B. M. (2000) *Deleuze and Cinema: The Aesthetics of Sensation*. Edinburgh: Edinburgh University Press.

Kim, S. (2004) 'Rereading David Morley's *The "Nationwide" Audience*', in *Cultural Studies*, 18 (1), pp. 84–108.

King, B. (2003) 'Embodying an Elastic Self: The Parametrics of Contemporary Stardom', in T. Austin and M. Barker (eds), *Contemporary Hollywood Stardom*. London: Arnold, pp. 45–61.

———(2004) 'Mass Media', in G. Taylor and S. Spencer (eds), *Social Identities: Multidisciplinary Approaches*. London and New York: Routledge, pp. 182–98.

Knight, P. (2000) *Conspiracy Culture*. London and New York: Routledge.

Knights, B. (1992) *From Reader to Reader: Theory, Text and Practice in the Study Group*. Hemel Hempstead: Harvester Wheatsheaf.

Kraniauskas, J. (1998) 'Globalization is Ordinary: The Transnationalization of Cultural Studies', in *Radical Philosophy*, 90, pp. 9–19.

Kuhn, T. S. (1970) *The Structure of Scientific Revolutions, Second Edition*. Chicago: University of Chicago Press.

Lacey, J. (2000) 'Discursive Mothers and Academic Fandom: Class, Generation and the Production of Theory', in S. R. Munt (ed.), *Cultural Studies and the Working Class: Subject to Change*. London: Cassell, pp. 36–50.

Lamont, M. (1987) 'How to Become a Dominant French Philosopher: The Case of Jacques Derrida', in *The American Journal of Sociology*, 93 (3), pp. 584–622.

Larsen, N. (1997) 'Theory at the Vanishing Point', in A. Kumar (ed.), *Class Issues: Pedagogy, Cultural Studies, and the Public Sphere*. New York: New York University Press, pp. 77–86.

Lash, S. (2002) *Critique of Information*. London: Sage.

Lechte, J. (2003) *Key Contemporary Concepts: From Abjection to Zeno's Paradox*. London: Sage.

Le Doeuff, M. (1989) *The Philosophical Imaginary*. London: Athlone Press.

Leenhardt, J. (1989) 'The Role of the Intellectuals in France', in L. Appignanesi (ed.), *Postmodernism: ICA Documents*. London: Free Association Books, pp. 199–207.

Lehtonen, M. (2000) *The Cultural Analysis of Texts*. London: Sage.

Levi-Strauss, C. (1972) *The Savage Mind*. London: Weidenfeld and Nicolson.

Lewis, James (2003) 'Academic Versus Audience Reading Formations of the Alien Saga', unpublished MA dissertation, JOMEC, Cardiff University.

Lewis, Jeff (2002) *Cultural Studies: The Basics*. London: Sage.

Lewis, Justin (1991) *The Ideological Octopus*. New York and London: Routledge.

———(2001) *Constructing Public Opinion*. New York: Columbia University Press.

Litvak, J. (1997) *Strange Gourmets: Sophistication, Theory, and the Novel*. Durham and London: Duke University Press.

Liu, A. (2004) *The Laws of Cool: Knowledge Work and the Culture of Information*. Chicago and London: University of Chicago Press.

Liu, C. (2003) 'Lacan's Afterlife: Jacques Lacan Meets A. Warhol', in J.-M. Rabaté (ed.), *The Cambridge Companion to Lacan*. Cambridge: Cambridge University Press, pp. 253–71.

Long, E. (1994) 'Textual Interpretation as Collective Action', in J. Cruz and J. Lewis (eds), *Viewing, Reading, Listening: Audiences and Cultural Reception*. Boulder, Colorado: Westview Press, pp. 181–211.

López, J. (2003) *Society and Its Metaphors: Language, Social Theory and Social Structure*. New York and London: Continuum.

Lury, C. (1996) *Consumer Culture*. Cambridge: Polity Press.

Lyotard, J.-F. (1984) *The Postmodern Condition: A Report on Knowledge*. Minneapolis: University of Minnesota Press.

Macdonald, N. (2001) *The Graffiti Subculture: Youth, Masculinity and Identity in London and New York*. London: Palgrave-Macmillan.

Macherey, P. (1978) *A Theory of Literary Production*. London: Routledge and Kegan Paul.

Mackay, H. (1995) 'Technological Reality: Cultured Technology and Technologized Culture', in B. Adam and S. Allan (eds), *Theorizing Culture: An Interdisciplinary Critique After Postmodernism*. London: UCL Press, pp. 236–48.

Maffesoli, M. (1996) *Time of the Tribes*. London: Sage.

Malefyt, T. D. and Moeran, B. (eds) (2003) *Advertising Cultures*. Oxford: Berg.

Marcus, G. E. (1998) *Ethnography Through Thick and Thin*. Princeton: Princeton University Press.

Marshall, P. D. (1997) *Celebrity and Power: Fame in Contemporary Culture*. Minneapolis and London: University of Minnesota Press.

———(2004) *New Media Cultures*. London: Arnold

Martin, P. J. (2004) 'Culture, Subculture and Social Organization', in A. Bennett and K. Kahn-Harris (eds), *After Subculture: Critical Studies in Contemporary Youth Culture*. London: Palgrave-Macmillan, pp. 21–35.

Martin, R. (2001) 'The Renewal of the Cultural in Sociology', in T. Miller (ed.), *A Companion to Cultural Studies*. Oxford: Blackwell Publishing, pp. 63–78.

Massumi, B. (1996) 'The Autonomy of Affect', in P. Patton (ed.), *Deleuze: A Critical Reader*. Oxford: Blackwell Publishing, pp. 217–39.

———(2002) *Parables for the Virtual: Movement, Affect, Sensation*. Durham and London: Duke University Press.

Maxwell, R. (2000) 'Cultural Studies', in G. Browning, A. Halci and F. Webster (eds), *Understanding Contemporary Society*. London: Sage, pp. 281–95.

McCracken-Flesher, C. (1994) 'Cultural Projections: The "Strange Case" of Dr. Jekyll, Mr. Hyde and Cinematic Response', in J. Carlisle and D. R. Schwarz (eds), *Narrative and Culture*. Athens: University of Georgia Press, pp. 179–99.

McGuigan, J. (1992) *Cultural Populism*. London and New York: Routledge.

McKee, A. (2002a) 'What Cultural Studies Needs is More Theory', in *Continuum*, 16 (3), pp. 311–16.

———(2002b) 'Fandom', in T. Miller (ed.), *Television Studies*. London: BFI Publishing, pp. 66–70.

———(2003a) *Textual Analysis: A Beginner's Guide*. London: Sage.

———(2003b) 'Review of *Fan Cultures*', in *International Journal of Cultural Studies*, 6 (1), pp. 126–8.

———(2004) 'Is *Doctor Who* Political?', in *European Journal of Cultural Studies*, 7 (2), pp. 201–17.

McLaughlin, T. (1996) *Street Smarts and Critical Theory: Listening to the Vernacular*. Wisconsin: University of Wisconsin Press.

McLellan, D. (ed.) (1977) *Karl Marx: Selected Writings*. Oxford: Oxford University Press.

McLuhan, M. (1962) *The Gutenberg Galaxy: The Making of Typographic Man*. London: Routledge and Kegan Paul.

———(1967) *Understanding Media: The Extensions of Man*. London: Sphere Books.

McQuail, D. (1987) *Mass Communication Theory: An Introduction, Second Edition*. London: Sage.

McQuillan, M., MacDonald, G., Purves, R. and Thomson, S. (1999) 'The Joy of Theory', in M. McQuillan, G. MacDonald, R. Purves and S. Thomson (eds), *Post-Theory: New Directions in Criticism*. Edinburgh: Edinburgh University Press, pp. ix–xx.

McRobbie, A. (1999) *In the Culture Society: Art, Fashion and Popular Music*. London and New York: Routledge.

Meehan, E. R. (2000) 'Leisure or Labor? Fan Ethnography and Political Economy', in I. Hagen and J. Wasko (eds), *Consuming Audiences? Production and Reception in Media Research*. New Jersey: Hampton Press, pp. 71–92.

Michael, J. (2000) *Anxious Intellects: Academic Professionals, Public Intellectuals, and Enlightenment Values*. Durham: Duke University Press.

Miklitsch, R. (1997) 'Punk Pedagogy, or Performing Contradiction: The Risks and Rewards of (Anti-) Transference', in H. A. Giroux and P. Shannon (eds), *Education and Cultural Studies*. New York and London: Routledge, pp. 259–70.

Miles, S. (2001) *Social Theory in the Real World*. London: Sage.

Miller, J. H. (1998) 'Literary and Cultural Studies in the Transnational University', in J. C. Rowe (ed.), *'Culture' and the Problem of the Disciplines*. New York: Columbia University Press, pp. 45–67.

Miller, T. (2001) 'What it is and What it isn't: Introducing . . . Cultural Studies', in T. Miller (ed.), *A Companion to Cultural Studies*. Oxford: Blackwell Publishing, pp. 1–19.

Miller, T. and McHoul, A. (1998) *Popular Culture and Everyday Life*. London: Sage.

Mills, B. (2004) 'Brass Eye', in G. Creeber (ed.), *Fifty Key Television Programmes*. London: Arnold.

Mills, C. W. (1970) *The Sociological Imagination*. London: Penguin.

Mills, S. (1994) 'Reading as/like a Feminist', in S. Mills (ed.), *Gendering the Reader*. Hemel Hempstead: Harvester Wheatsheaf, pp. 25–46.

Milner, A. (2002) *Re-Imagining Cultural Studies: The Promise of Cultural Materialism*. London: Sage.

Milner, A. and Browitt, J. (2002) *Contemporary Cultural Theory: An Introduction, Third Edition*. London and New York: Routledge.

Modleski, T. (1986) 'Introduction', in T. Modleski (ed.), *Studies In Entertainment: Critical Approaches to Mass Culture*. Bloomington and Indianapolis: Indiana University Press, pp. ix–xix.

Moores, S. (1993) *Interpreting Audiences: The Ethnography of Media Consumption*. London: Sage.

Moorhouse, H. F. (1991) *Driving Ambitions: An Analysis of the American Hot-rod Enthusiasm*. Manchester: Manchester University Press.

Moran, J. (2000) *Star Authors*. London: Pluto Press.

Morley, D. (1992) *Television, Audiences and Cultural Studies*. London: Routledge.

———(1996) 'Media Dialogue: Reading the Readings of the Readings . . .', in J. Curran, D. Morley and V. Walkerdine (eds), *Cultural Studies and Communications*. London: Arnold, pp. 300–305.

———(1997) 'Theoretical Orthodoxies: Textualism, Constructivism and the "New Ethnography" in Cultural Studies', in M. Ferguson and P. Golding (eds), *Cultural Studies in Question*. London: Sage, pp. 121–37.

———(1998) 'So-called Cultural Studies: Dead Ends and Reinvented Wheels', in *Cultural Studies*, 12 (4), pp. 476–97.

Morley, D. and Chen, K.-H. (eds) (1996) *Stuart Hall: Critical Dialogues in Cultural Studies*. London and New York: Routledge.

Morris, M. (1990) 'Banality in Cultural Studies', in P. Mellencamp (ed.) (1990) *Logics of Television: Essays in Cultural Criticism*. London: BFI Publishing.

———(1998a) *Too Soon Too Late: History in Popular Culture*. Bloomington: Indiana University Press.

———(1998b) 'Publishing Perils, and How to Survive them: A Guide for Graduate Students', in *Cultural Studies*, 12 (4), pp. 498–512.

Morrison, D. E. (1998) *The Search for a Method*. Luton: University of Luton Press.

Morton, A. (2004) *On Evil*. New York and London: Routledge.

Morton, D. (2004) 'Transforming Theory: Cultural Studies and the Public Humanities', in I. Callus and S. Herbrechter (eds), *Critical Studies: Post-Theory, Culture, Criticism*. Amsterdam and New York: Rodopi, pp. 25–47.

Mowitt, J. (1992) *Text: The Genealogy of an Antidisciplinary Object*. Durham and London: Duke University Press.

Muggleton, D. (2000) *Inside Subculture: The Postmodern Meaning of Style*. Oxford: Berg.

Muggleton, D. and Weinzierl, R. (eds) (2003) *The Post-Subcultures Reader*. Oxford: Berg.

Mulhall, S. (2002) *On Film*. London and New York: Routledge.

Mulligan, K. (2003) 'Searle, Derrida, and the Ends of Phenomenology', in B. Smith (ed.), *John Searle*. Cambridge: Cambridge University Press, pp. 261–86.

Mulvey, L. (1999[originally 1975]) 'Visual Pleasure and Narrative Cinema', in S. Thornham (ed.), *Feminist Film Theory: A Reader*. Edinburgh: Edinburgh University Press, pp. 58–69.

Mungham, G. and Pearson, G. (eds) (1976) *Working Class Youth Culture*. London: Routledge and Kegan Paul.

Murdock, G. (1994) 'Tales of Expertise and Experience: Sociological Reasoning and Popular Representation', in C. Haslam and A. Bryman (eds), *Social Scientists Meet the Media*. London: Routledge, pp. 108–22.

———(2003) 'Back to Work: Cultural Labor in Altered Times', in A. Beck (ed.), *Cultural Work: Understanding the Cultural Industries*. London and New York: Routledge, pp. 15–36.

Murray, S. (2004a) *Mixed Media: Feminist Presses and Publishing Politics*. London: Pluto Press.

———(2004b) ' "Celebrating the Story the Way It Is": Cultural Studies, Corporate Media and the Contested Utility of Fandom', in *Continuum*, 18 (1), pp. 7–25.

Nash, C. (2001) *The Unravelling of the Postmodern Mind*. Edinburgh: Edinburgh University Press.

Nealon, J. and Searls Giroux, S. (2003) *The Theory Toolbox: Critical Concepts for the Humanities, Arts and Social Sciences*. Lanham, Maryland: Rowman and Littlefield.

Nell, V. (1988) *Lost in a Good Book: The Psychology of Reading for Pleasure*. New Haven and London: Yale University Press.

Norris, C. (1982) *Deconstruction: Theory and Practice*. London and New York: Routledge.

O'Dair, S. (2000) 'Stars, Tenure, and the Death of Ambition', in P. C. Herman (ed.), *Day Late, Dollar Short: The Next Generation and the New Academy*. New York: SUNY Press, pp. 45–61.

Ong, W. J. (1982) *Orality and Literacy: The Technologizing of the Word*. London and New York: Methuen.

Osborne, P. (2000) *Philosophy in Cultural Theory*. London and New York: Routledge.

O'Shaughnessy, M. (1999) *Media and Society: An Introduction*. Oxford: Oxford University Press.

O'Shea, A. (1998) 'A Special Relationship? Cultural Studies, Academia and Pedagogy', in *Cultural Studies*, 12 (4) pp. 513–27.

Parham, J. (2002) 'Teaching Pleasure: Experiments in Cultural Studies and Pedagogy', in *International Journal of Cultural Studies*, 5 (4), pp. 461–78.

Parker, I. (2004) *Slavoj Žižek: A Critical Introduction*. London: Pluto Press.

Parkin, F. (1971) *Class Inequality and Political Order*. London: MacGibbon and Kee.

Payne, M. (ed.) (1997) *A Dictionary of Cultural and Critical Theory*. Oxford: Blackwell Publishing.

Pearce, L. (1997) *Feminism and the Politics of Reading*. London: Arnold.

Pfister, J. (1996) 'The Americanization of Cultural Studies', in J. Storey (ed.), *What Is Cultural Studies?* London: Arnold, pp. 287–99.

Philo, G. and Miller, D. (eds) (2001) *Market Killing: What the Free Market Does and What Social Scientists Can Do About It.* Harrow: Pearson Education Limited.

Porter, D. (ed.) (1997) *Internet Culture.* London: Routledge.

Poster, M. (1998) 'Textual Agents: History at "The End of History" ', in J. C. Rowe (ed.) *'Culture' and the Problem of the Disciplines.* New York: Columbia University Press, pp. 199–227.

Postman, N. (1985) *Amusing Ourselves to Death.* London: Methuen.

Powell, R. and Clarke, J. (1976) 'A Note on Marginality', in S. Hall and T. Jefferson (eds), *Resistance Through Rituals: Youth Subcultures in Post-war Britain.* London: Hutchinson, pp. 223–29.

Procter, J. (2004) *Stuart Hall: Routledge Critical Thinkers.* London and New York: Routledge.

Purdie, S. (1992) 'Janice Radway, *Reading the Romance*', in M. Barker and A. Beezer (eds), *Reading Into Cultural Studies.* London and New York: Routledge, pp. 148–64.

Pustz, M. J. (1999) *Comic Book Culture: Fanboys and True Believers.* Jackson: University Press of Mississippi.

Rabaté, J.-M. (2002) *The Future of Theory.* Oxford: Blackwell Publishing.

Radway, J. (1984) *Reading the Romance.* Chapel Hill and London: University of North Carolina Press.

———(1987) *Reading the Romance.* London: Verso.

———(1991) *Reading the Romance, With a New Introduction by the Author.* Chapel Hill and London: University of North Carolina Press.

Readings, B. (1996) *The University in Ruins.* Massachusetts and London: Harvard University Press.

Real, M. (1996) *Exploring Media Culture: A Guide.* London: Sage.

———(2001) 'Cultural Theory in Popular Culture and Media Spectacles', in J. Lull (ed.), *Culture in the Communication Age.* London: Routledge, pp. 167–78.

Richardson, L. (1997) *Fields of Play: Constructing an Academic Life.* New Jersey: Rutgers University Press.

Ritzer, G. (1998) *The McDonaldization Thesis: Explorations and Extensions.* London: Sage.

———(2001) *Explorations in Social Theory: From Metatheorizing to Rationalization.* London: Sage.

Robbins, B. (1993) *Secular Vocations: Intellectuals, Professionalism, Culture.* London: Verso.

———(1996) 'Double Time: Durkheim, Disciplines, and Progress', in C. Nelson and D. P. Gaonkar (eds), *Disciplinarity and Dissent in Cultural Studies.* New York and London: Routledge, pp. 185–200.

———(1999) 'Celeb-Reliance: Intellectuals, Celebrity, and Upward Mobility', available online at www.iath.virginia.edu/pmc/text-only/issue.199/9.2robbins.txt

Rojek, C. (2001) *Celebrity.* London: Reaktion Books.

———(2003) *Stuart Hall: Key Contemporary Thinkers.* Cambridge: Polity Press.

Roustang, F. (1982) *Dire Mastery: Discipleship from Freud to Lacan.* Baltimore and London: Johns Hopkins University Press.

Rowlands, M. (2005) *Everything I Know I Learned from TV: Philosophy Explained Through Our Favourite TV Shows.* London: Ebury Press.

Royle, N. (2003) *The Uncanny.* New York and London: Routledge.

Rubinstein, D. (2001) *Culture, Structure and Agency: Toward a Truly Multidimensional Society.* London: Sage.

Ruddock, A. (2001) *Understanding Audiences: Theory and Method.* London: Sage.

Rutsky, R. L. and Macdonald, B. J. (2003) 'Introduction', in R. L. Rutsky and B. J. Macdonald (eds), *Strategies for Theory: From Marx to Madonna.* New York: SUNY Press, pp. vii–xvi.

Sage, L. (1998) 'Living on Writing', in J. Treglown and B. Bennett (eds), *Grub Street and the Ivory Tower*. Oxford: Oxford University Press, pp. 262–76.

Salamensky, S. I. (2001) 'Dangerous Talk: Phenomenology, Performativity, Cultural Crisis', in S. I. Salamensky (ed.), *Talk Talk Talk: The Cultural Life of Everyday Conversation*. New York and London: Routledge , pp. 15–35.

Salih, S. (2002) *Judith Butler: Routledge Critical Thinkers*. London and New York: Routledge.

Sandvoss, C. (2003) *A Game of Two Halves: Football, Television and Globalization*. London and New York: Routledge.

———(2005) *Fans: The Mirror of Consumption*. Cambridge: Polity Press.

Saukko, P. (2003) *Doing Research in Cultural Studies*. London: Sage.

Saussure, F. D. (1983) *Course in General Linguistics*. London: Duckworth.

Schlesinger, P. (2001) 'Media Research and the Audit Culture', in G. Philo and D. Miller (eds), *Market Killing: What the Free Market Does and What Social Scientists Can Do About It*. Harrow: Pearson Education Limited, pp. 179–90.

Scholes, R. (1985) *Textual Power: Literary Theory and the Teaching of English*. New Haven and London: Yale University Press.

Sconce, J. (2003) 'Tulip Theory', in A. Everett and J. T. Caldwell (eds), *New Media: Theories and Practices of Digitextuality*. New York and London: Routledge, pp. 179–93.

Sedgwick, E. K. (2003) *Touching Feeling: Affect, Pedagogy, Performativity*. Durham: Duke University Press.

Seigworth, G. J. (2000) 'Banality for Cultural Studies', in *Cultural Studies*, 14 (2) pp. 227–68.

Seigworth, G. J. and Wise, J. Macgregor (2000) 'Introduction: Deleuze and Guattari in Cultural Studies', in *Cultural Studies*, 14 (2) pp. 139–46.

Shiach, M. (1989) *Discourse on Popular Culture*. Stanford: Stanford University Press.

Shotter, J. (1993) *Cultural Politics of Everyday Life*. Buckingham: Open University Press.

Shukin, N. (2000) 'Deleuze and Feminisms: Involuntary Regulators and Affective Inhibitors', in I. Buchanan and C. Colebrook (eds), *Deleuze and Feminist Theory*. Edinburgh: Edinburgh University Press, pp. 144–55.

Shumway, D. R. (1997) 'The Star System in Literary Studies', in *PMLA*, 112, pp. 85–100.

Silverstone, R. (1994) *Television and Everyday Life*. London and New York: Routledge.

Simon, K. (2004) 'Inside the Idea Factory', in M. S. Prelinger and J. Schalt (eds), *Collective Action, A Bad Subjects Anthology*. London and Ann Arbor: Pluto Press, pp. 113–17.

Simpson, D. (2002) *Situatedness, or, Why We Keep Saying Where We're Coming From*. Durham and London: Duke University Press.

Skovmand, M. and Schrøder, K. C. (eds) (1992) *Media Cultures: Reappraising Transnational Media*. London and New York: Routledge.

Smith, M. J. (2000) *Culture: Reinventing the Social Sciences*. Buckingham: Open University Press.

Smith, P. (2001) *Cultural Theory: An Introduction*. Oxford: Blackwell Publishing.

South, J. B. (ed.) (2003) *Buffy the Vampire Slayer and Philosophy: Fear and Trembling in Sunnydale*. Chicago: Open Court.

Spigel, L. (1992) *Make Room for TV*. Chicago: University of Chicago Press.

Spillman, L. (ed.) (2002) *Cultural Sociology*. Oxford: Blackwell Publishing.

Stahl, G. (2003) 'Tastefully Renovating Subcultural Theory: Making Space for a New Model', in D. Muggleton and R. Weinzierl (eds), *The Post-Subcultures Reader*. Oxford: Berg, pp. 27–40.

Stebbins, R. A. (1992) *Amateurs, Professionals, and Serious Leisure*. Montreal and Kingston: McGill-Queen's University Press.

Stewart, S. (1993) *On Longing: Narratives of the Miniature, the Gigantic, the Souvenir, the Collection*. Durham and London: Duke University Press.

Stokes, J. (2003) *How To Do Media and Cultural Studies*. London: Sage.

Stones, R. (1996) *Sociological Reasoning: Towards a Past-Modern Sociology*. London: Macmillan.

Storey, J. (2001) *Cultural Theory and Popular Culture: An Introduction, 3rd Edition*. Harrow: Pearson Education Limited.

———(2003) *Inventing Popular Culture*. Oxford: Blackwell Publishing.

Strathern, M. (2000) 'Afterword: Accountability . . . and Ethnography', in M. Strathern (ed.), *Audit Cultures: Anthropological Studies in Accountability, Ethics and the Academy*. London and New York: Routledge, pp. 279–304.

Strinati, D. (2000) *An Introduction to Studying Popular Culture*. London and New York: Routledge.

———(2004) *An Introduction to Theories of Popular Culture: Second Edition*. London and New York: Routledge.

Striphas, T. (1998) 'Introduction – the Long March: Cultural Studies and its Institutionalization', in *Cultural Studies*, 12 (4), pp. 453–75.

———(2002) 'Banality, Book Publishing and the Everyday Life of Cultural Studies', in *International Journal of Cultural Studies*, 5 (4), pp. 438–60.

Swingewood, A. (1998) *Cultural Theory and the Problem of Modernity*. London: Macmillan.

Thomas, L. (1995) 'In Love with *Inspector Morse*: Feminist Subculture and Quality Television', in *Feminist Review* No. 51, pp. 1–25.

———(2002) *Fans, Feminisms and 'Quality' Media*. London and New York: Routledge.

Thompson, J. B. (1995) *Media and Modernity*. Cambridge: Polity Press.

Thornham, S. (2000) *Feminist Theory and Cultural Studies: Stories of Unsettled Relations*. London: Arnold.

Thornton, S. (1995) *Club Cultures*. Cambridge: Polity Press.

———(1997) 'General Introduction', in K. Gelder and S. Thornton (eds), *The Subcultures Reader*. London and New York: Routledge, pp. 1–7.

Threadgold, T. (1997) *Feminist Poetics: Poesis, Performance, Histories*. London and New York: Routledge.

Thwaites, T., Davis, L. and Mules, W. (2002) *Introducing Cultural and Media Studies: A Semiotic Approach*. London: Palgrave.

Tolson, A. (1996) *Mediations: Text and Discourse in Media Studies*. London: Arnold.

———(1997) 'Social Surveillance and Subjectification: The Emergence of "Subculture" in the Work of Henry Mayhew', in K. Gelder and S. Thornton (eds), *The Subcultures Reader*. London and New York: Routledge, pp. 302–11.

Tompkins, J. P. (1980) *Reader-Response Criticism: From Formalism to Post-structuralism*. Baltimore and London: Johns Hopkins University Press.

Tudor, A. (1999) *Decoding Culture: Theory and Method in Cultural Studies*. London: Sage.

Tulloch, J. (1999) *Performing Culture*. London: Sage.

———(2000) *Watching Television Audiences: Cultural Theories and Methods*. London: Arnold.

Tulloch, J. and Alvarado, M. (1983) Doctor Who: *The Unfolding Text*. London: Macmillan.

Tulloch, J. and Jenkins, H. (1995) *Science Fiction Audiences: Watching* Doctor Who *and* Star Trek. London and New York: Routledge.

Turner, G. (2003) *British Cultural Studies: Third Edition*. London and New York: Routledge.

———(2004) *Understanding Celebrity*. London: Sage.

Turner, G., Bonner, F. and Marshall, P. D. (2000) *Fame Games: The Production of Celebrity in Australia*. Melbourne: Cambridge University Press.

Van Maanen, J. (1988) *Tales of the Field*. Chicago: University of Chicago Press.

Vieth, E. (2000) 'The Future is Present: American Cultural Studies on the Net', in J. Hartley and R. E. Pearson (eds), *American Cultural Studies: A Reader*. Oxford: Oxford University Press, pp. 427–36.

Wallen, J. (1998) *Closed Encounters: Literary Politics and Public Culture*. Minneapolis: University of Minnesota Press.

Webster, F. (2001) 'Sociology, Cultural Studies, and Disciplinary Boundaries', in T. Miller (ed.), *A Companion to Cultural Studies*. Oxford: Blackwell Publishing, pp. 79–100.

Wernick, A. (1991) *Promotional Culture*. London: Sage.

Wicke, J. (1994) 'Celebrity Material: Materialist Feminism and the Culture of Celebrity', in *South Atlantic Quarterly*, 93 (4) pp. 751–78.

Widdicombe, S. and Wooffitt, R. (1995) *The Language of Youth Subcultures: Social Identity in Action*. Hemel Hempstead: Harvester-Wheatsheaf.

Williams, J. (1992) Letter in *PMLA*, 107, pp. 1280–1.

———(1997) 'The Romance of the Intellectual and the Question of Profession', in H. A. Giroux and P. Shannon (eds), *Education and Cultural Studies*. New York and London: Routledge, pp. 49–64.

———(2000) 'The Posttheory Generation', in P. C. Herman (ed.), *Day Late, Dollar Short: The Next Generation and the New Academy*. New York: SUNY Press, pp. 25–43.

Williams, N. (2004) *How to Get a 2:1 in Media, Communication and Cultural Studies*. London: Sage.

Williams, R. (1983[1976]) *Keywords: A Vocabulary of Culture and Society: Second Edition*. London: Fontana.

———(1997[1958]) 'Culture is Ordinary', in Ann Gray and J. McGuigan (eds), *Studying Culture: An Introductory Reader*. London: Arnold, pp. 5–14.

Williams, S. (2001) *Emotion and Social Theory*. London: Sage.

Willis, P. (1977) *Learning to Labour: How Working Class Kids Get Working Class Jobs*. Farnborough: Gower Press.

———(1978) *Profane Culture*. London: Routledge and Kegan Paul.

———(1980) 'Notes on method', in S. Hall, D. Hobson, A. Lowe and P. Willis (eds), *Culture, Media, Language*. London: Hutchinson, pp. 88–95.

———(2000) *The Ethnographic Imagination*. Cambridge: Polity Press.

Wilson, S. (2004) 'The Joy of Things', in I. Callus and S. Herbrechter (eds), *Critical Studies: Post-Theory, Culture, Criticism*. Amsterdam and New York: Rodopi, pp. 167–88.

Winnicott, D. W. (1992) *Through Paediatrics to Psychoanalysis: Collected Papers*. London: Karnac Books.

Wise, S. (1990) 'Sexing Elvis', in S. Frith and A. Goodwin (eds), *On Record: Rock, Pop and the Written Word*. London: Routledge, pp. 390–8.

Wolff, J. (1995) *Resident Alien: Feminist Cultural Criticism*. Cambridge: Polity Press.

Wood, H. (2004) 'What *Reading the Romance* Did for us' in *European Journal of Cultural Studies*, 7 (2), pp. 147–54.

Wood, R. (1986) *Hollywood from Vietnam to Reagan.* New York: Columbia University Press.

Wren-Lewis, J. (1983) 'The Encoding/Decoding Model: Criticisms and Redevelopments for Research on Decoding', in *Media, Culture and Society*, 5 (2), pp. 179–97.

Wright Wexman, V. (1999) 'The Critic as Consumer: Film Study in the University, *Vertigo*, and the Film Canon', in B. Henderson and A. Martin (eds), *Film Quarterly: Forty Years – A Selection.* Berkeley: University of California Press, pp. 76–90.

Žižek, S. (2001) *The Fright of Real Tears.* London: BFI Publishing.

Index